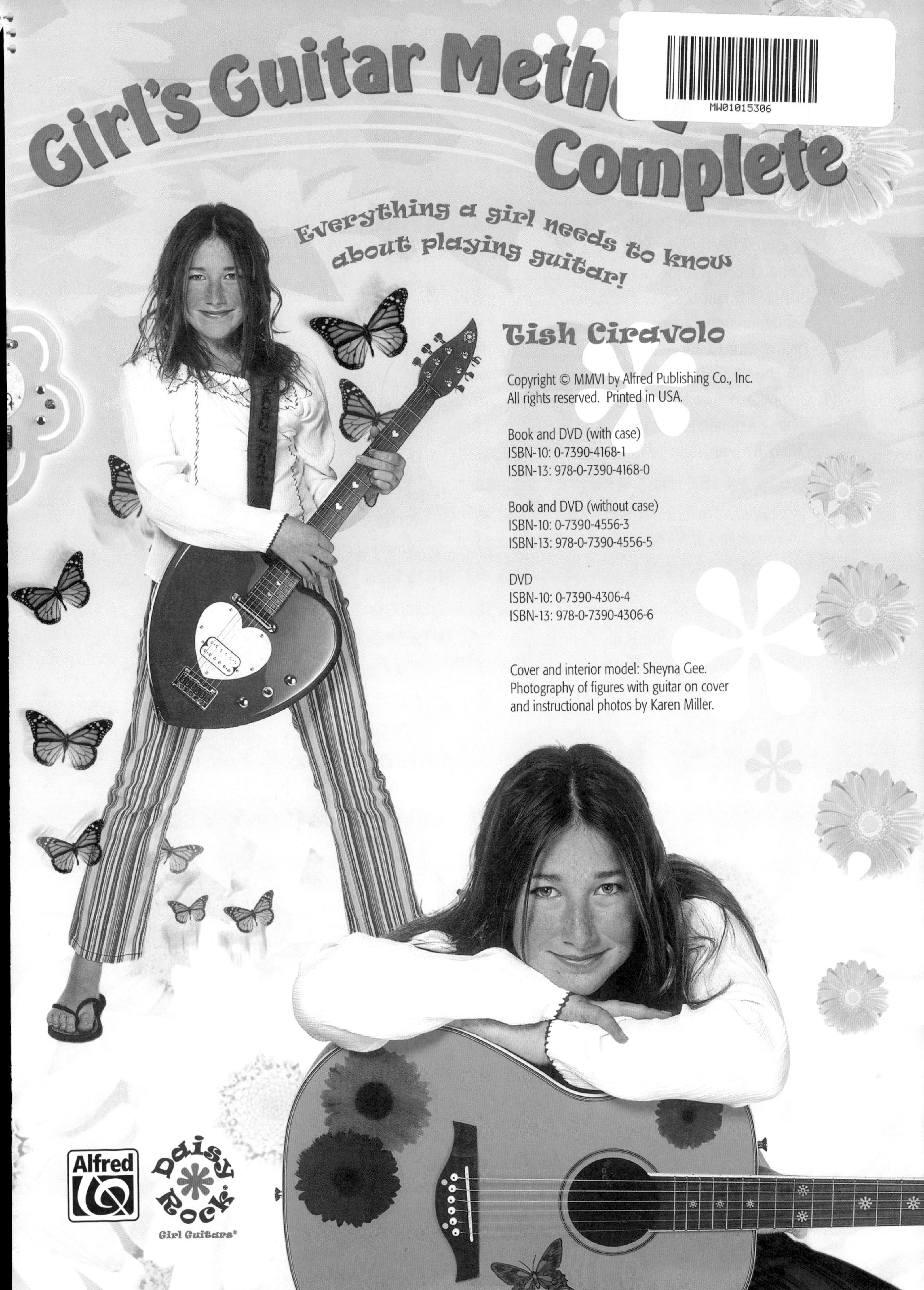

Girl's Guitar Method Complete

Everything a girl needs to know about playing guitar!

Tish Ciravolo

Book and DVD (with case)
ISBN-10: 0-7390-4168-1
ISBN-13: 978-0-7390-4168-0

Book and DVD (without case)
ISBN-10: 0-7390-4556-3
ISBN-13: 978-0-7390-4556-5

DVD
ISBN-10: 0-7390-4306-4
ISBN-13: 978-0-7390-4306-6

Cover and interior model: Sheyna Gee.
Photography of figures with guitar on cover and instructional photos by Karen Miller.

Contents

Types of Guitars

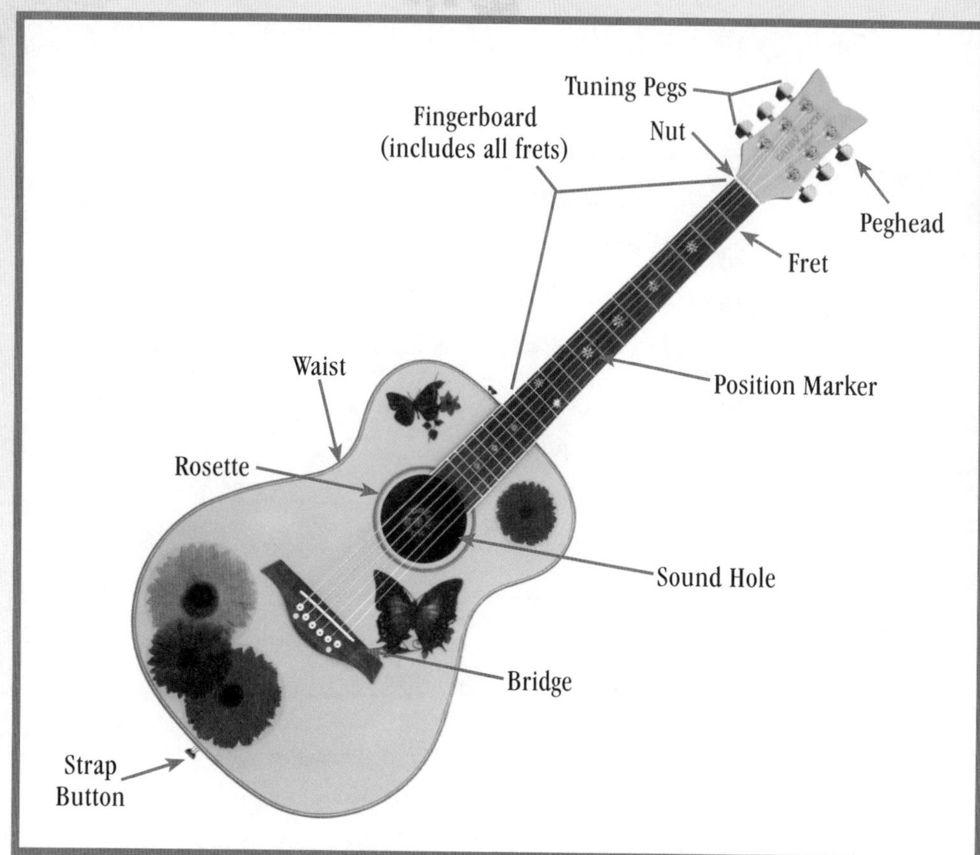

Acoustic Flat Top Guitar

Acoustic Flat Top guitars have narrow necks and steel strings. They're either strummed with a flat pick or played with one or more finger picks. They have a bright, crisp sound. They're used in rock, blues, country and folk playing.

Strings: Steel
Gauge: Light or Medium

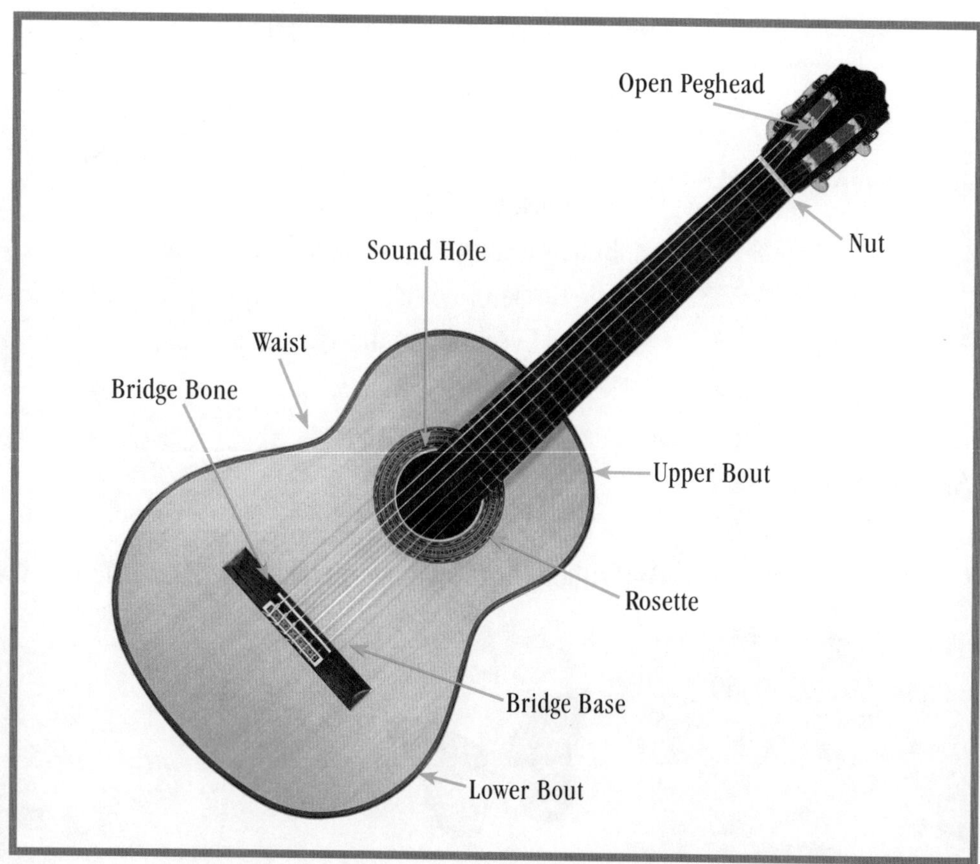

Classical Guitar

Classical guitars have flat tops, wide necks, and nylon strings. They have a mellow, warm sound. Picks are rarely used on classical guitars.

Strings: Nylon
Gauge: Varied

Solid-Body Electric Guitar

Solid-body electrics have narrow necks, light-gauge strings and one or more electrical pickups. The output of these pickups is fed through an amplifier and is sometimes modified further by using wah-wah pedals, distortion pedals, choruses or other means of altering the tone. Solid body electrics are used for rock, heavy metal, blues, country and jazz music.

Strings: Steel
Gauge: Light

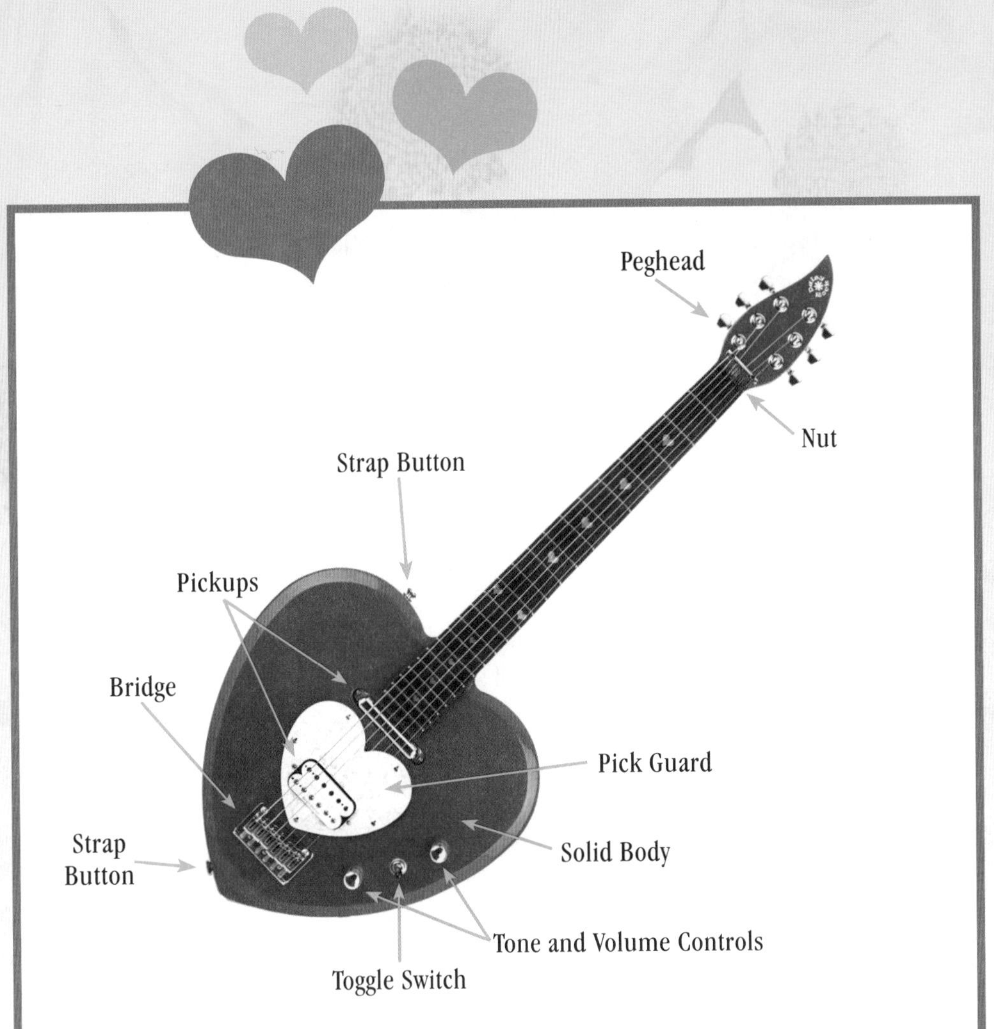

Hollow-Body Electric Guitar

Hollow-body electrics are semi-hollow guitars with electrical pickups. This gives the guitar a warm, rich sound. They're good for jazz, blues, rock and fusion.

Strings: Steel
Gauge: Medium

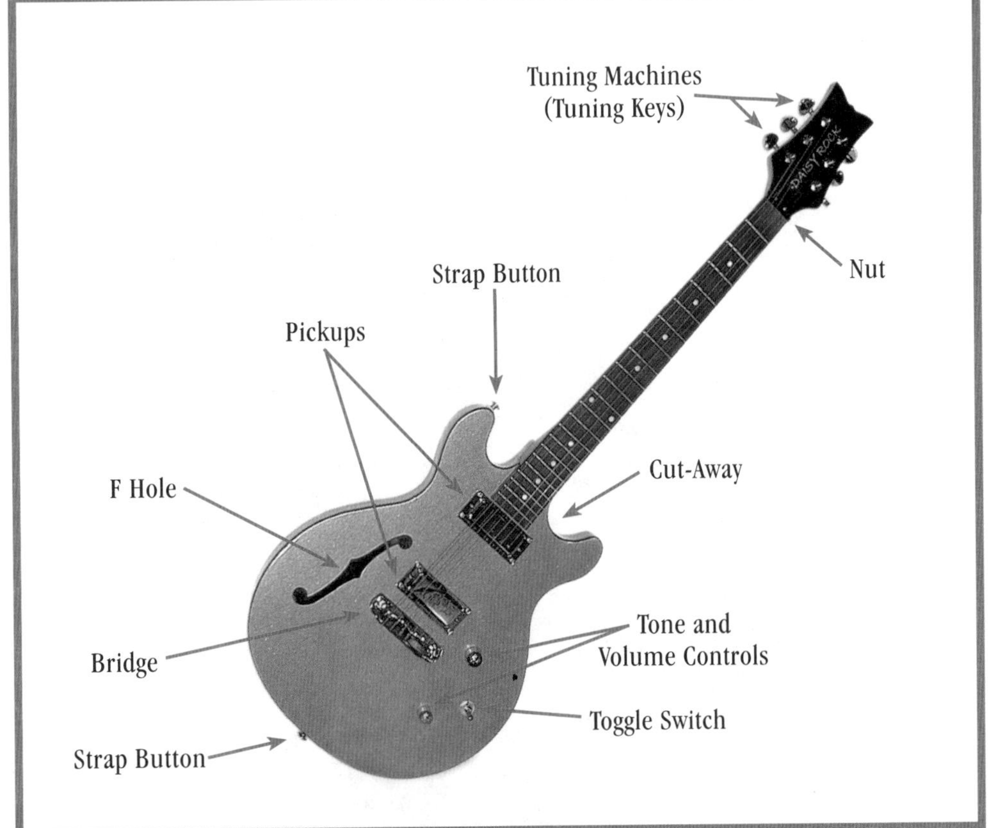

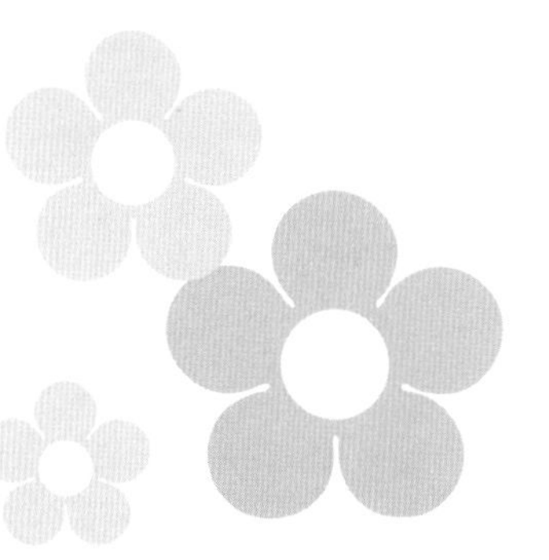

A Short History of the Guitar

Instruments related to the guitar have been in existence since ancient times. The idea of stretching strings across a vibrating chamber of air, called a sound box, dates back to prehistoric times, and is found in virtually every culture in the world.

In the late 1940s engineers realized that the hollow wood body of the guitar was no longer necessary as the sole generator of a musical signal, so the sound box was eliminated and the result was the solid body electric guitar. Since then there have been many modifications in the design of guitars, but basically they are either acoustic or electric.

Using this book you can learn how to play the guitar if you have either type.

Buying a Guitar

First, ask yourself what kind of music you like the most. Then choose the model from pages 4 and 5 that is recommended for that style.

Caring for Your Guitar

Most guitar care is simply common sense.

- Rule one is never to expose the instrument to extremes of heat or cold. This means if you take your guitar outside, keep it out of the sun. It also means that you don't leave it in the unheated trunk of a car in the winter.
- Rule two is to make sure the strings are tuned to an accurate pitch. Tuning the strings too high can have serious consequences for the instrument, causing the neck to bow or the bridge to rip out of the top.

Other things you can do are to wipe the strings off after playing and to polish the instrument using guitar polish, which you can get at any music store. It won't hurt to ask your repairman to check over the instrument twice a year—just before the summer and winter.

Photo: Jay Blakesberg

Liz Phair

Her 1993 debut album, "Exile in Guyville," became an instant classic with Phair's raw, sparse production and lyrical candor. The guitar plays a major role in Phair's sound. Straight forward rhythms executed with a ragged, in-your-face performance compliment her conversational singing style.

Tuning Your Guitar

First make sure the strings are wound properly around the tuning pegs. They should go from inside to outside. See below:

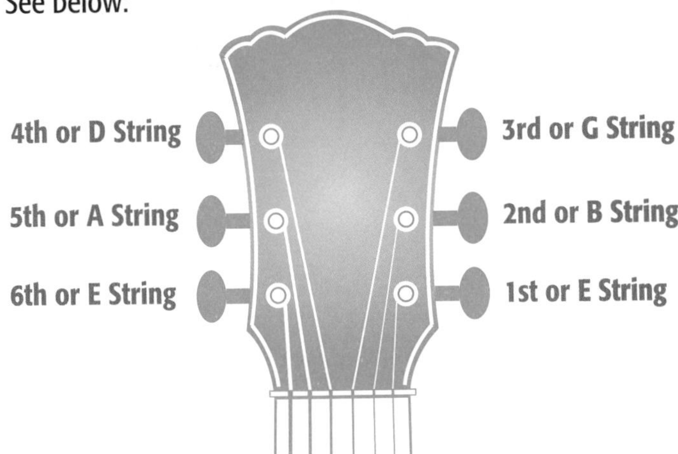

Turning the tuning key counter-clockwise (always from the point of view of the player) raises the pitch. Turning the tuning key clockwise lowers the pitch.

Some guitars have the six tuning pegs on the same side of the head. Make sure all six strings are wound the same way, from inside out.

Once your strings are stretched across the guitar properly, use the DVD for this book, and follow the directions to get the guitar in perfect tune.

IMPORTANT: Always remember that the thinnest, highest string—the one closest to the floor—is the first string. The thickest, lowest string—the one closest to the ceiling—is the sixth string. When guitarists say "the highest string," they mean the one highest in pitch, not the one highest in position.

How to Tune Your Guitar Without Using the DVD

The six strings of your guitar have the same pitches as the six notes shown on the piano in the following illustration:

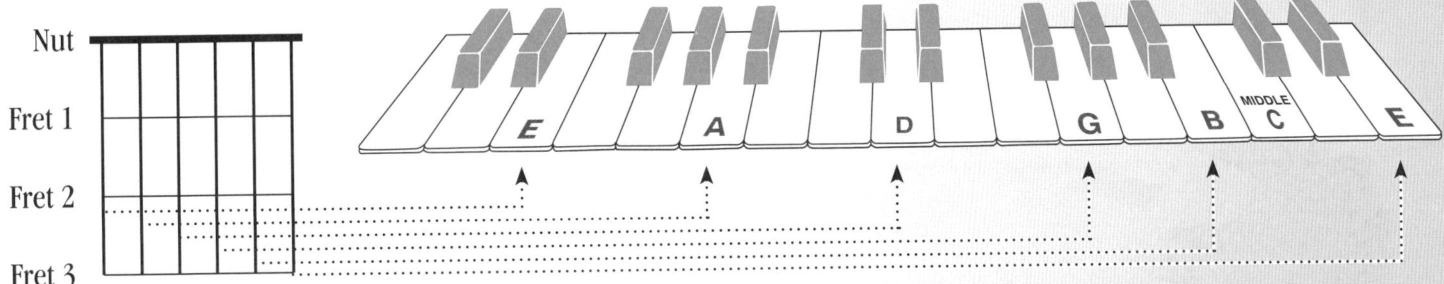

Tune the sixth string to E on the piano. If no piano is available, we recommend you buy a tuner from your local music store.

Press 5th fret of 6th string to get pitch of 5th string (A).

Press 5th fret of 5th string to get pitch of 4th string (D).

Press 5th fret of 4th string to get pitch of 3rd string (G).

Press 4th fret of 3rd string to get pitch of 2nd string (B).

Press 5th fret of 2nd string to get pitch of 1st string (E).

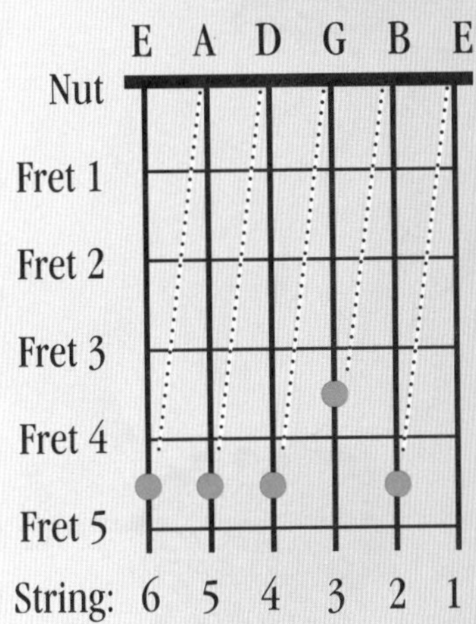

Holding Your Guitar

▲ *Holding the pick*

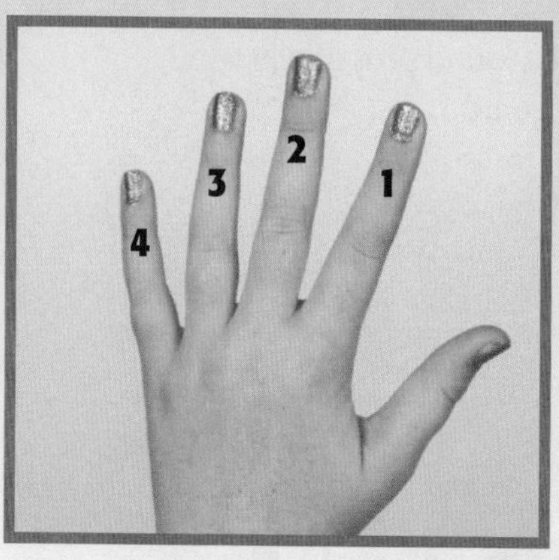

▲ *Numbering the left-hand fingers*

▲ *Standing, with strap*

▲ *Sitting on the floor with legs crossed*

▲ *Sitting*

▲ *Sitting with right leg crossed over left*

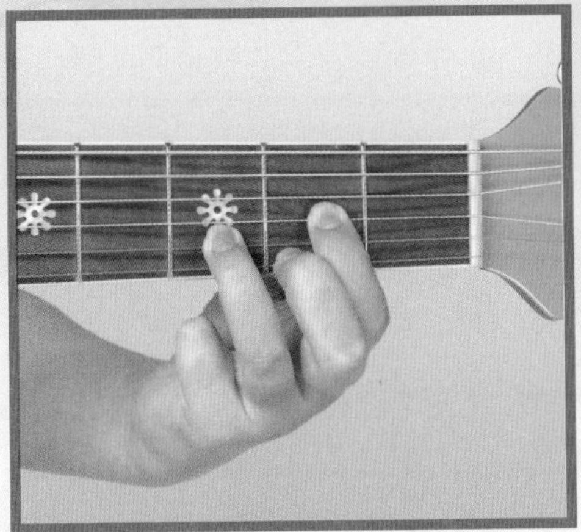

▲ *The left hand position from the front*

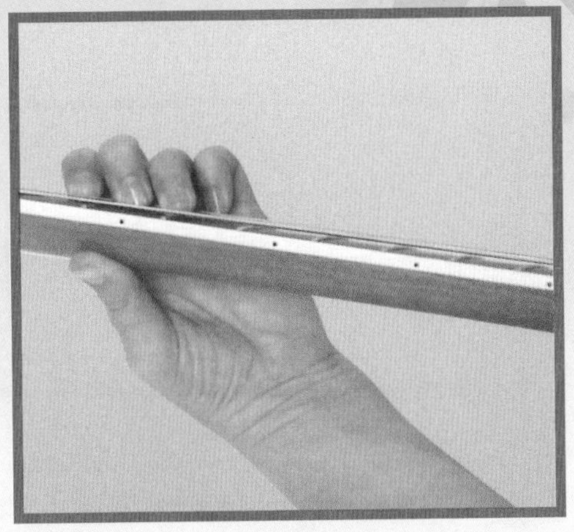

▲ *The left hand position from the back*

The Left-Hand Position

Note that the thumb falls about opposite the joint of the second and third fingers. Keep the elbow in and the fingers curved.

▲ *Position of the right arm*

▲ *Motion of the pick*

The Right-Hand Position

The pick is held firmly, but without squeezing it hard enough to cause tension in the right arm. The motion is a relaxed downward sweep of the wrist, not the entire arm.

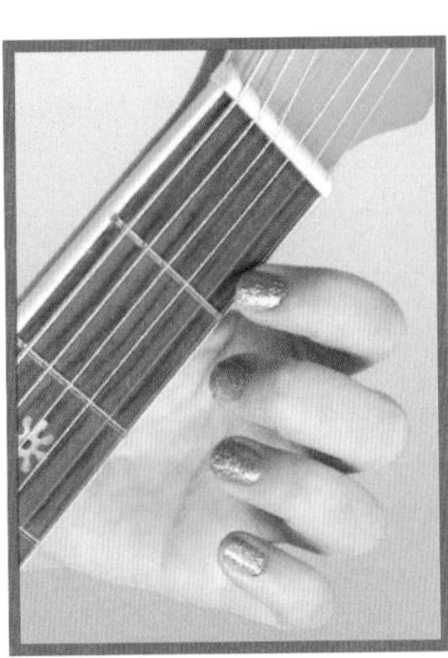

▲ *THIS*
Finger presses the string down near the fret without actually being on it.

▲ *NOT THIS*
Finger is too far from fret wire; tone is "buzzy" and indefinite.

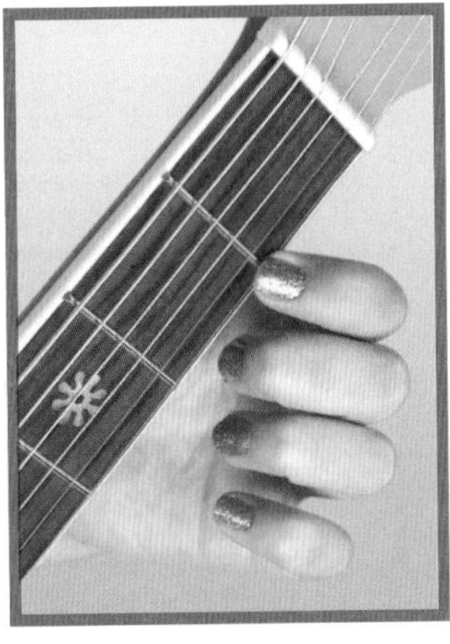

▲ *NOT THIS*
Finger is on top of fret wire; tone is muffled and unclear.

Placing the Finger on a String

When you place a left-hand finger on a string, make sure you press firmly and as close to the fret wire as you can without actually being right on it. This will ensure a clean, bright tone.

Getting Acquainted with Music

Notes

Musical sounds are indicated by symbols called NOTES. Their time value is determined by their color (white or black) and by stems and flags attached to the note.

The Staff (Stave)

The name and pitch of the notes are determined by the note's position on a graph made of five horizontal lines, and the spaces in between, called the staff. The notes are named after the first seven letters of the alphabet (A–G), repeated to embrace the entire range of musical sound.

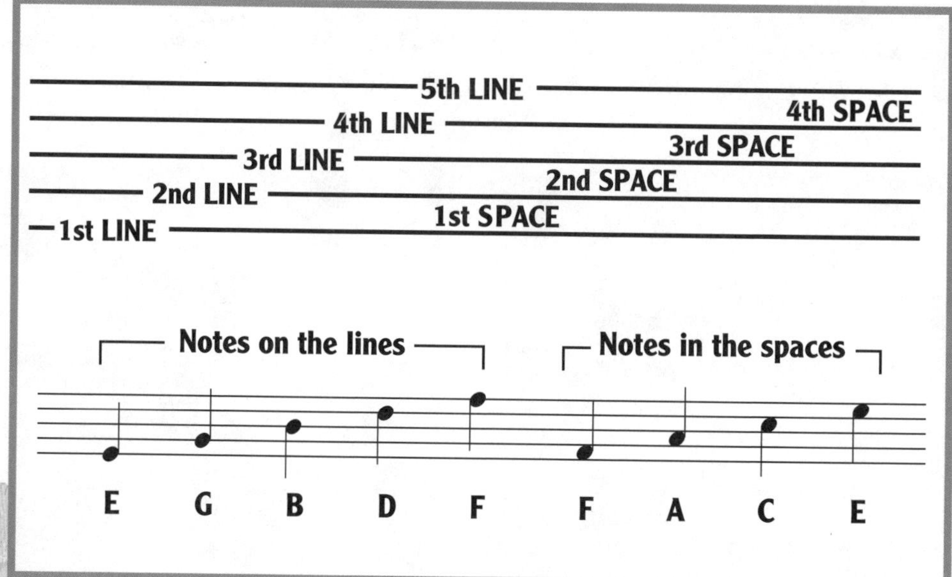

Measures (Bars) and Bar Lines

Music is also divided into equal parts, called MEASURES. One measure is divided from another by a BAR LINE.

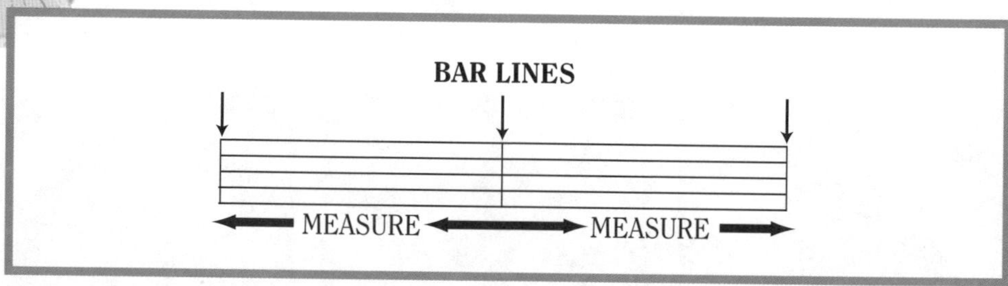

Clefs

During the evolution of music notation, the staff had from two to twenty lines, and symbols were invented to locate a reference line, or pitch, by which all other pitches were determined. These symbols were called clefs.

Music for the guitar is written in the G or treble clef. Originally the Gothic letter G was used on a four-line staff to establish the pitch of G.

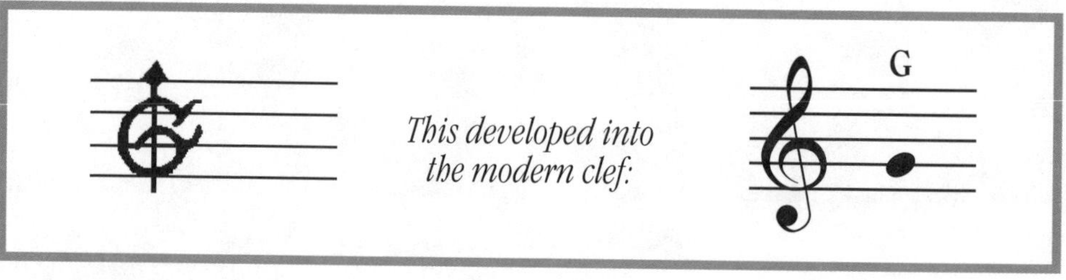

Getting Acquainted with Tablature

Tablature is a graphic method of showing how to play notes and chords on the guitar. It uses a six-line staff, each line representing one string of the guitar.

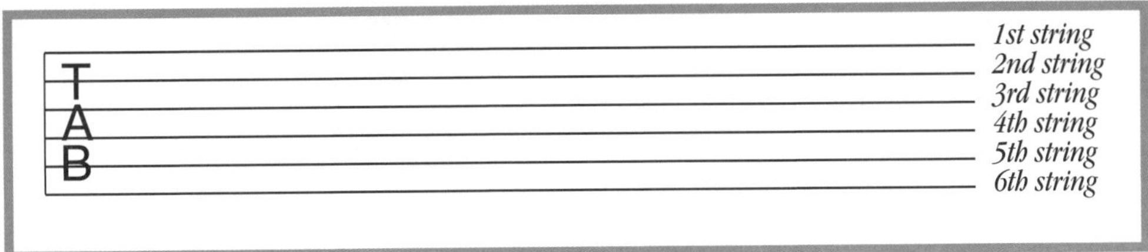

A number placed on a line means to play that fret on the corresponding string.

Play the 1st string, 3rd fret — 2nd string, 1st fret — 3rd string, open — 4th string, 2nd fret

Numbers placed one on top of the other are played simultaneously.

1st string open, 2nd string, 1st fret — 2nd, 3rd, and 4th strings open — 1st string, 1st fret + three open strings — A five-note C chord

Chord Diagrams

Chord diagrams are used to indicate fingering for chords. The example to the right means to place your first finger on the first fret, second string and second finger on the second fret, fourth string. Then strum the first four strings only. The x's on the fifth and sixth strings indicate not to play these.

To make it as clear as possible, all the material in this book appears both in traditional music and in tablature. Chord diagrams are included where appropriate.

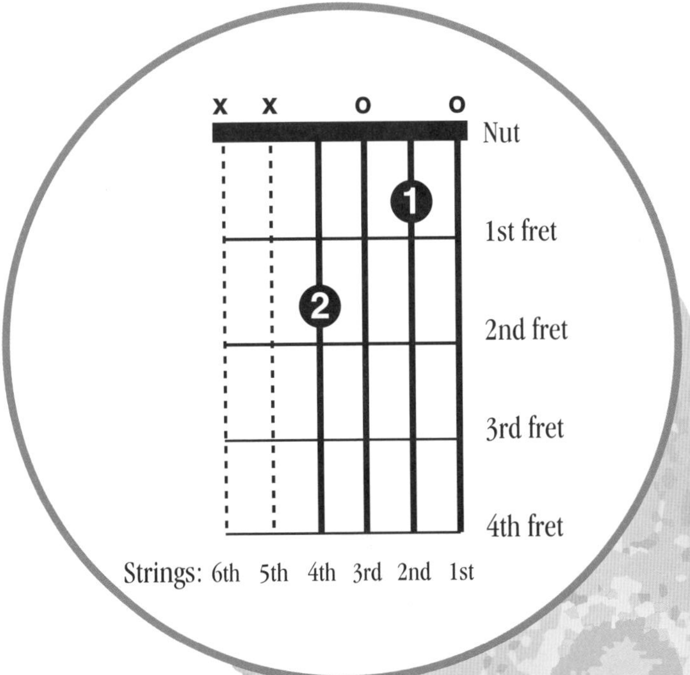

Notes on the First String E

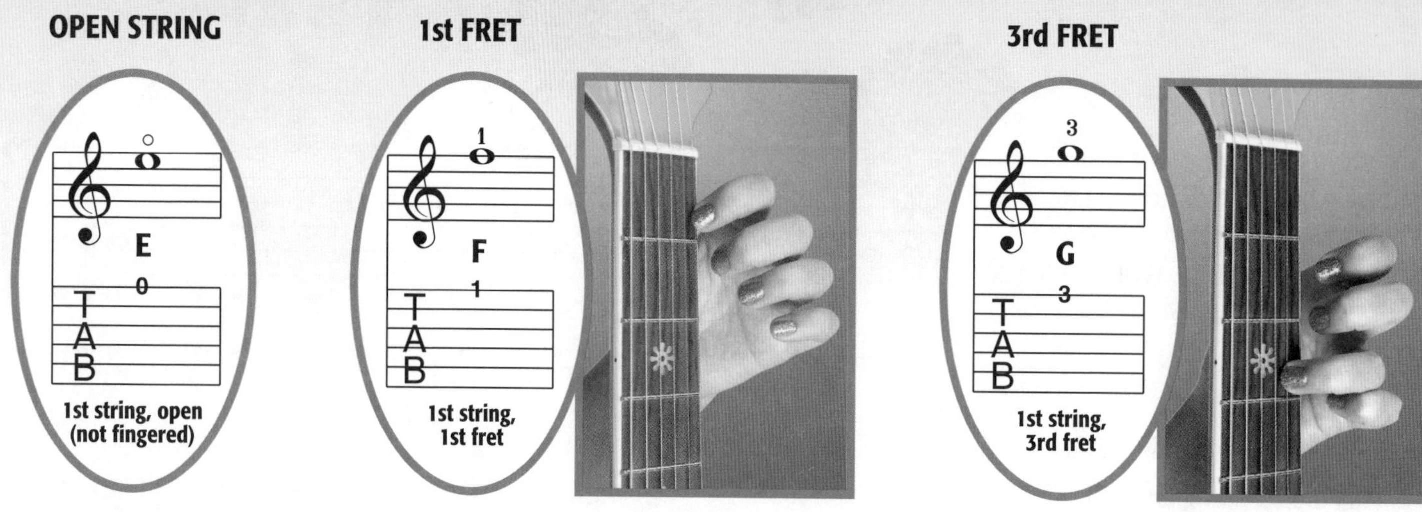

Playing the first string open (the note E):

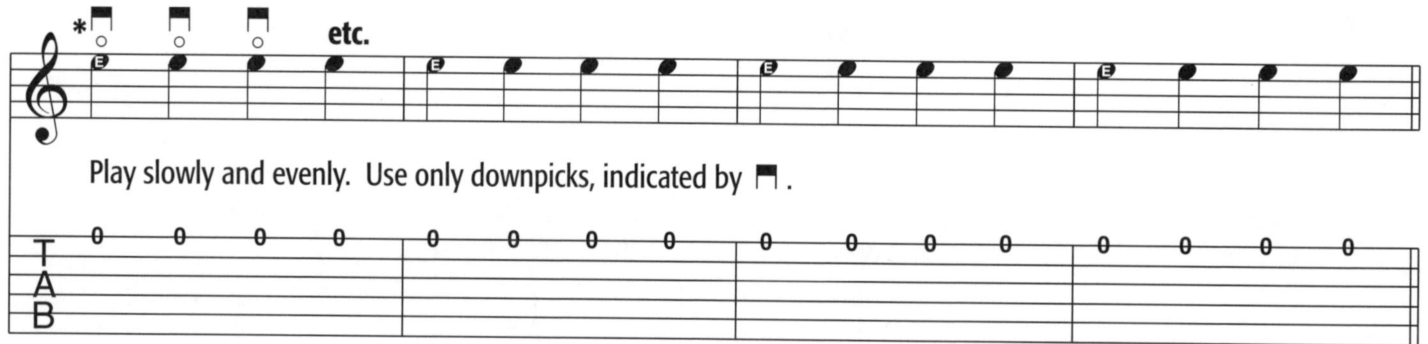

Combining the fingered notes F and G with the open string E:

*o means OPEN STRING

Sophia's Smile

Left-hand fingers: When playing from the first to the third fret, keep the first finger down. Only the G will sound, but when you go back to the F, your finger will already be in place, making the transition sound smoother.

A double bar line marks the end of a piece.

The Ballad of Nicole

Left-hand fingers: Place as close to the fret wires as possible without actually touching them.

How to Count Time
4 Kinds of Notes:

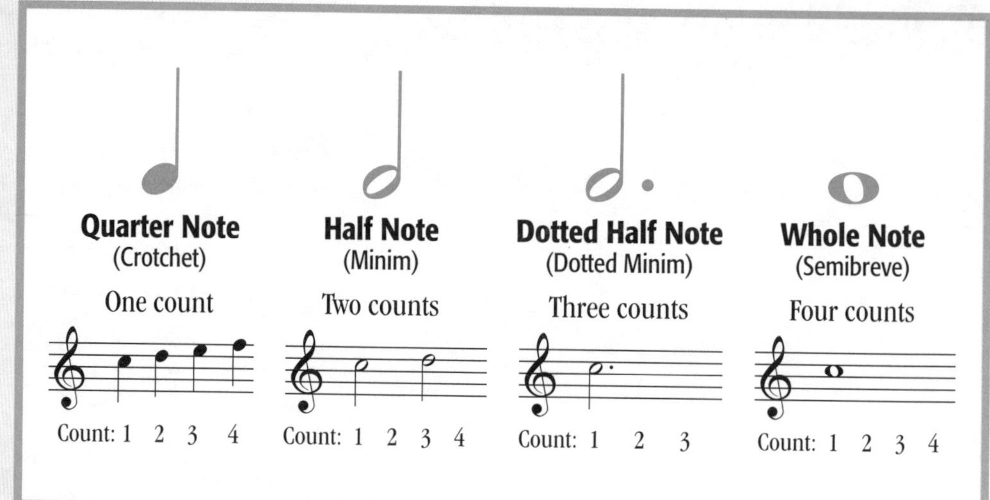

Time Signatures

Each piece of music has two numbers at its beginning called a time signature. These numbers tell us how to count time for that particular piece.

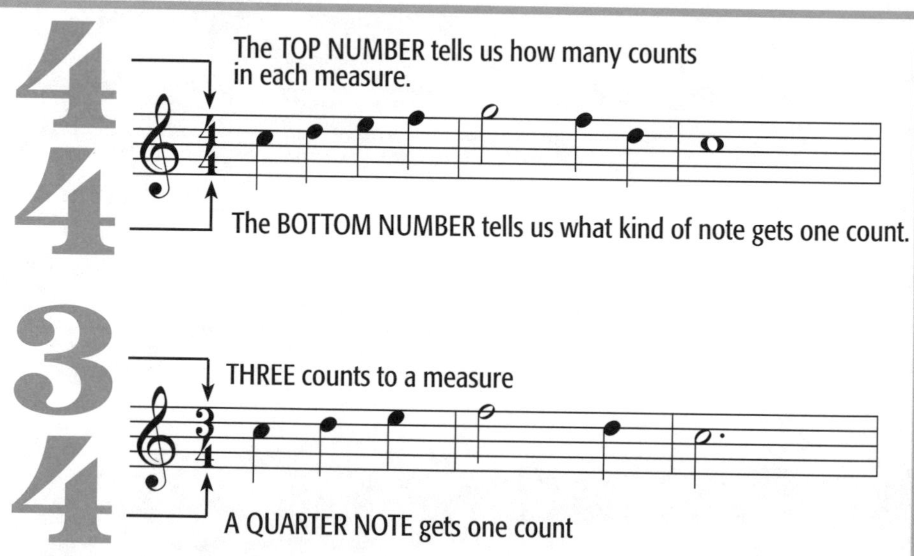

Important:

Fill in the missing time signatures of the songs already learned. Even though tablature players do not read standard music notation, it is still important to become familiar with the concept of time signatures.

Sarah McLachlan

Canadian Sarah McLachlan is probably best known as the organizer and headliner of the Lilith Fair. The idea came from her frustration about lack of radio airplay and the desire to perform with women she admired. She recorded her first album, "Touch," at the age of 19.

Photo: Jeffrey Mayer/Star File

Playing Different Kinds of Notes and Time Signatures

Half Notes (two counts)

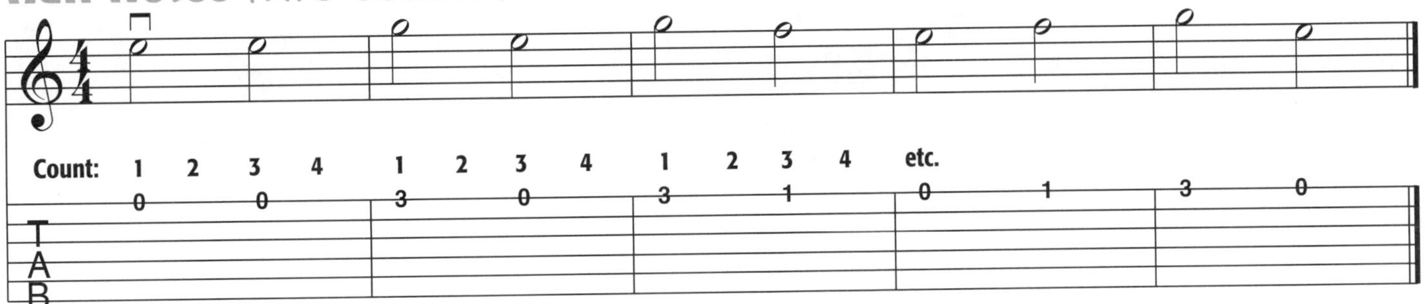

Dotted Half Notes (three counts)

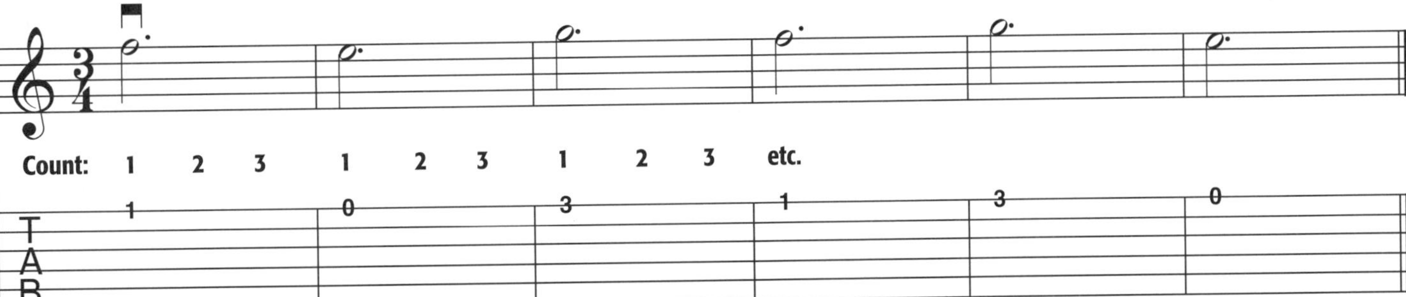

Whole Notes (four counts)

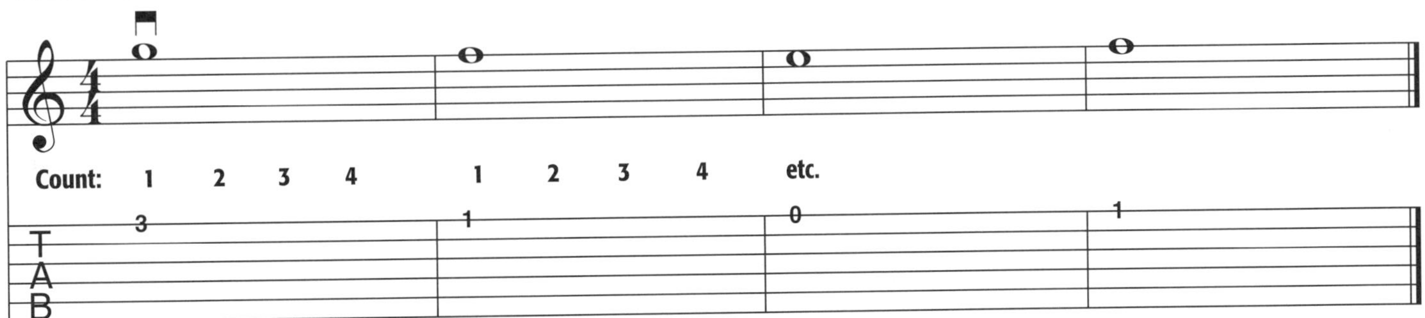

Mixed Notes (review)

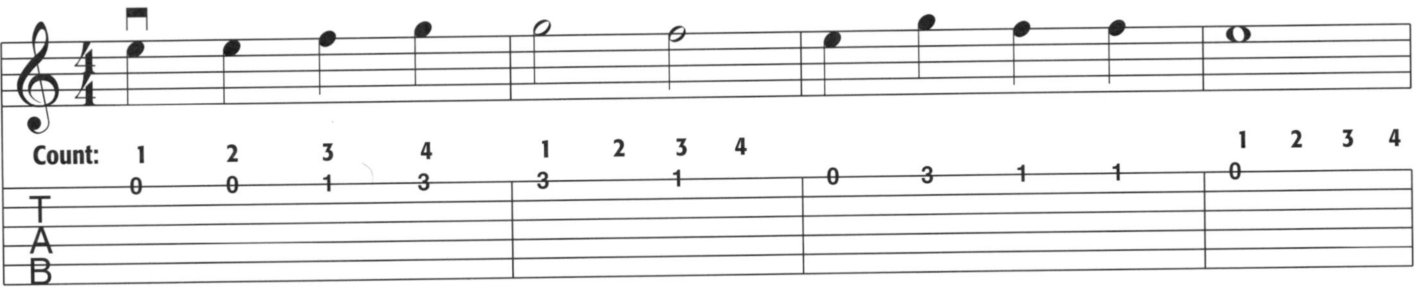

Notes on the Second String B

OPEN STRING

B

T 0
A
B

2nd string, open

1st FRET

1

C

T 1
A
B

2nd string, 1st fret

3rd FRET

3

D

T 3
A
B

2nd string, 3rd fret

B				C				D				B			
0	0	0	0	1	1	1	1	3	3	3	3	0	0	0	0

B		C		D										
0	0	1	1	3	3	1	1	0	0	1	3	1	3	0

"My brother played keyboards and his best friend played drums. They wanted to start a band and they needed a guitarist. So, my mom thought the best thing would be for me to play the guitar and off we went to the music store. After a few music lessons and lots of jam sessions in the garage, we started playing at fairs and festivals where having a female guitarist in the band was indeed something to see." —Dana

Beautiful Brown Eyes

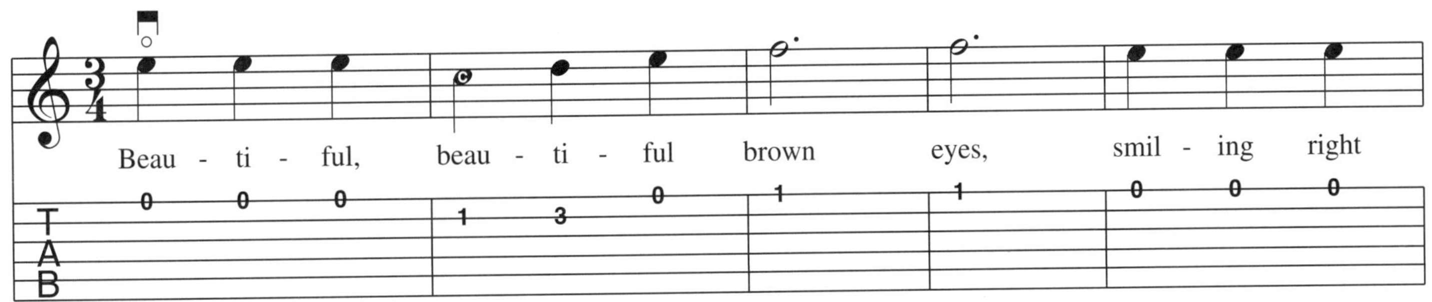

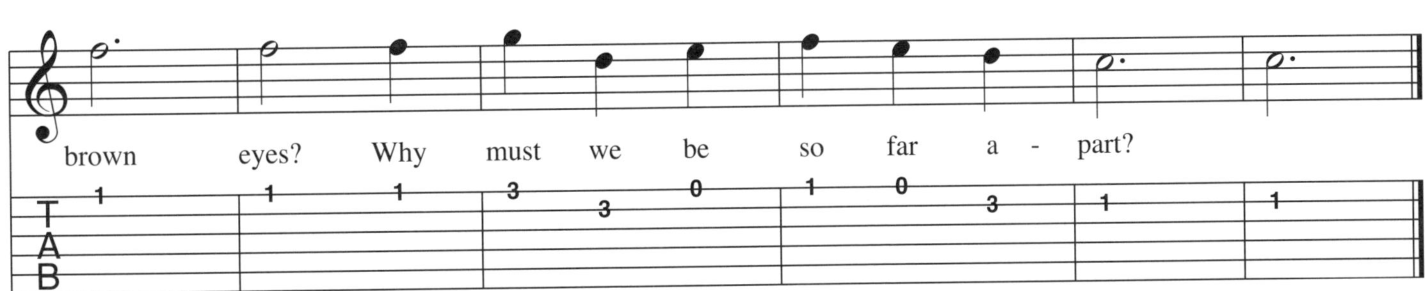

Daisy Rock

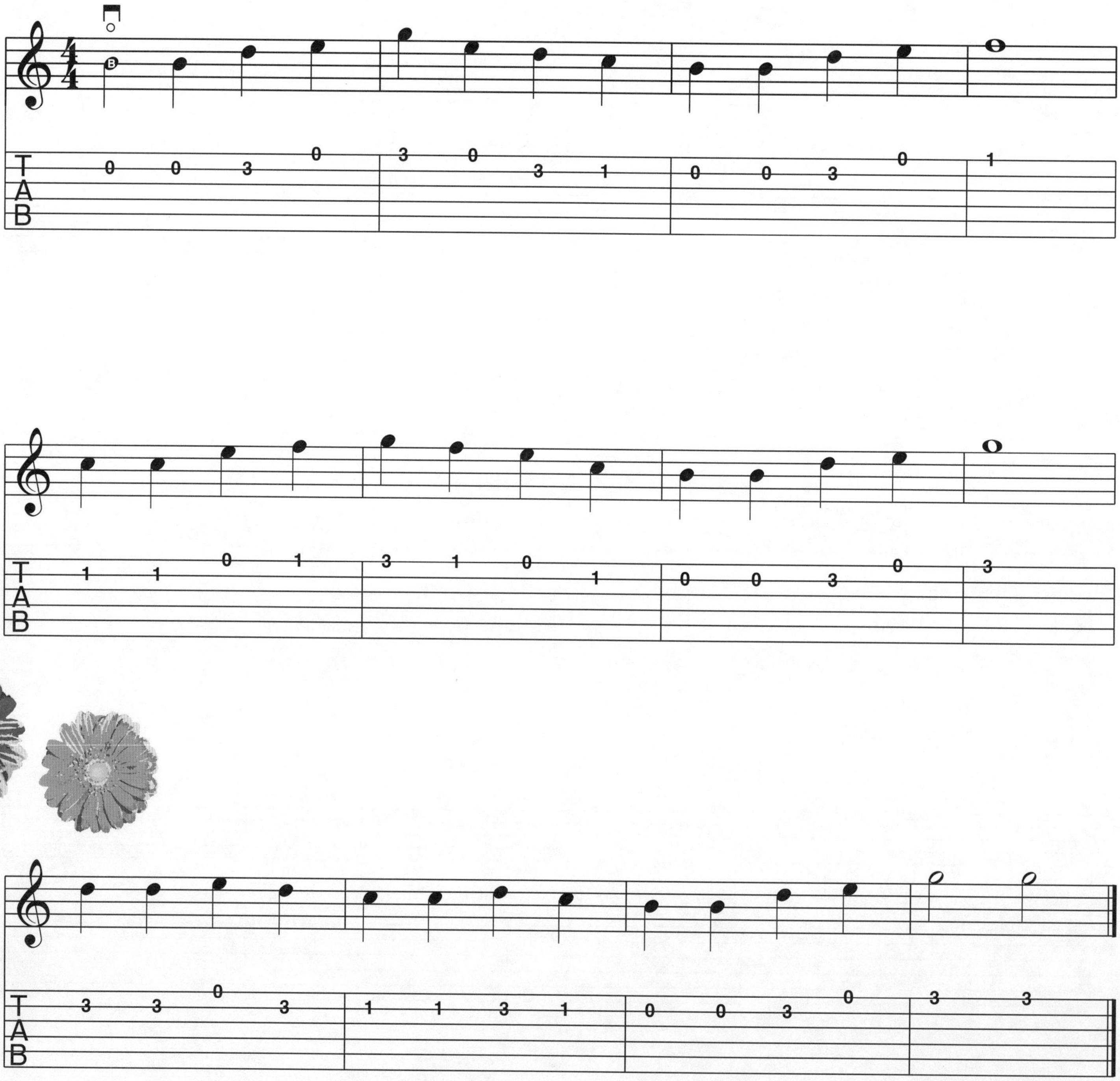

Jingle Bells

J. Pierpont

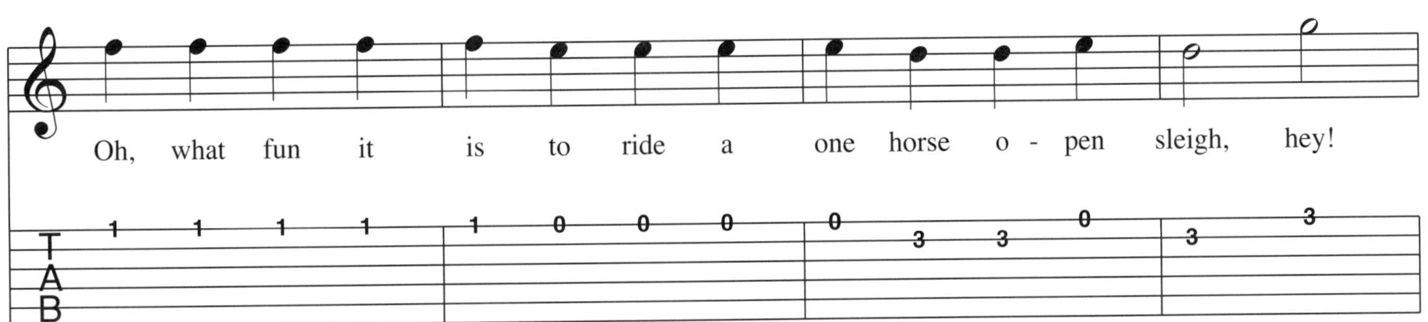

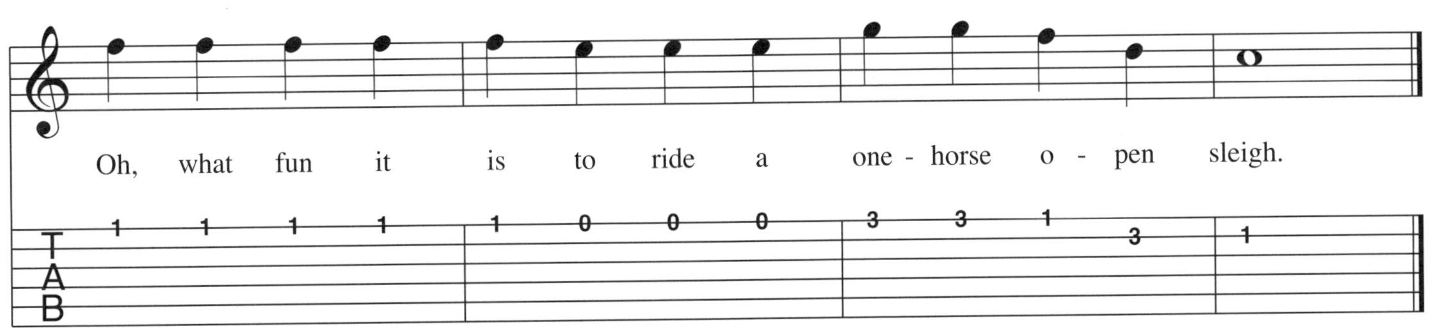

Notes on the Third String G

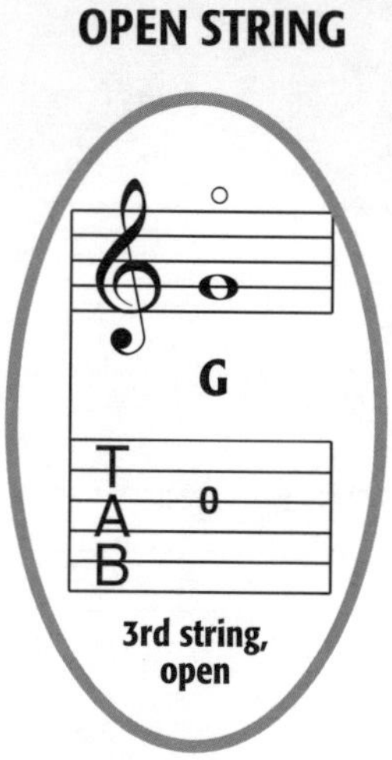
OPEN STRING
G
TAB
0
3rd string, open

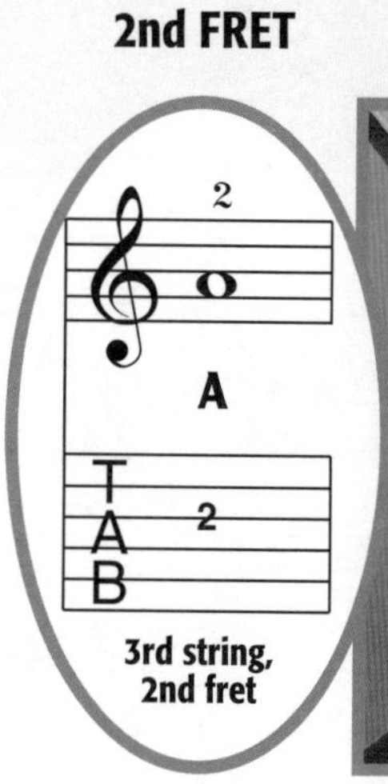
2nd FRET
2
A
TAB
2
3rd string, 2nd fret

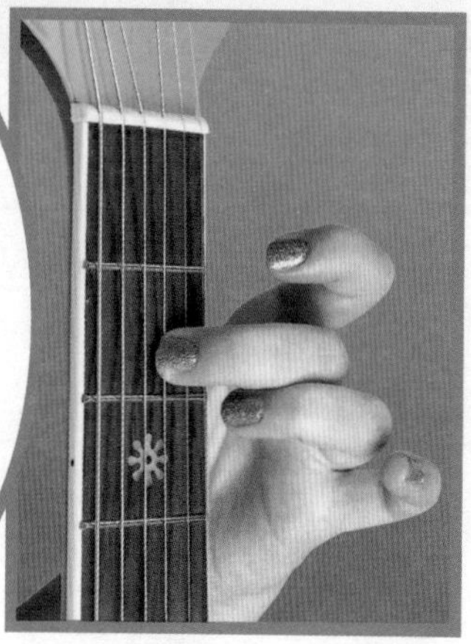

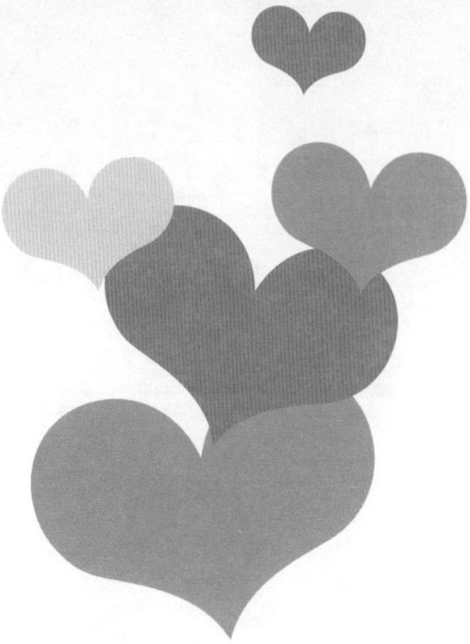

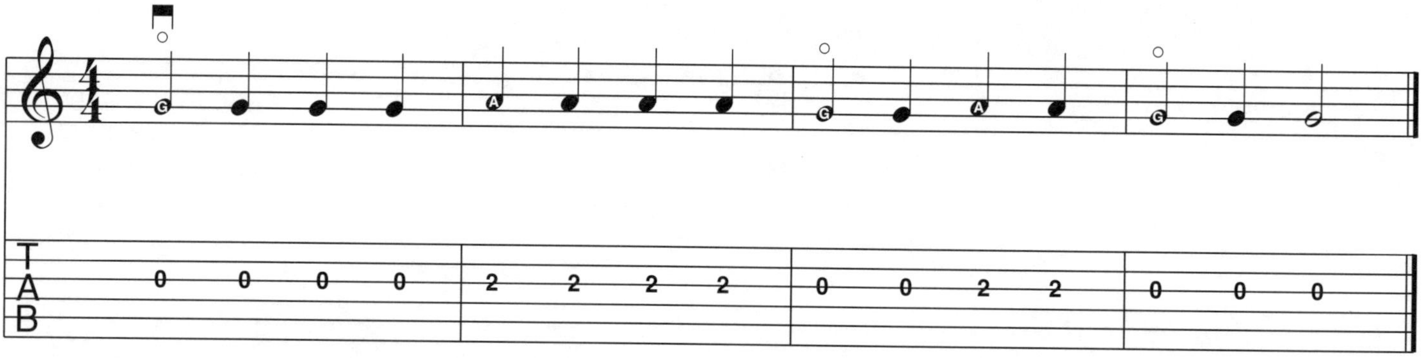

Au Clair de la Lune

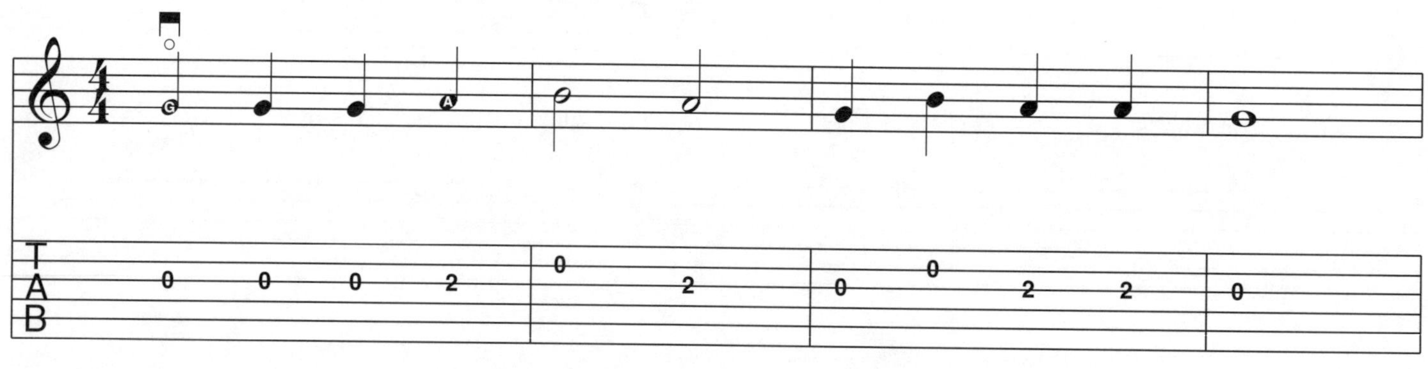

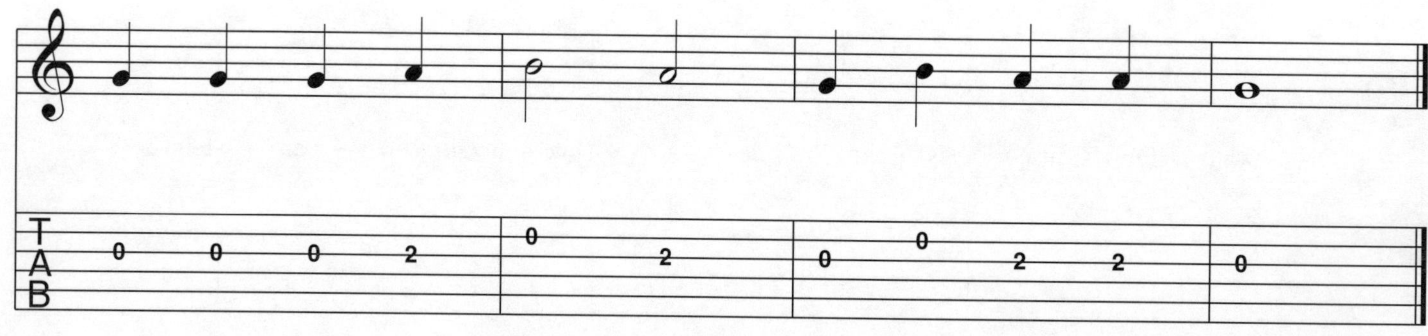

Three-String Rock

Aura Lee

Elvis Presley recorded this folk song in a modern version called "Love Me Tender."

*The double dots on the inside of the double bars indicate that everything between the double bars must be REPEATED.

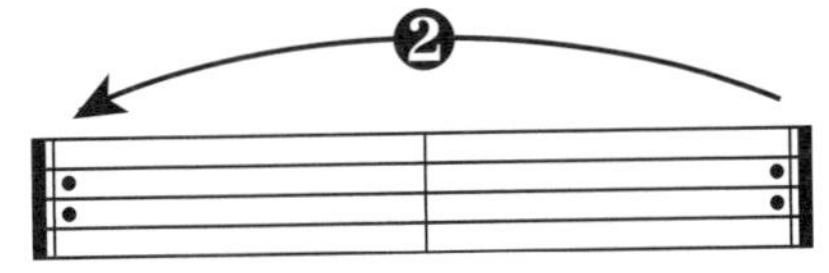

Largo from the New World Symphony
Dvořák

Introducing Chords

A CHORD is a combination of two or more harmonious notes. All notes except the whole note have a stem going up or down.

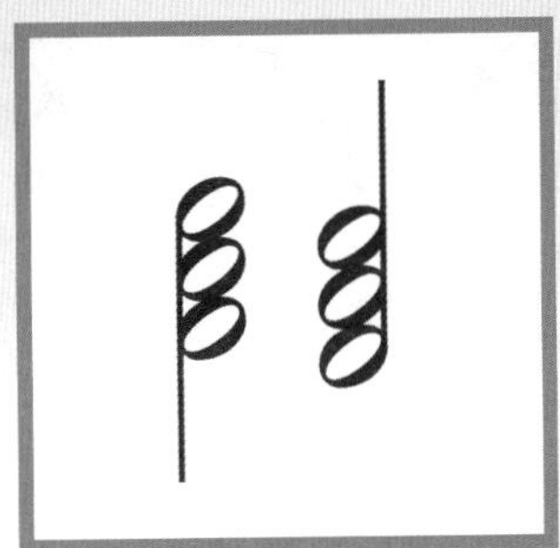

When notes are to be struck together as a CHORD, they are connected by the same stem.

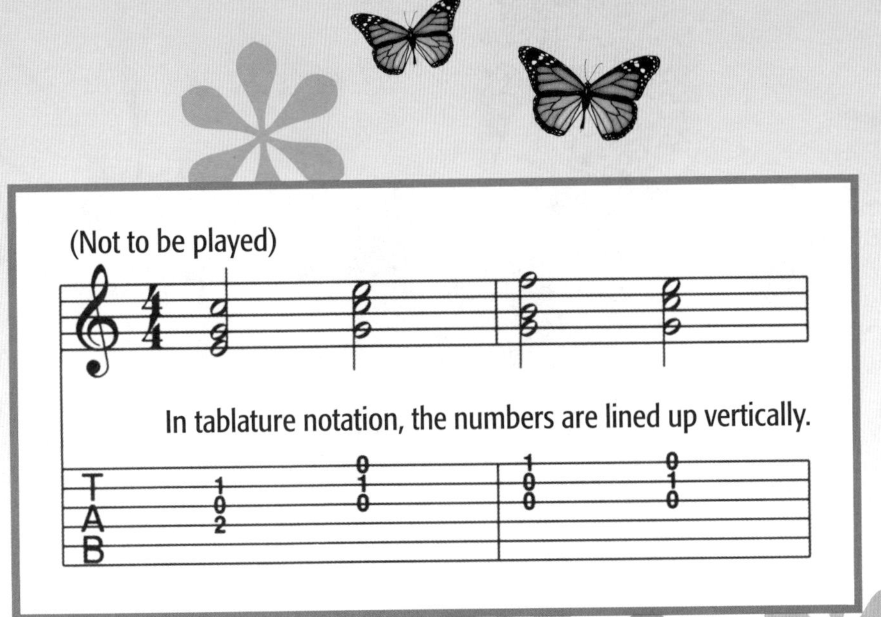

Meet the Chords

Two-note chords on the open B and E strings.

Two-note chords on the open G and B strings.

Three-note chords on the open G, B and E strings.

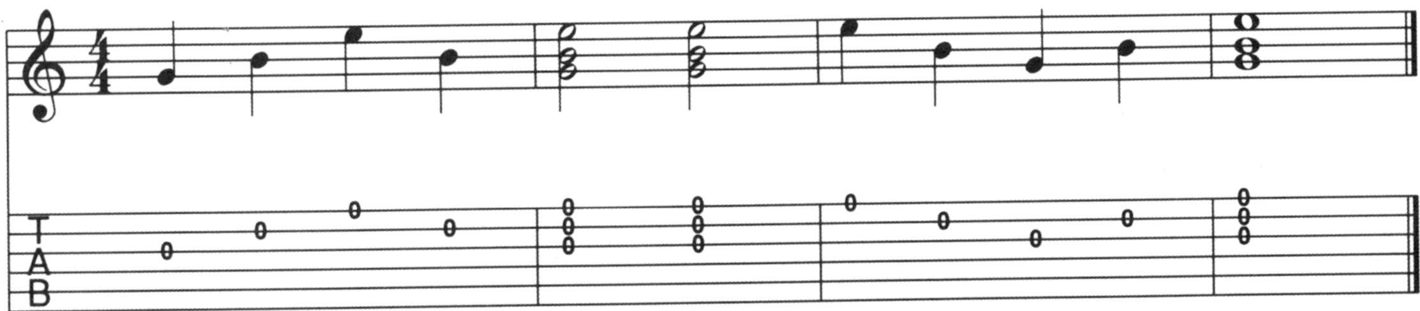

The Three-String C Chord

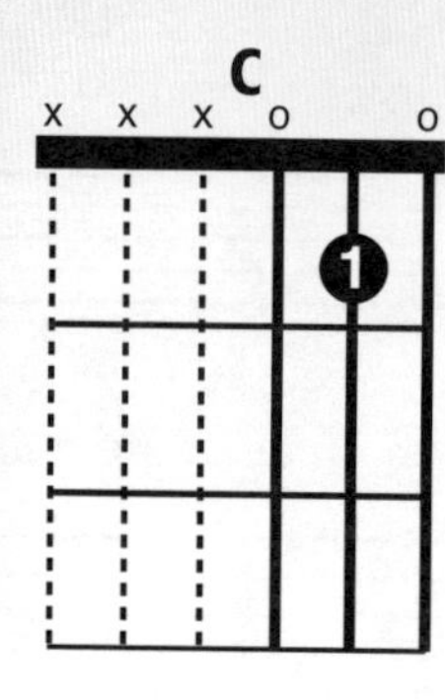

Do not play dashed strings.

The chords you played on page 23 use only combinations of open strings. The next chord is called the C chord. It uses one finger plus the 1st and 3rd open strings.

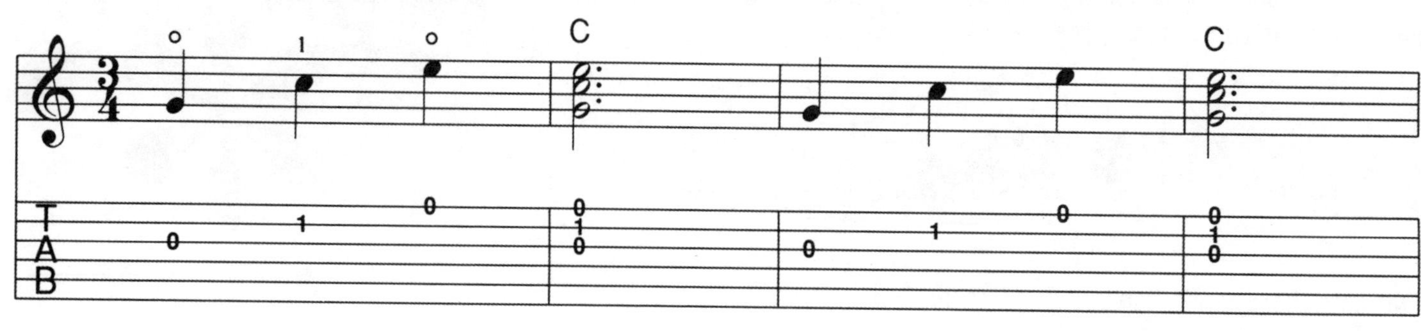

Ode to Joy from the 9th Symphony

Beethoven

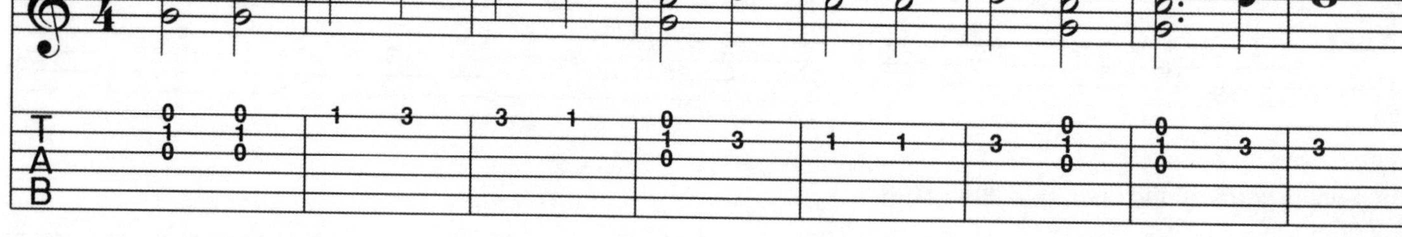

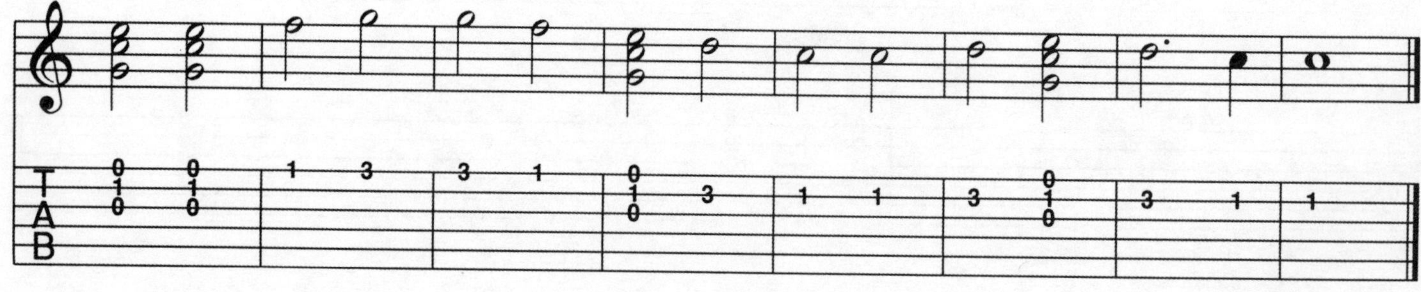

Introducing the Quarter Rest (Crotchet Rest)

This strange-looking rest is used in music notation to mean one beat of silence. First play the exercise, then try the song.

For a cleaner effect when an open-string note is followed by a rest, you may stop the sound of the strings by touching them lightly with the "heel" of the right hand.

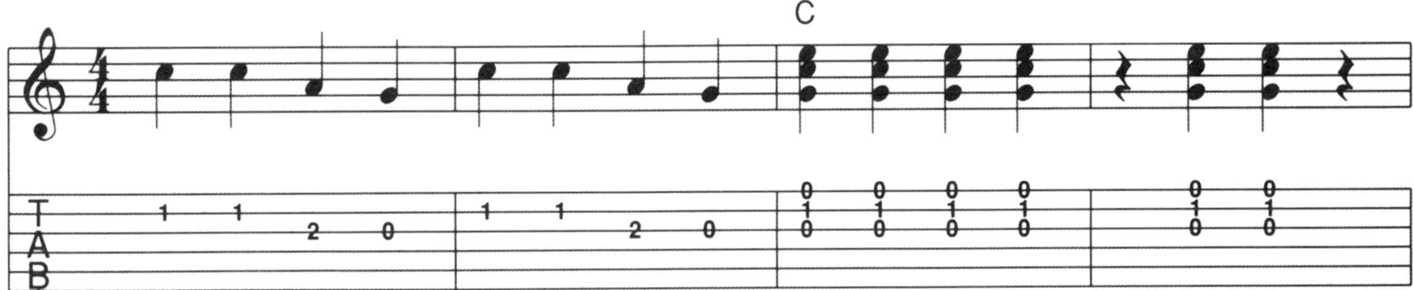

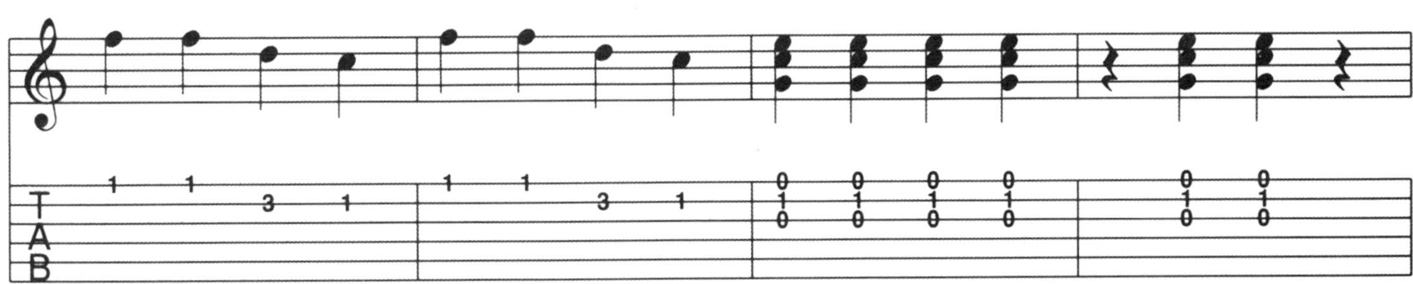

The Three-String G7 Chord

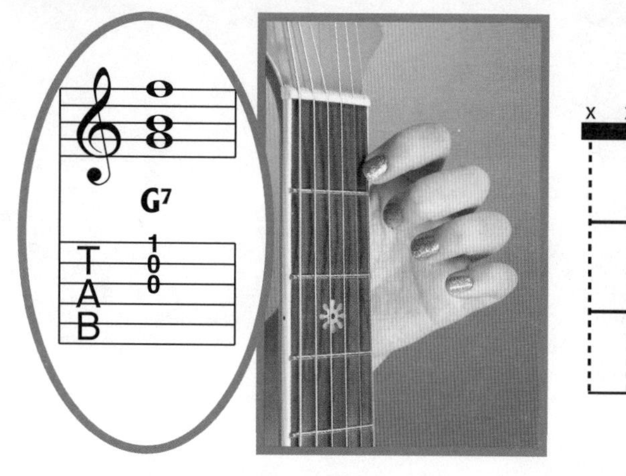

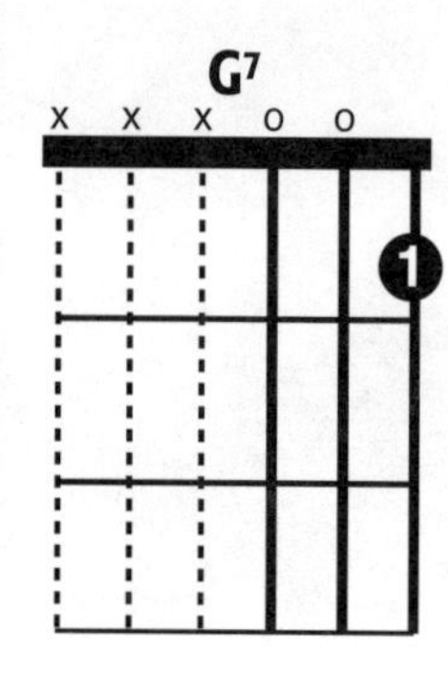

Summer camp was no fun except for counselor Trudy playing guitar every night by the fire. Soon Trudy had taught us basic chords and we were writing songs about our crushes on the boys in camp. We would sing so loud and laugh so hard that the boys eventually wandered over to see what all the commotion was about. —Amber

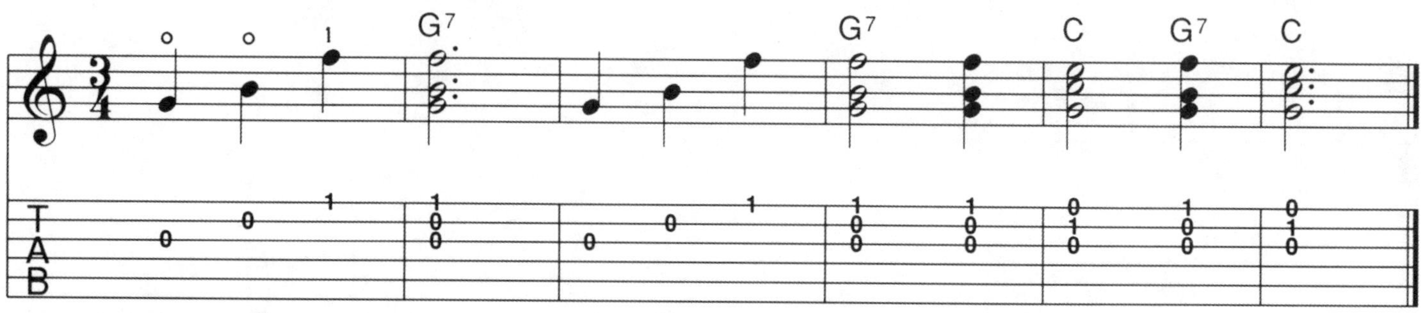

Down in the Valley

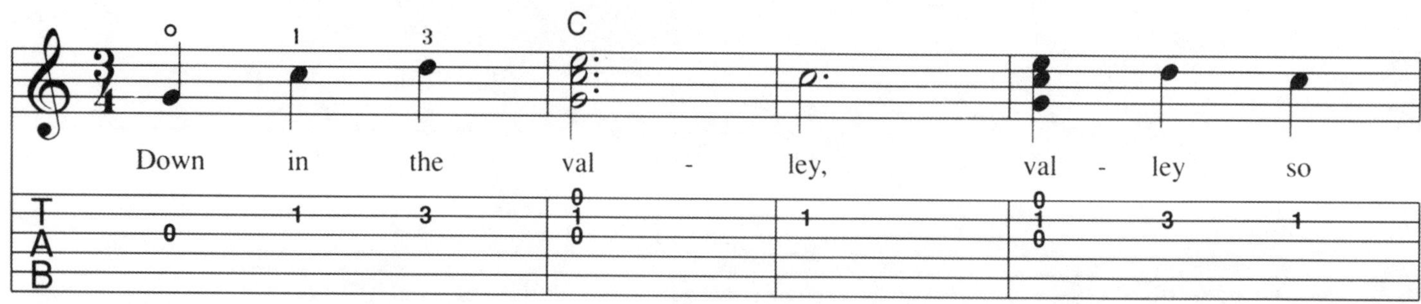

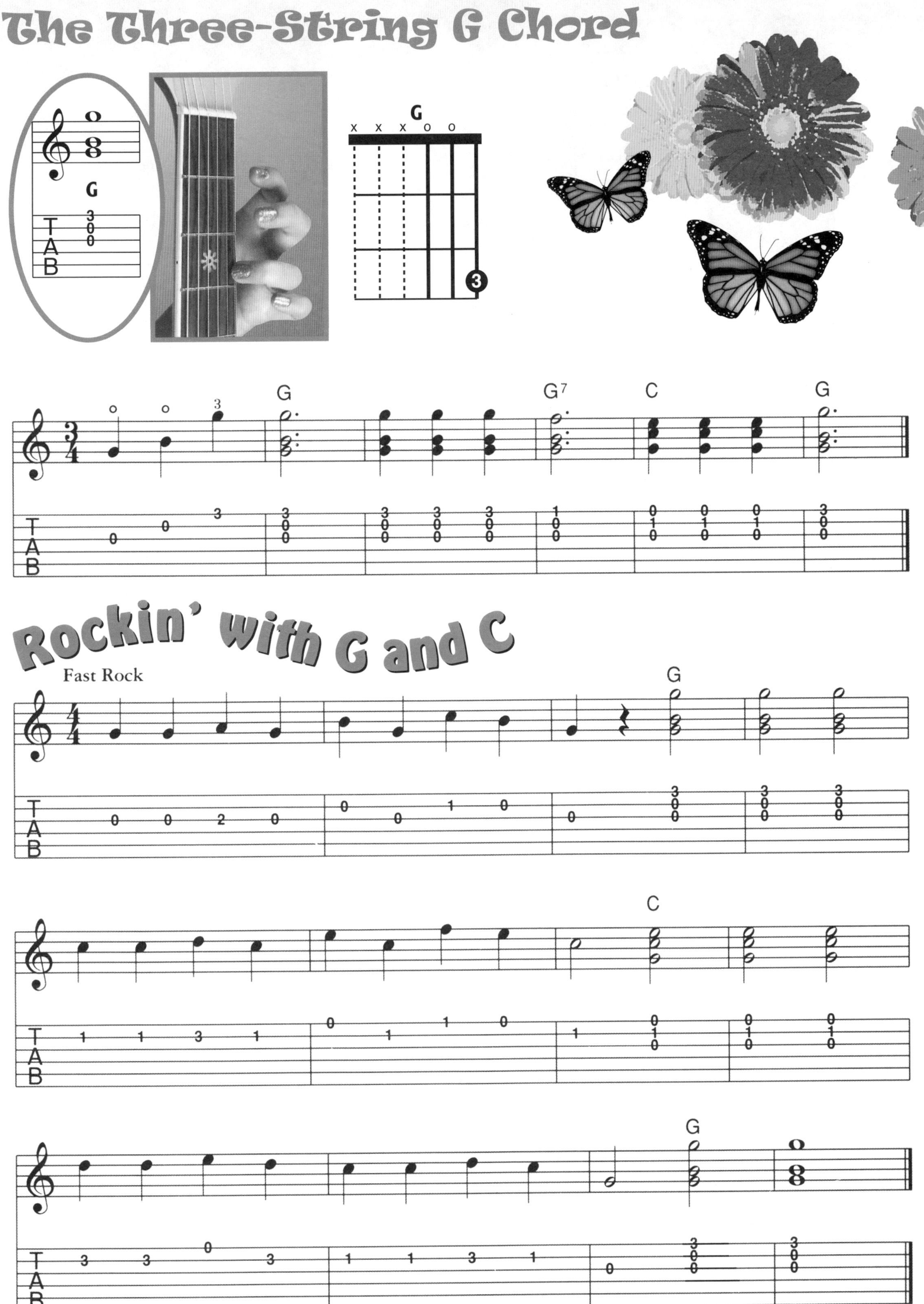
The Three-String G Chord
G
T
A
B
G
x x x o o
3
G
G7
C
G
Rockin' with G and C
Fast Rock
G
C
G

Notes on the Fourth String D

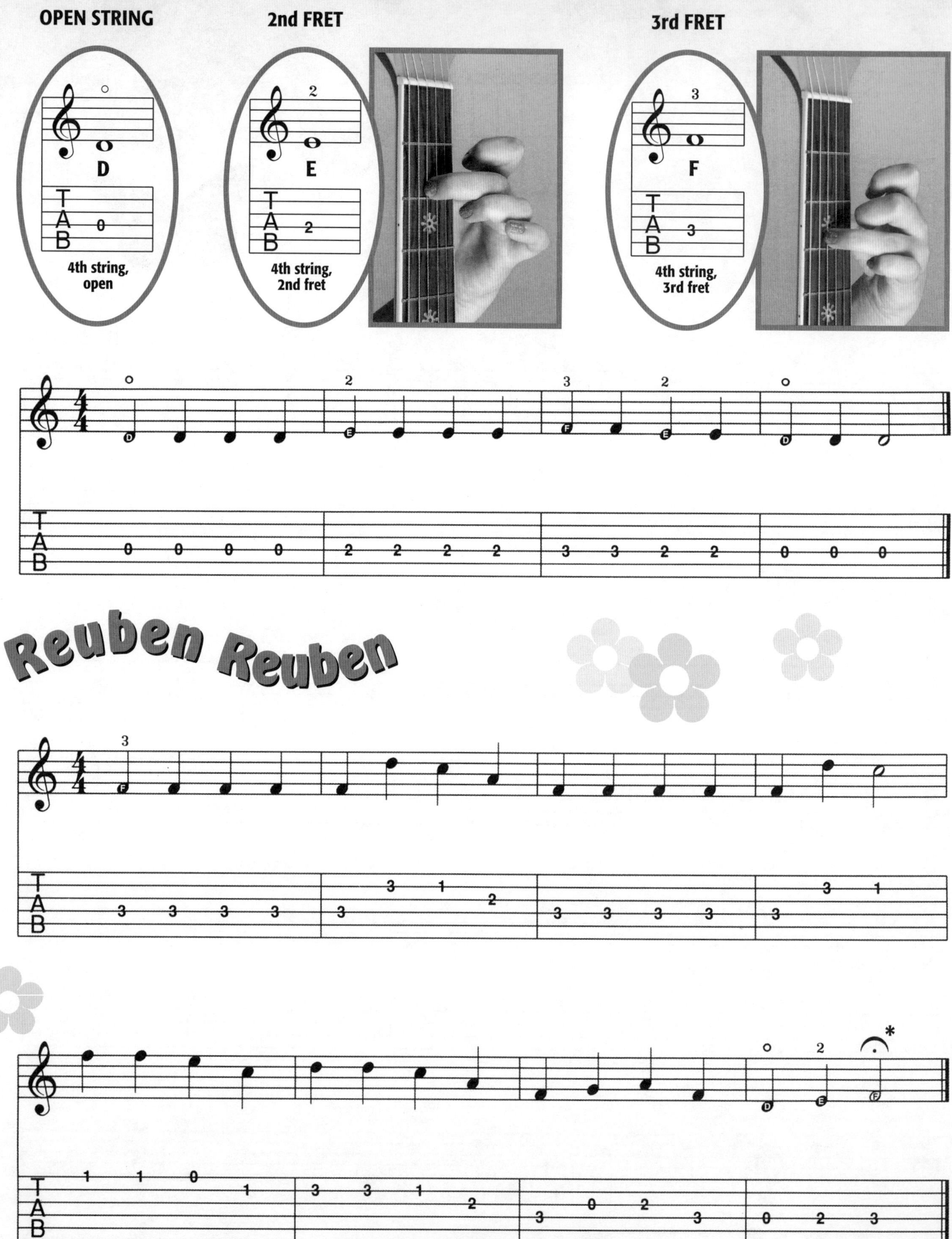

* HOLD SIGN (Fermata or Pause Sign): This sign indicates that the time value of the note is lengthened at the discretion of the player (approximately 1½ times).

Old MacDonald Had a Farm

Merry-Go-Round

C means "common time" (the same as $\frac{4}{4}$ time)

Daisy Bell (A Bicycle Built for Two)

Not all guitar solos are played using only one form of the 3-note chords already learned. Some songs use various combinations of 2- and 3-note chords.

Music continues on next page.

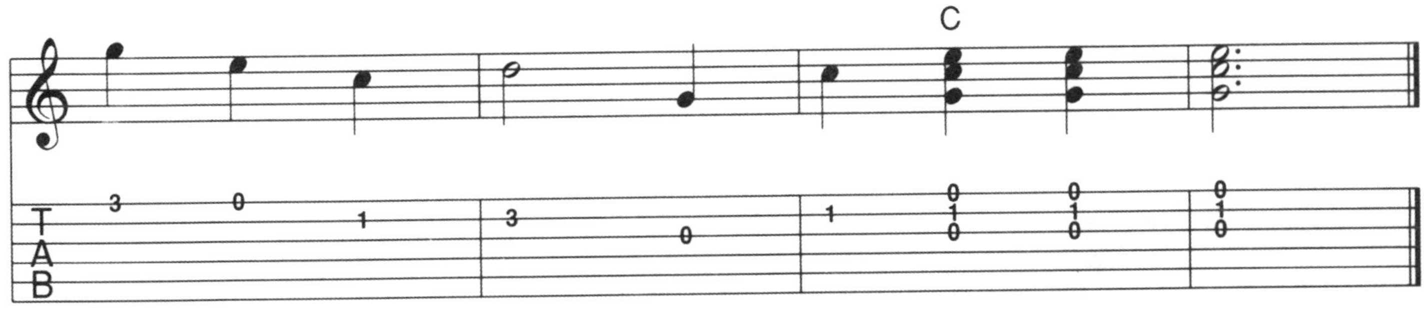

"My best friend in high school was Barbara Haughey. I met her in Algebra class in the 9th grade. I was sitting in the back of class with my other friend Nardo (a girl) and we were practicing Dancing Queen by Abba for the local gong show. Barbara got so mad at us for not studying, she threw her book at us and hit me in the head! After we won the contest, Barbara told me in no uncertain terms that I didn't have a very good singing voice, but she would help me by teaching me how to play acoustic guitar. She taught me "Rocky Raccoon" and that's how we became best friends." —Tish

Annette Conlon from Eden Automatic

The Four-String G & G7 Chords

The three-note G and G7 chords you have learned can be expanded to fuller and richer sounding four-note chords simply by adding the open 4th string.

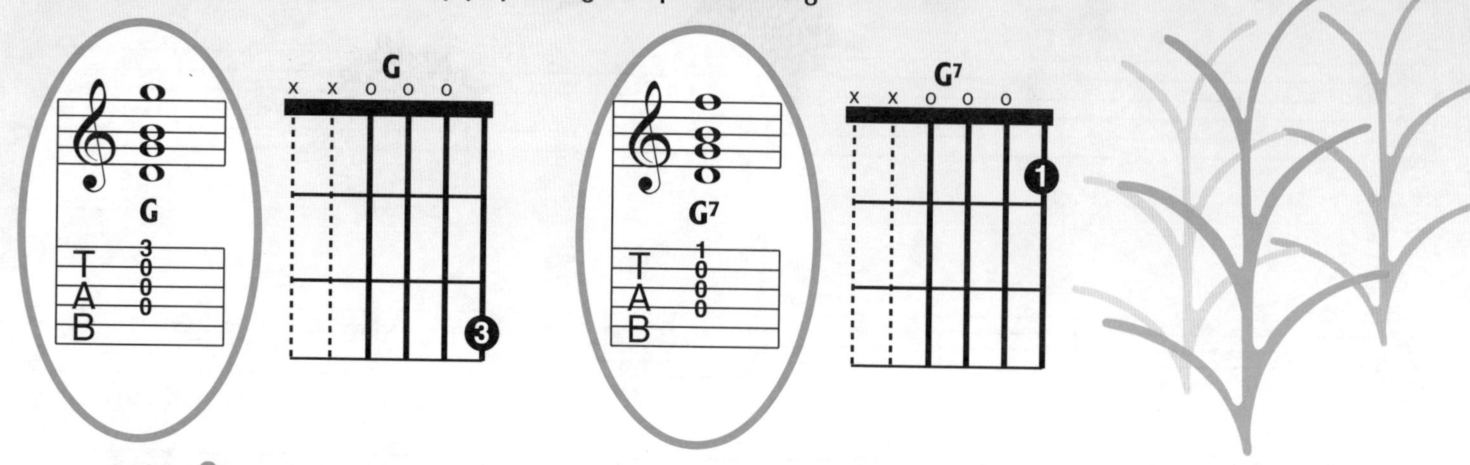

Rockin' the Chimes

The next song uses the four-note G and G7 chords. Sometimes the notes are played one at a time (called an arpeggio) instead of being played together (as a chord).

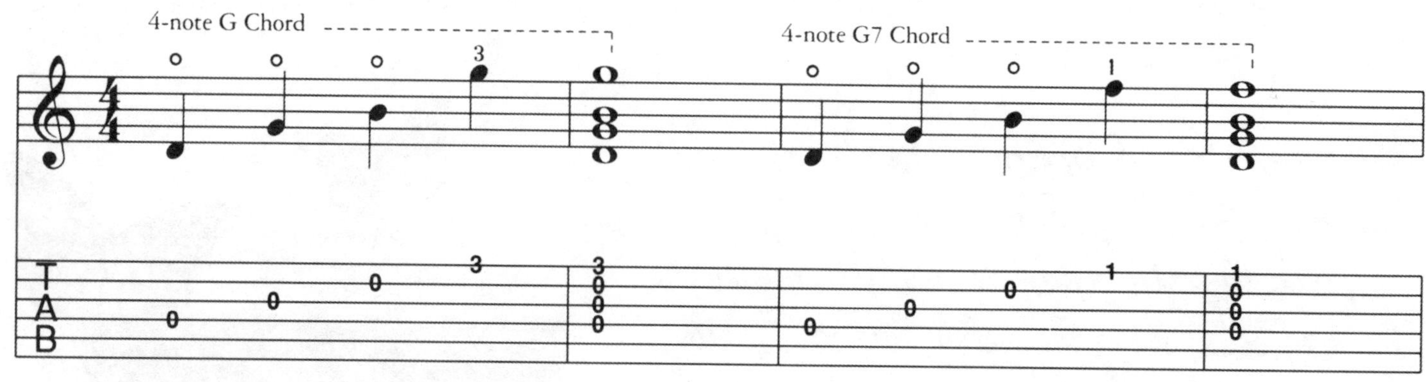

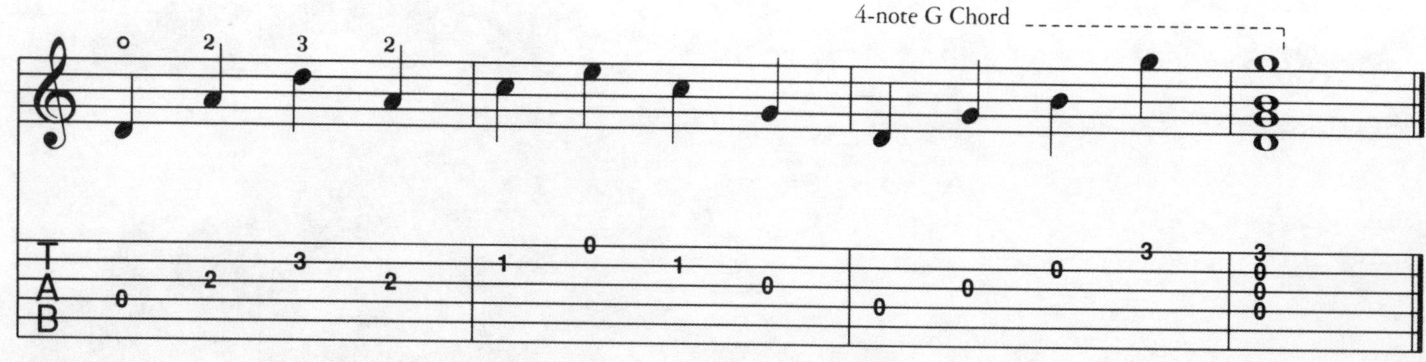

Laughing Hannah

Notes on the Fifth String A

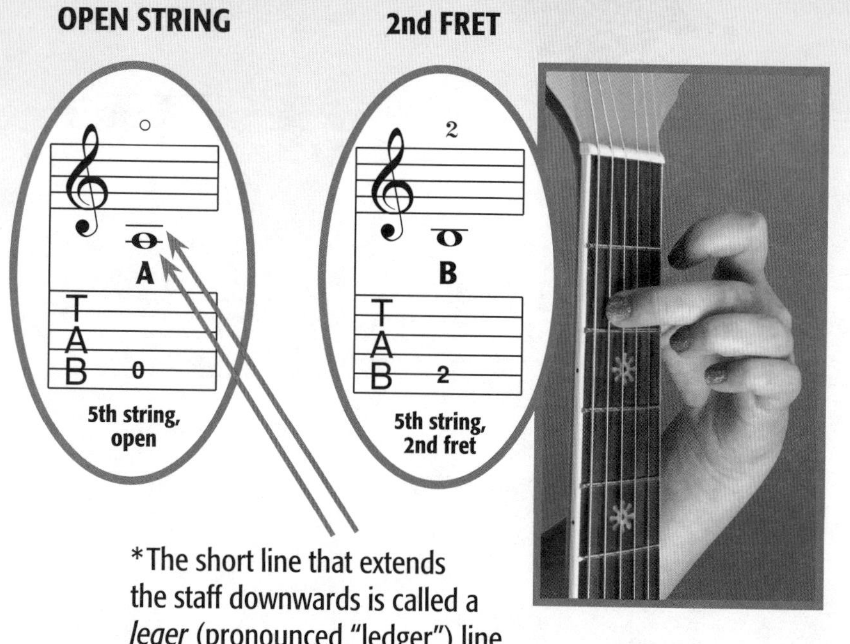

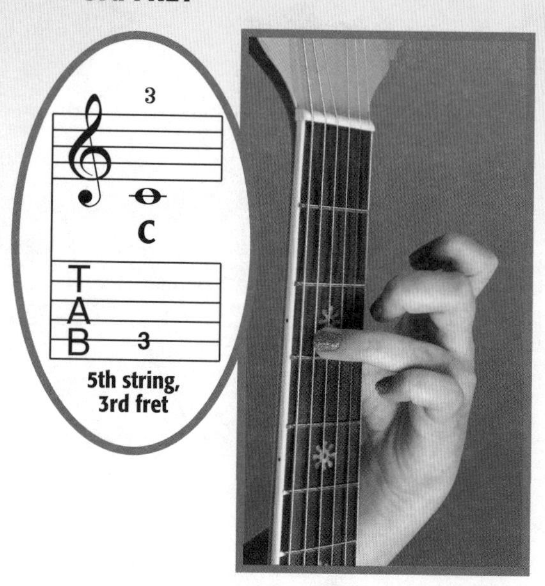

*The short line that extends the staff downwards is called a *leger* (pronounced "ledger") line.

Jewel

Jewel Kilcher grew up in a musical household in Anchorage, Alaska. She performed with her parents throughout her childhood. Her debut album, "Pieces of You," was released in 1995. This collection of heartfelt folk songs became a huge success. Her plaintive fingerstyle playing creates a style that is timeless.

Photo: Todd Kaplan/Star File

Rock On!

T
A
B
0 0 2 0
3 0
2 2 2 2
0 3
0 0 2 0
3 0

T
A
B
0 0
0
0 0 2 0
3 0
2 2 2 2
0 3
0 0 2 0
3 0
0 0
0
2 2 0 2
0 2

T
A
B
0 0 3 0
3 0
0 0 2 0
3 0
0 0
0

Introducing High A

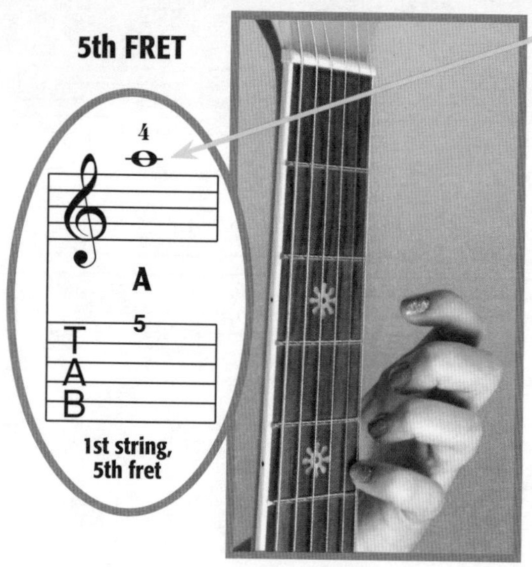

Leger lines can also extend the staff upwards.

Notice that high A is played on the 5th fret, but the 4th finger is used. Slide your hand up the fret-board so the 4th finger can reach the 5th fret.

Pink Fuzzy Slippers

Incomplete Measures

Not every piece of music begins on the first beat. Music sometimes begins with an incomplete measure, called the UPBEAT or PICKUP. If the upbeat is one beat, the last measure will sometimes have only three beats in $\frac{4}{4}$, or two beats in $\frac{3}{4}$ to make up for the extra beat at the beginning.

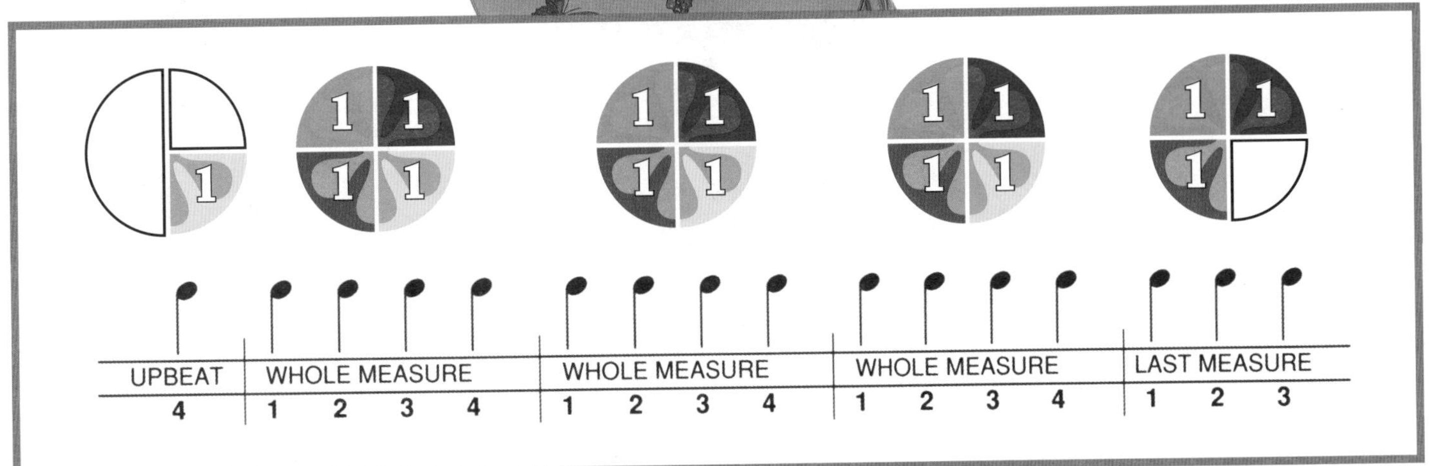

A-Tisket, A-Tasket

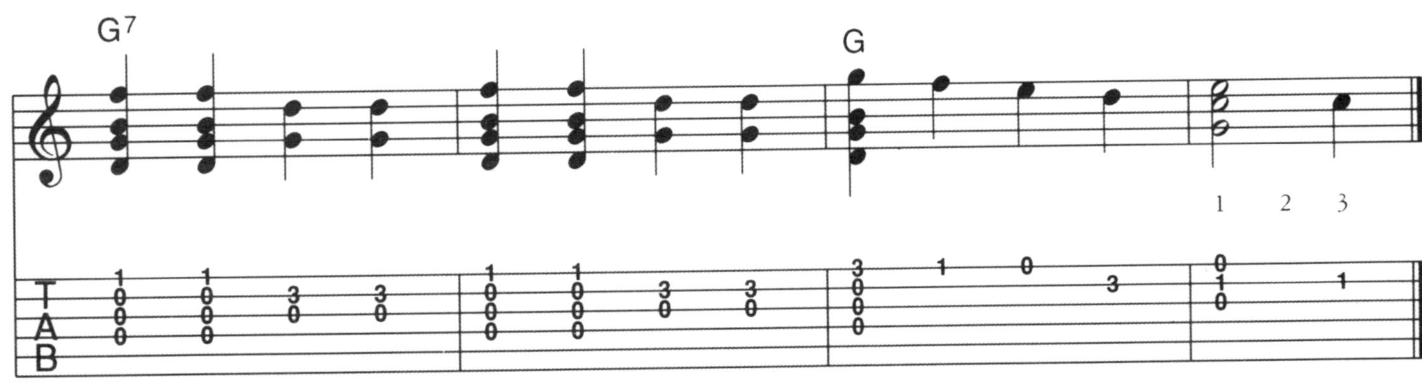

Notes on the Sixth String E

OPEN STRING

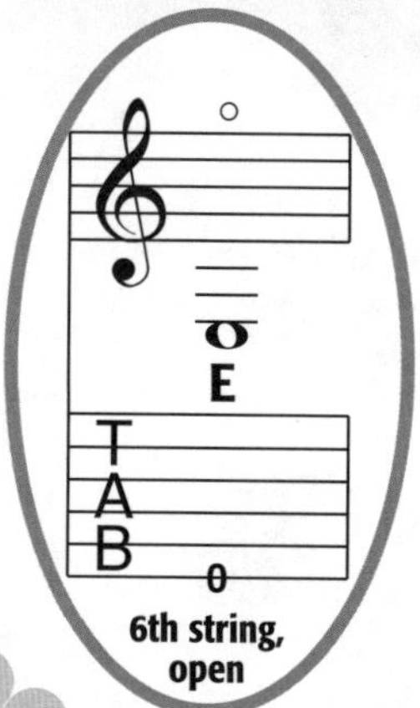

E

6th string, open

1st FRET

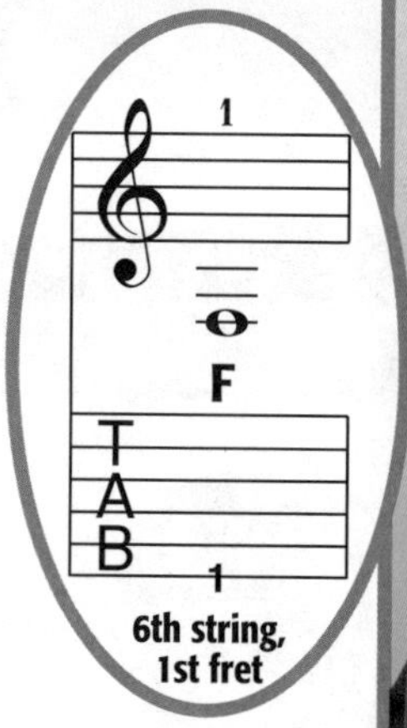

F

6th string, 1st fret

3rd FRET

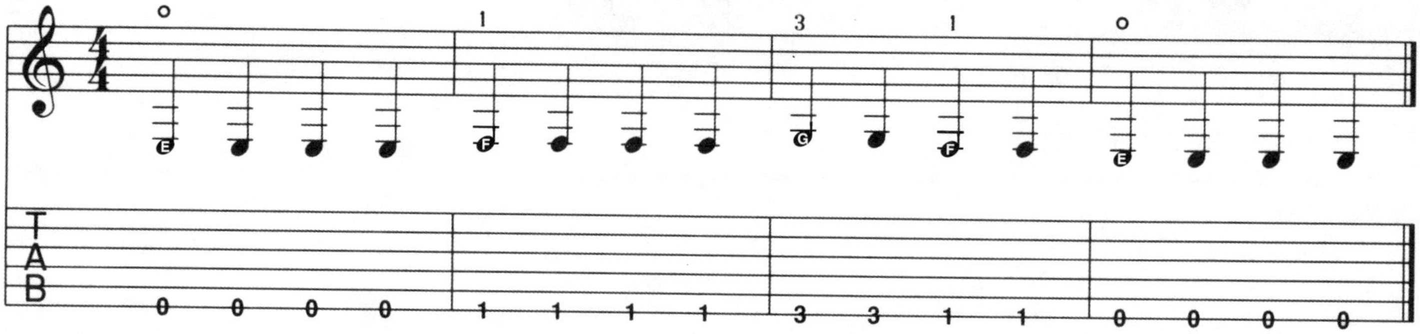

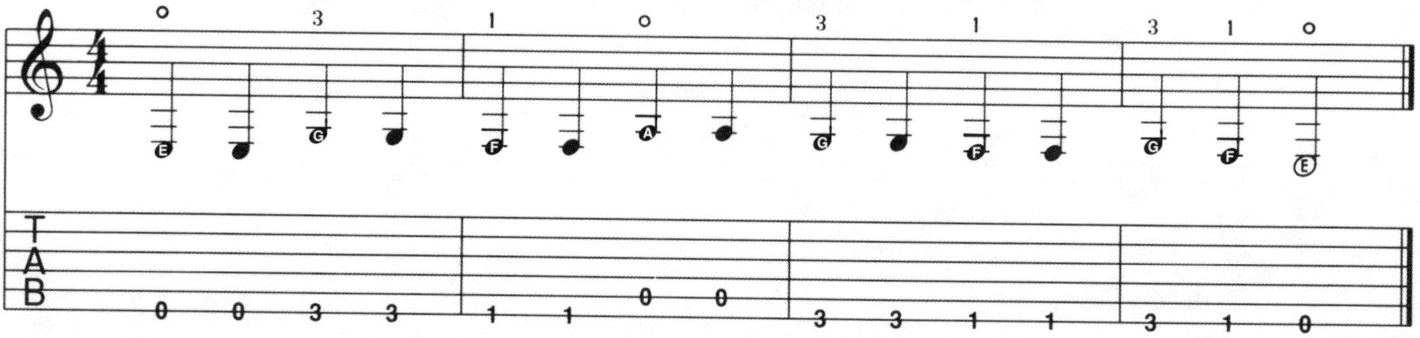

G

6th string, 3rd fret

The Natural Scale

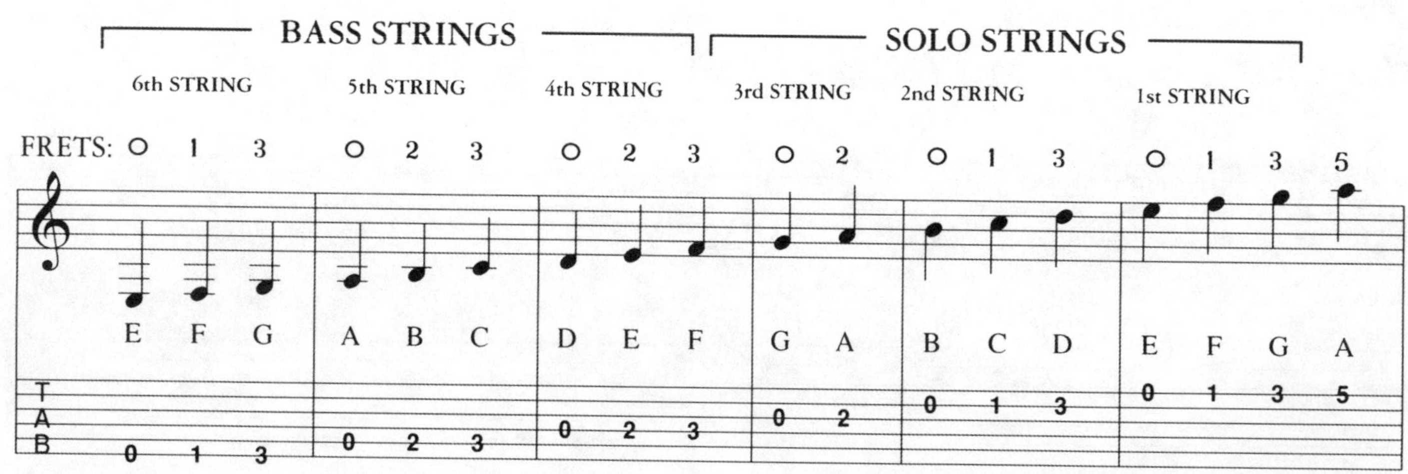

Silver Threads Among the Gold

Fast

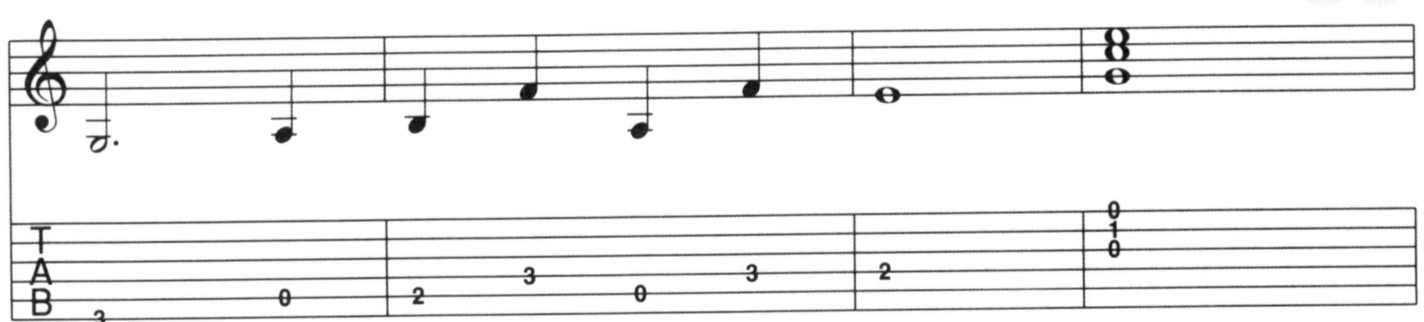

Tempo Signs

Tempo signs tell how fast or slow to play.

The three principal TEMPO SIGNS are:

say:

Andante (slow)	**Moderato** (moderately)	**Allegro** (fast)
on-*don*-tay	**Mah-duh-*rah*-toe**	**Al-*lay*-grow**

Three-Tempo Rock

Play three times: 1st time *Andante,* 2nd time *Moderato,* 3rd time *Allegro.*

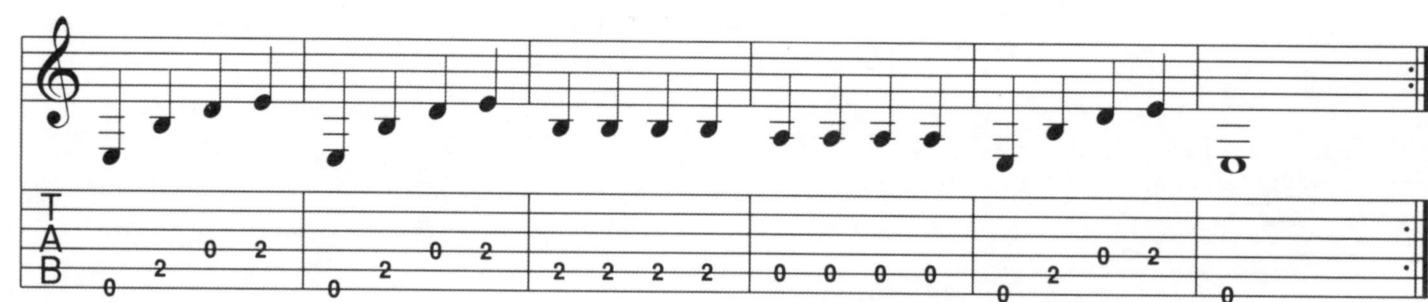

Courtney Love

Her band Hole began in 1988 and has gone on to international stardom. The aggressive guitar styles of Courtney Love power her songs with a frenetic energy, but underneath her raw guitar delivery lays an obvious talent for songwriting.

Photo: Bob Gruen/Star File

The Joy of Love (Plaisir d'amour)

You can do two things to get the most out of the next song arrangement.

First, play accented notes (those marked with a >) a little louder than unmarked notes. Also, keep your finger(s) down where indicated. This will make your playing sound smoother and more professional.

"My brother was taking guitar lessons at our local music store and I would go with him. I started dating one of the guys who worked there. One day, this girl came in the store to buy an amp when she got in a fight with my boyfriend. His comment was "girls don't play guitar!" The next day I signed up for lessons and dropped him as my boyfriend. Later he became my roadie when we were touring and I always thanked him for helping me pick up the guitar. Hah!" —Katie

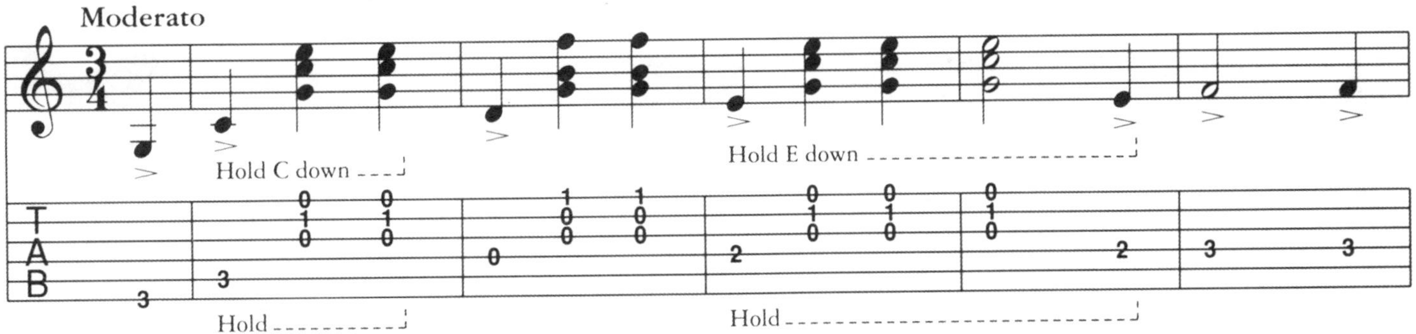

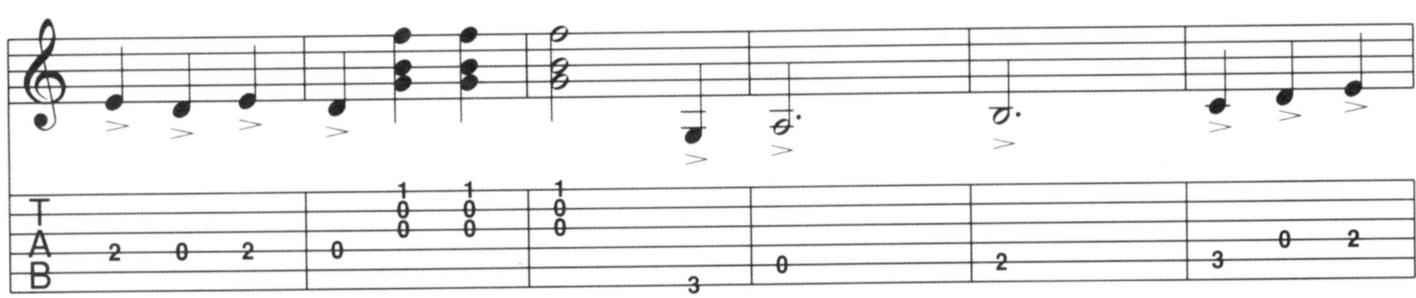

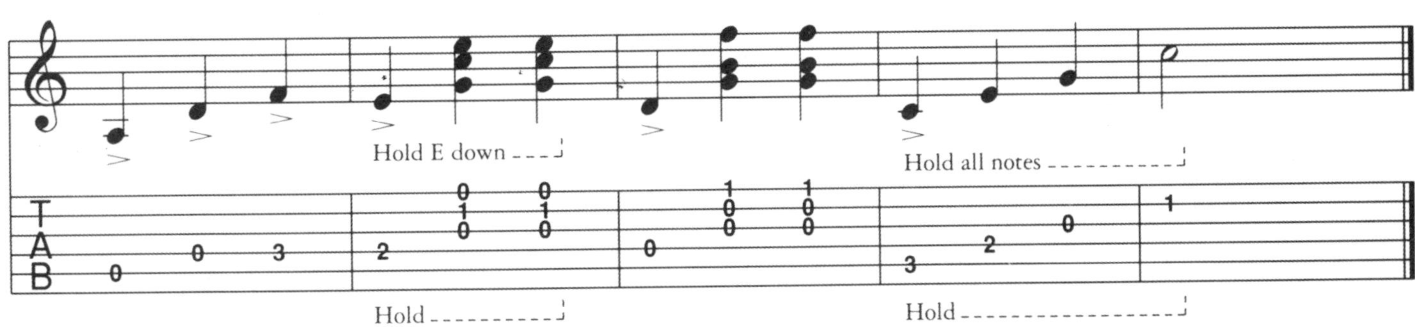

Bass-Chord Accompaniments

A popular style of playing chord accompaniments in $\frac{4}{4}$ time breaks the chord into two parts: a single bass note followed by a chord made up of the remaining notes. On the 1st beat play only the lowest note (called the bass note). Then play the rest of the chord (usually the three highest strings) on the 2nd, 3rd and 4th beats. The complete pattern is:

Bass note–chord–chord–chord.

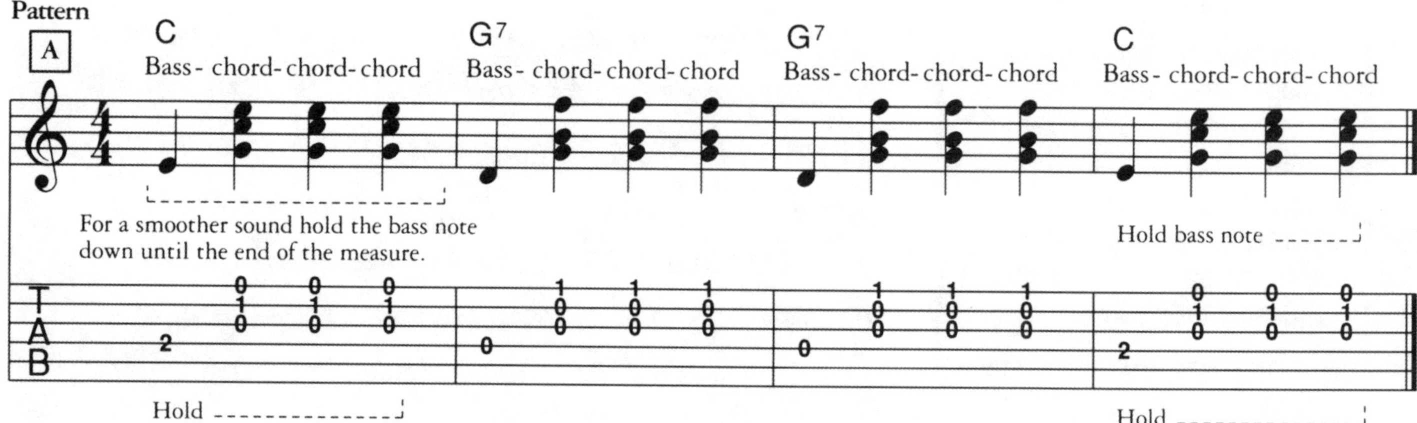

Another style of playing chord accompaniments in $\frac{4}{4}$ time uses a bass note on the 1st and 3rd beats and three-string chords on the 2nd and 4th beats.

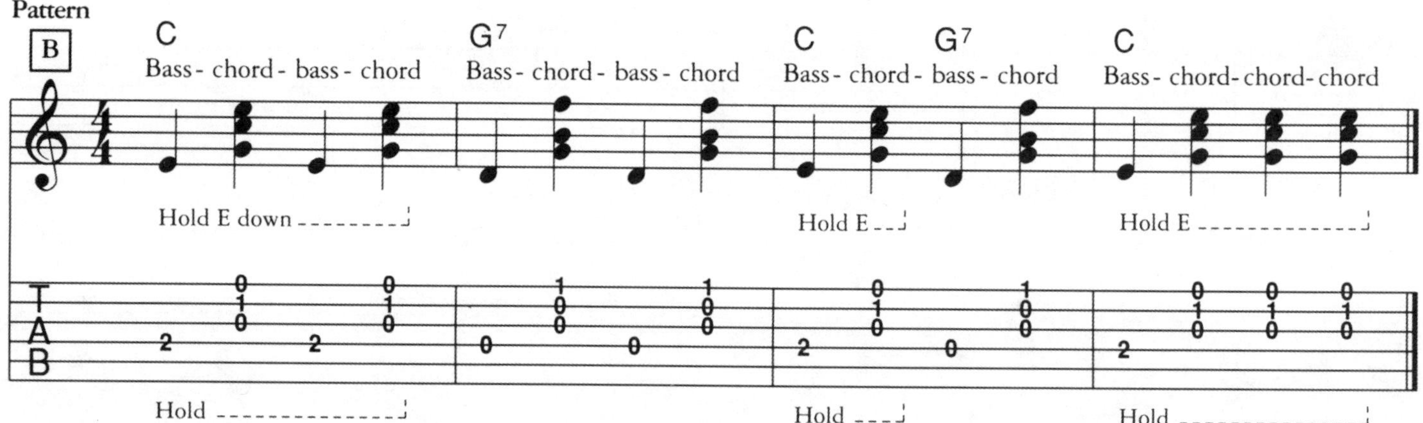

This style of playing chord accompaniments can be adapted to $\frac{3}{4}$ time by playing a bass note on the 1st beat, and three-string chords on the 2nd and 3rd beats.

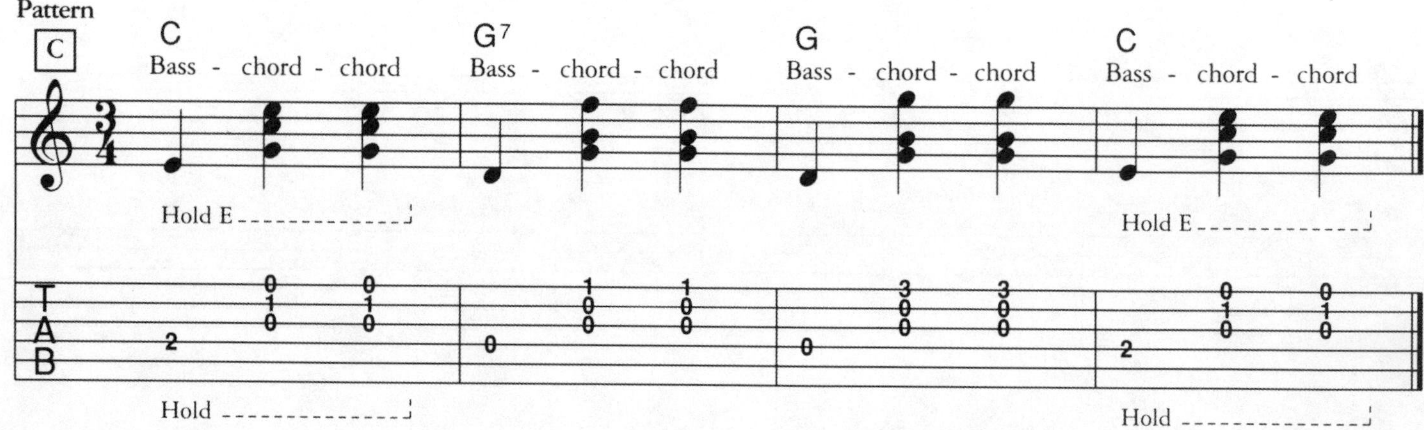

Can-Can (Duet)

This famous melody, often associated with the Cabaret *Moulin Rouge*, should be learned two different ways. First, play the solo part as written. Then find a friend to play the solo part or listen to it on your recording while you play a chord accompaniment using either pattern [A] or [B] on page 42.

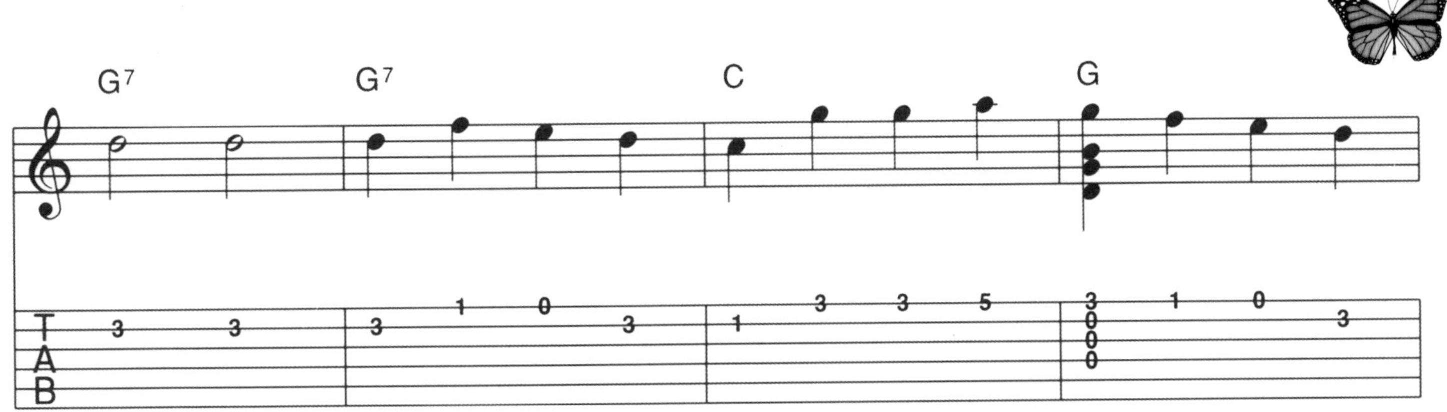

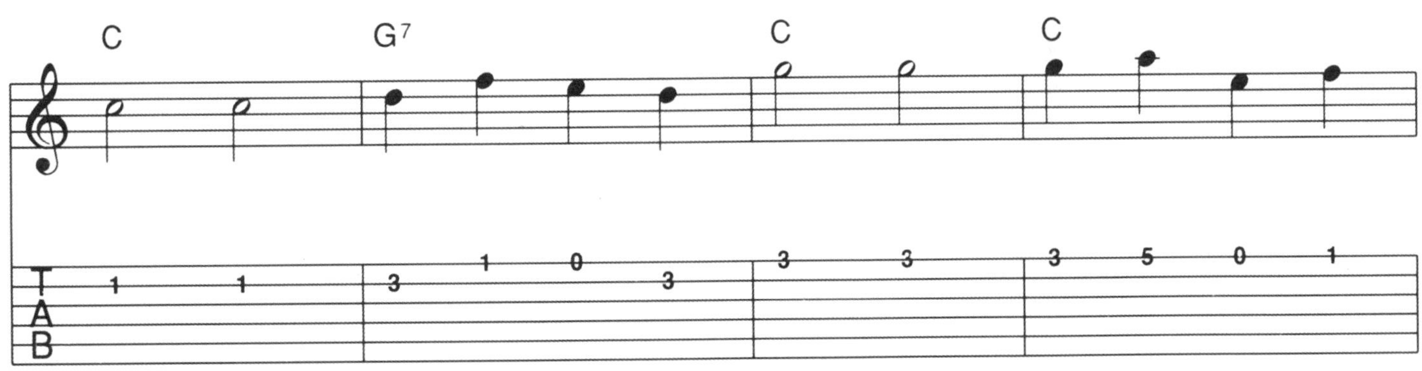

Dynamics

Signs showing how SOFT or LOUD to play are called DYNAMICS. The principal dynamics are:

p	***mf***	***f***	***ff***
(piano)	*(mezzo-forte)*	*(forte)*	*(fortissimo)*
SOFT	**MODERATELY LOUD**	**LOUD**	**VERY LOUD**

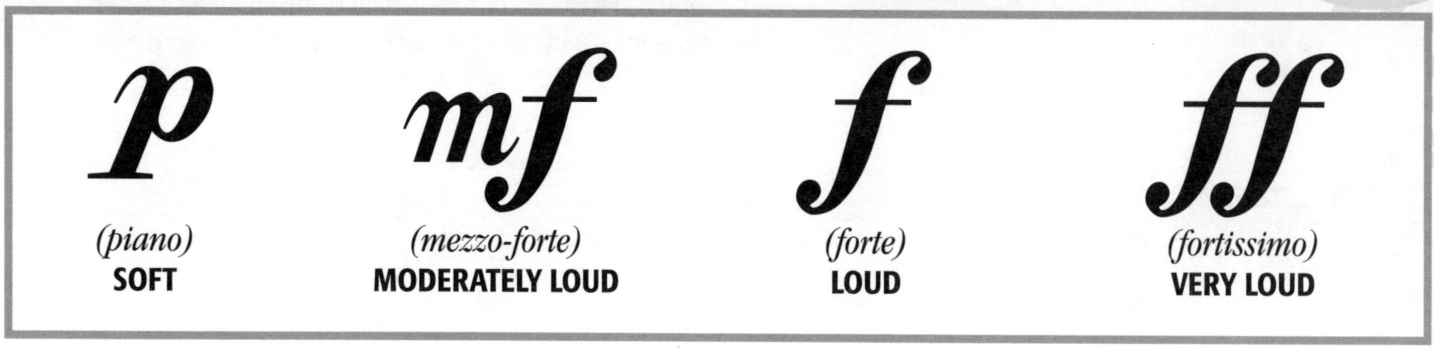

Castles in the Sand

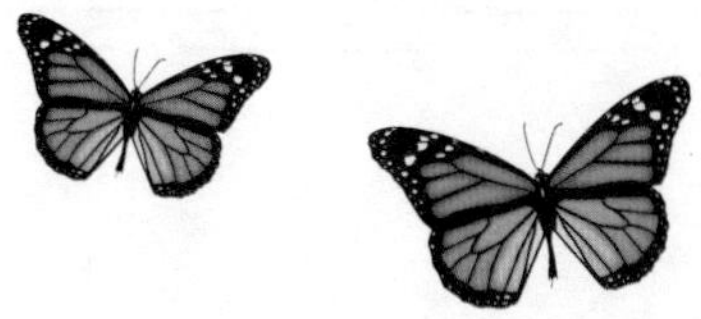

Moderato

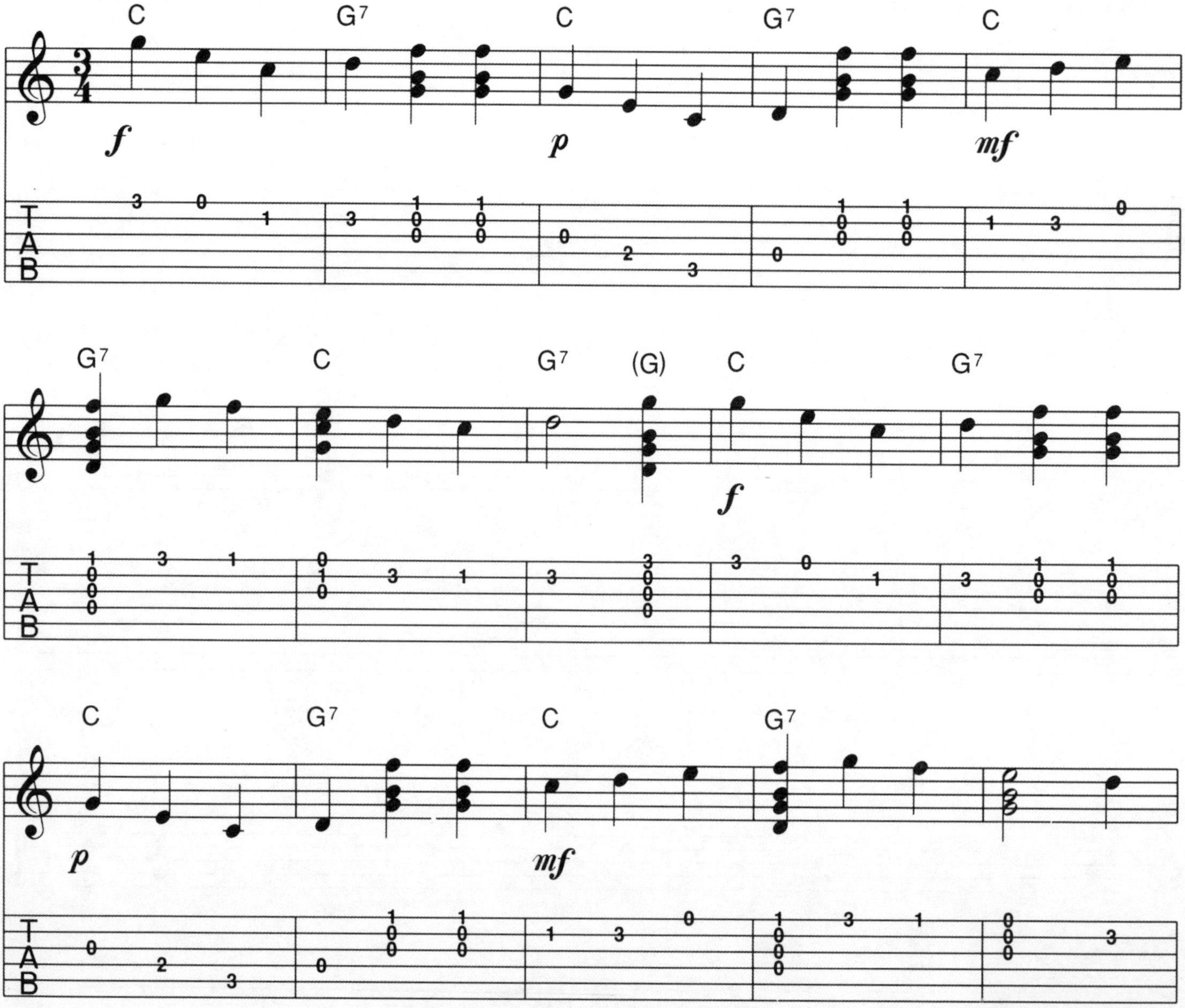
C G7 C G7 C
f p mf
G7 C G7 (G) C G7
f
C G7 C G7
p mf

Music continues on next page.

C G7 C
f
TAB

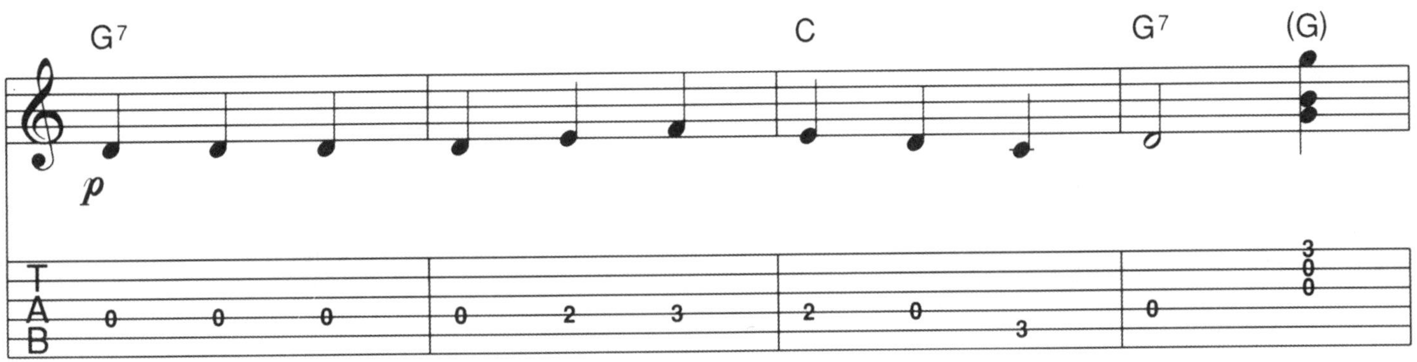
G7 C G7 (G)
p
TAB

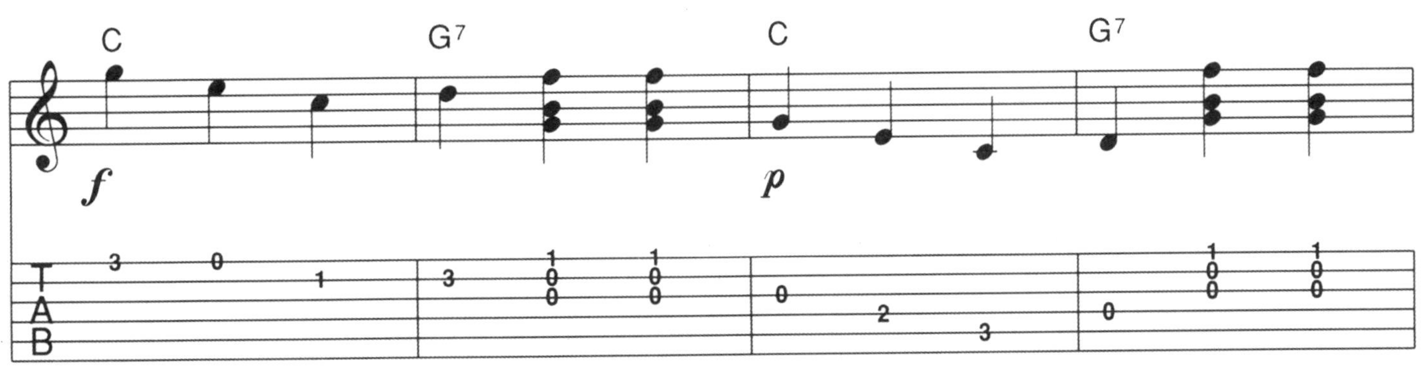
C G7 C G7
f p
TAB

C G7 C
mf
TAB

Signs of Silence

 **QUARTER REST (Crotchet Rest) = 1 COUNT**

HALF REST (Minim Rest) = 2 COUNTS

WHOLE REST (Semibreve Rest) = 4 COUNTS IN $\frac{4}{4}$ TIME

3 COUNTS IN $\frac{3}{4}$ TIME

Mermaids Never Rest

The Four-String C Chord

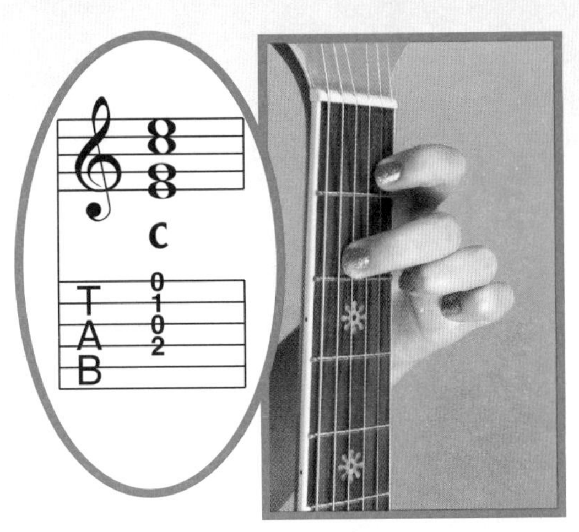

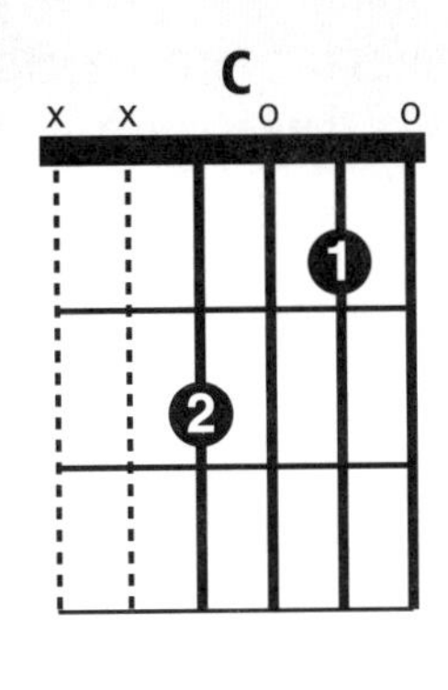

"The boy I had the biggest crush on in the 8th grade put a flier up in the cafeteria looking for a guitar player for his band. Having played the guitar at home for a few years, I worked up the courage to respond. We never went out, but playing music with other people proved to be more fun than I could have imagined."

—Bella

When the Saints Go Marching In

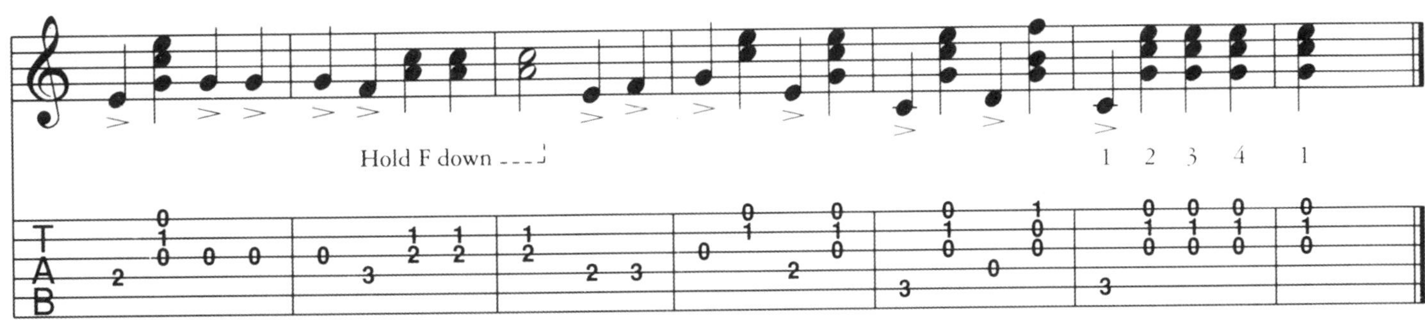

"I've been trying to learn guitar with my boyfriend's father's guitar, which has WAY too wide of a neck for me. And I always wanted a cool, stylish-looking guitar with a heart shape . . . or another shape that was personalized to me. So when I was watching the news and saw the cool girl guitars I was thrilled." —Jessica

Ties

TIES are curved lines connecting two or more successive notes of the same pitch.
When two notes are tied, the second one is not picked, but its time value is added to the value of the first note.

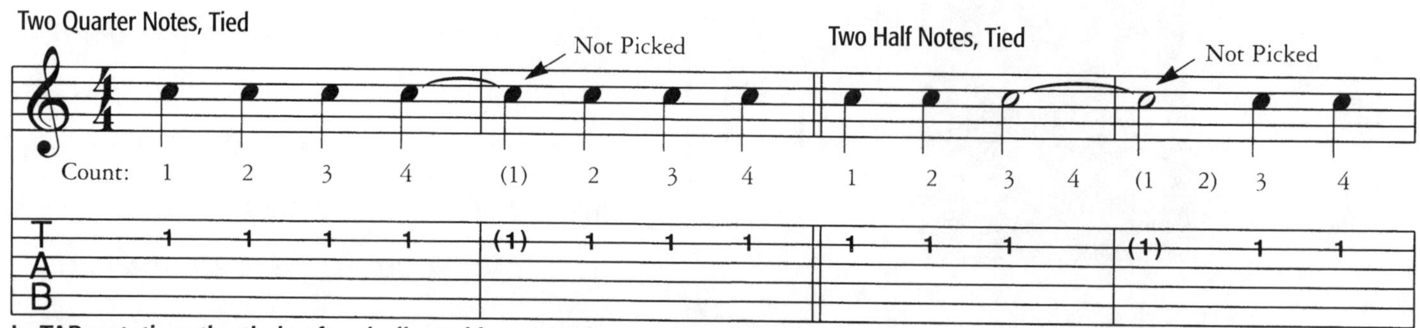

In TAB notation, the tie is often indicated by parentheses around the fret number—do not pick that note again.

The Sidewalks of New York (East Side, West Side)

* Chords may also be tied.

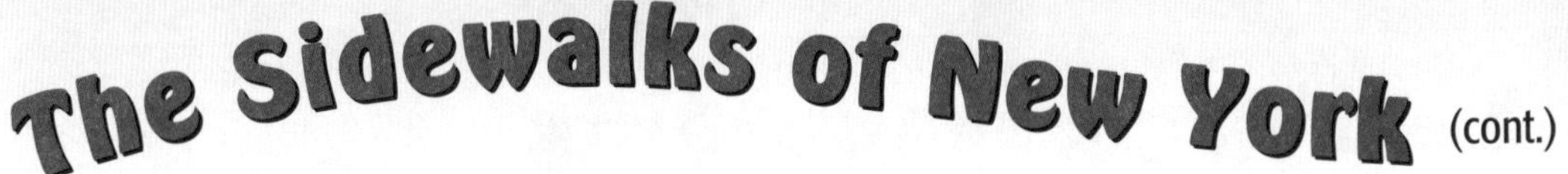

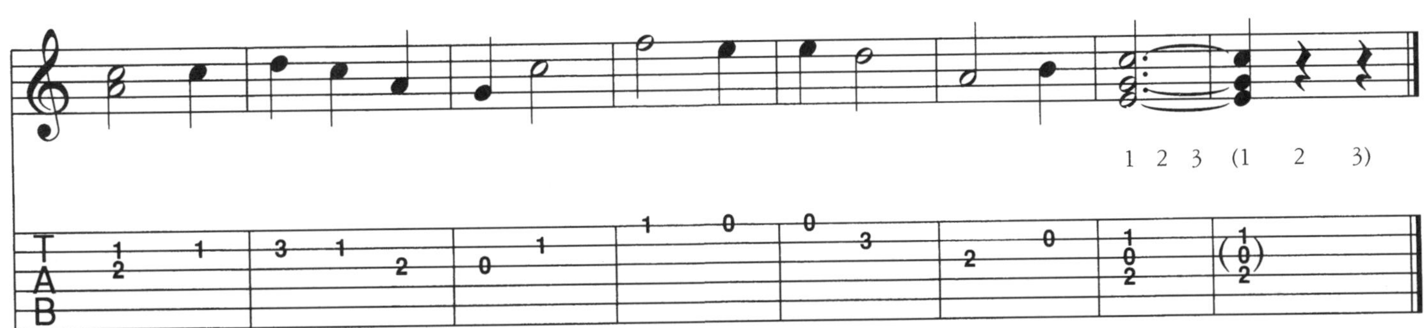

O Happy Day

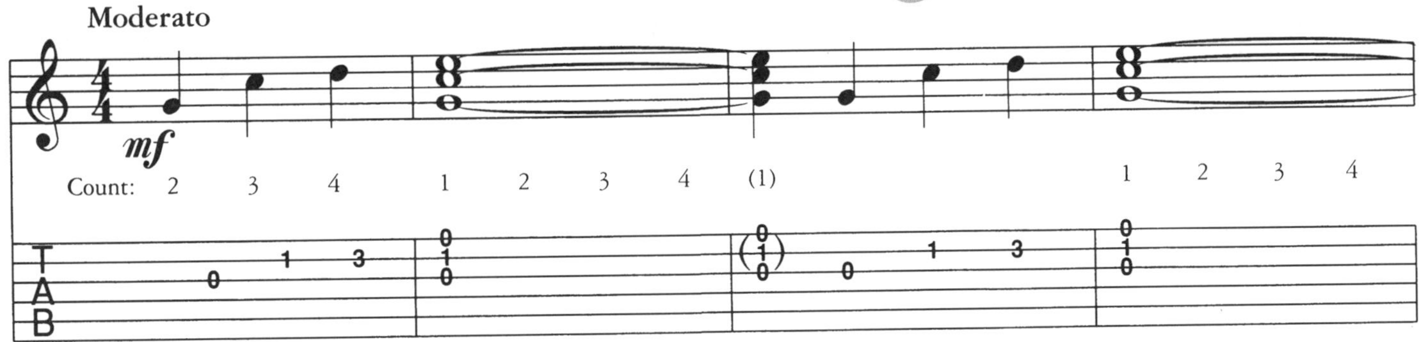

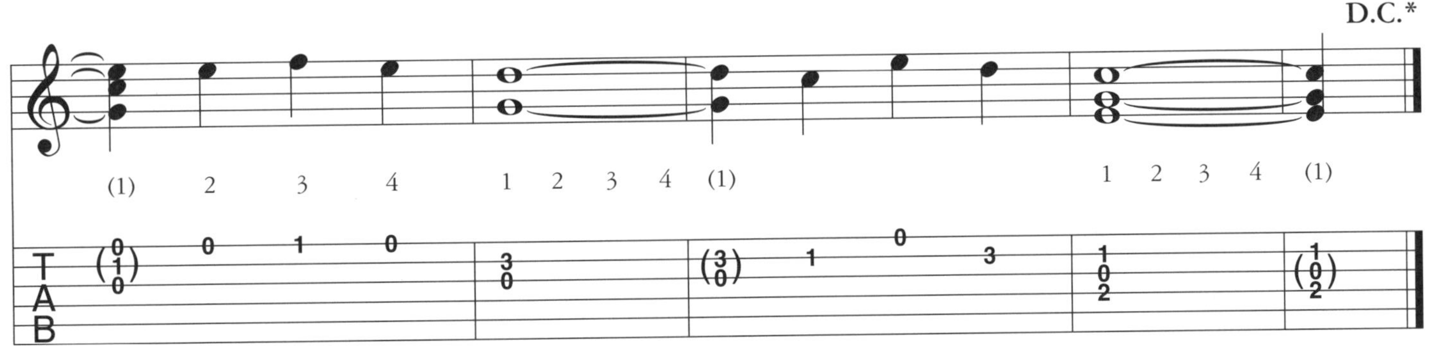

* D.C. = Da Capo (dah CAH-poe) This Italian expression, which means "from the beginning," indicates that you should go back to the beginning of the piece and play through a second time. Notice that the last measure of "O Happy Day" contains only one beat. Beats 2, 3 and 4 are made up in the first measure.

More Bass-Chord Accompaniments

When a piece is in $\frac{3}{4}$ time, a popular style of chord accompaniment is found in the pattern **bass–chord–chord, chord–chord–chord**. The bass note is the note that names the chord: C for the C chord, G for the G and G7 chords. Also, the bass note is usually the lowest note when the chord is played. In the following exercises, play the bass note alone first, then the rest of the chord on beats 2 and 3.

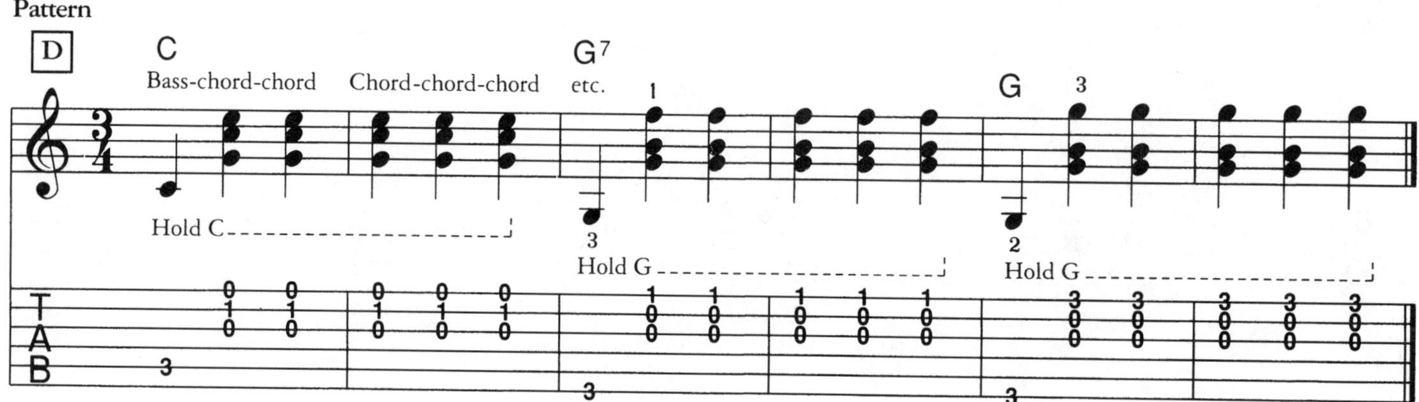

A variation of the above accompaniment uses a bass note on the first beat of each measure.

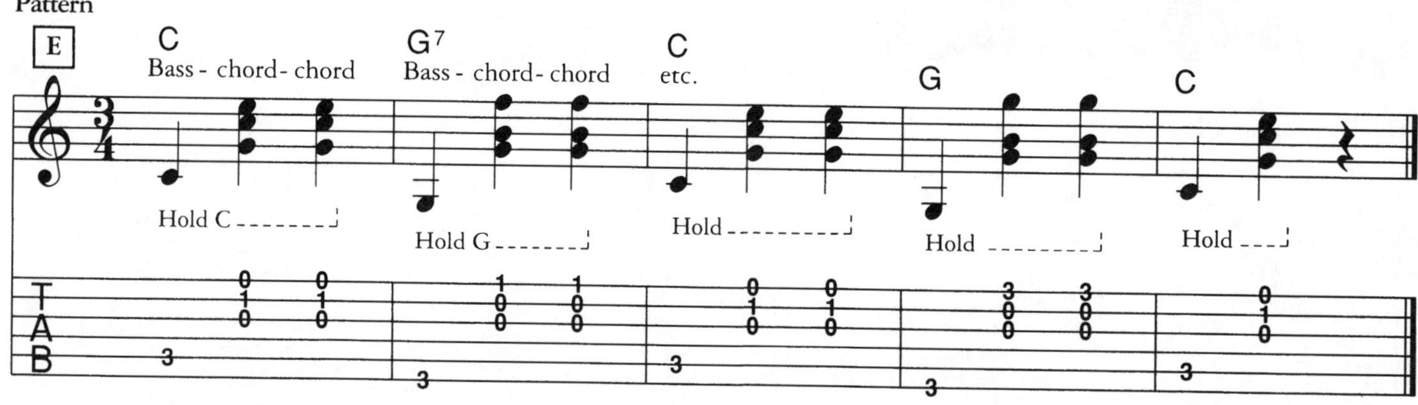

If a chord is repeated for two or more measures, using any other notes of the chord as *alternate bass notes* can create a greater variety of sound. In $\frac{4}{4}$ time, you may use alternate bass notes every other measure or within a single measure.

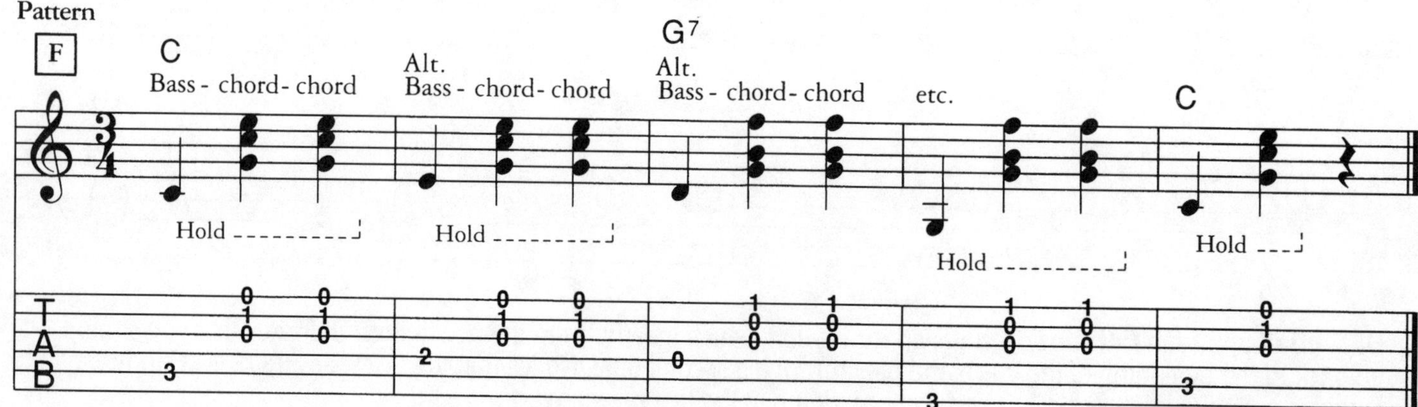

Cielito Lindo

Using the patterns you have just learned, play chord accompaniments to this famous Mexican folk song using bass and alternate bass notes. Then learn the melody as a guitar solo (the melody is on your recording).

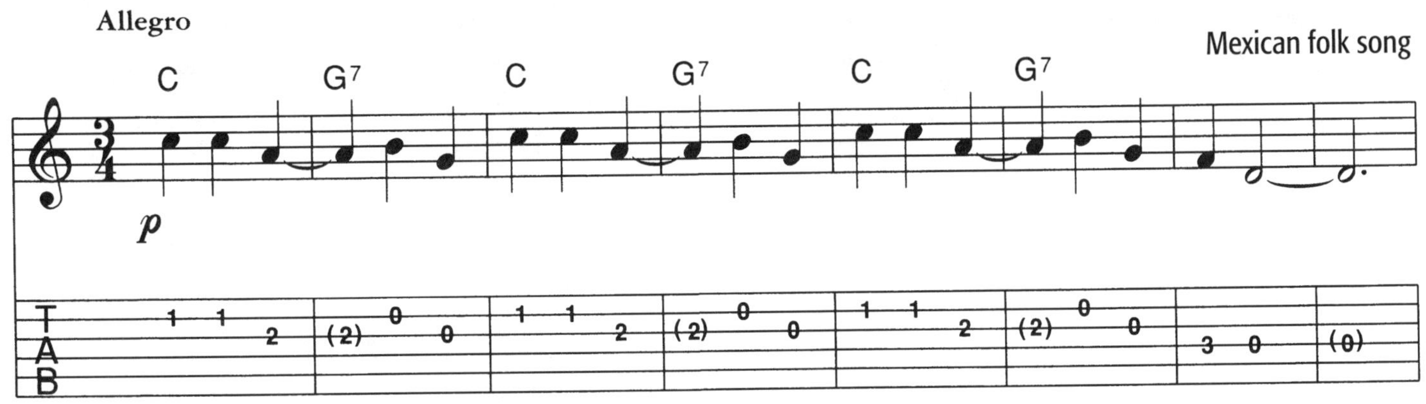

Eighth Notes

EIGHTH NOTES are black notes that have a flag added to the stem: ♪ or ♪.

Two or more eighth notes are written with connecting stems: ♫ or ♫.

This is an eighth rest 𝄾.

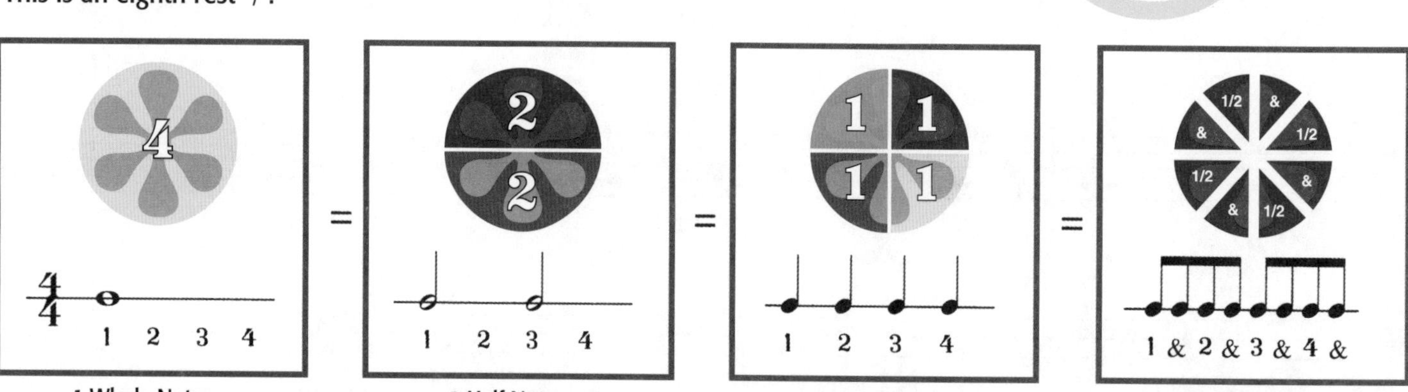

1 Whole Note = 2 Half Notes = 4 Quarter Notes = 8 Eighth Notes

Up until now, you have played only using downstrokes. To be able to play more quickly, we will now use UPSTROKES.

Use alternating downstrokes ⊓ and upstrokes V on eighth notes.

Imagine Eighth Notes

Allegro moderato

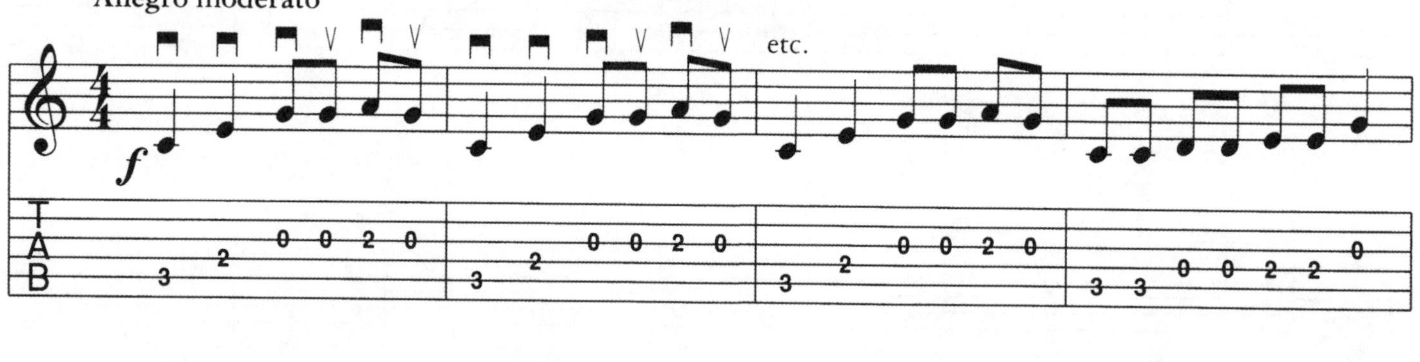

* Fill in the rest of the page with downstrokes and upstrokes.

Flower Drill

Speed drills are for the development of technique and should be practiced daily. Start all speed drills slowly, and be sure that each note is clear and distinct. On each repetition, increase the tempo a little. We recommend that you practice with a metronome to maintain an even tempo.

Chrissie Hynde

Hynde grew up in Akron, Ohio, the daughter of a secretary mother and an adman father. She admits, "I was not the model teenage girl that anybody's parents would have wanted. I didn't date boys and I was a lousy student. All I wanted to do was go out and see bands." She taught herself the harmonica, ukulele and guitar, and at 16 made her local debut fronting for a band. "I don't think of myself as a girl guitar player," she says. "I just think of myself as a guitar player."

Photo: Ken Settle

Sharps ♯, Flats ♭, and Naturals ♮

The distance from one fret to the next fret, up or down, is a HALF STEP.
Two half steps make a WHOLE STEP.

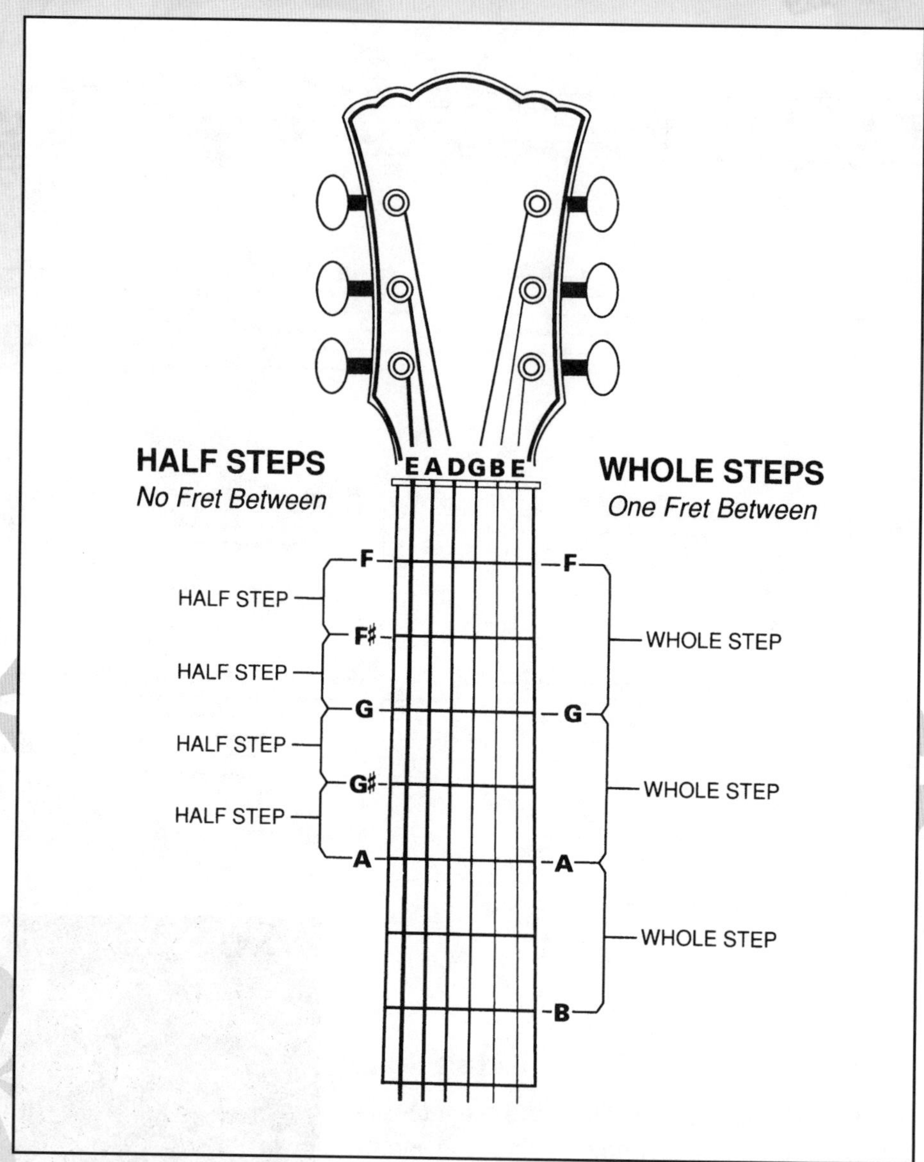

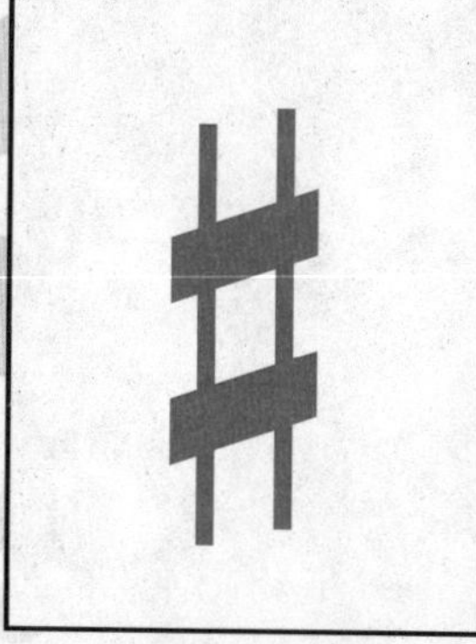

A sharp *raises* the note a half step. Play the next higher fret.

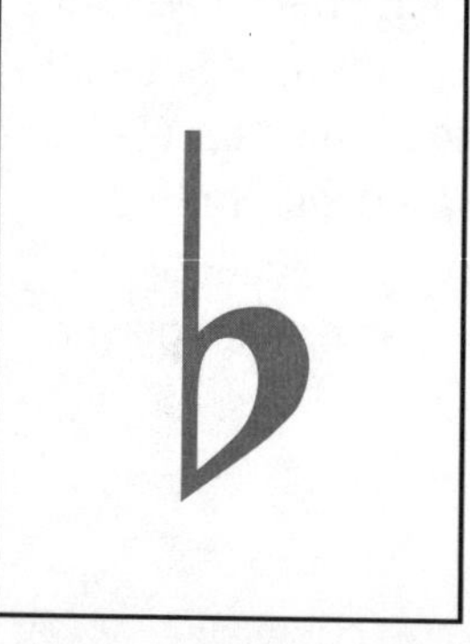

A flat *lowers* the note a half step. Play the next fret lower if the note is fingered. If the note is open, play the 4th fret of the next lower string unless that string is G (3rd string)—then play the 3rd fret.

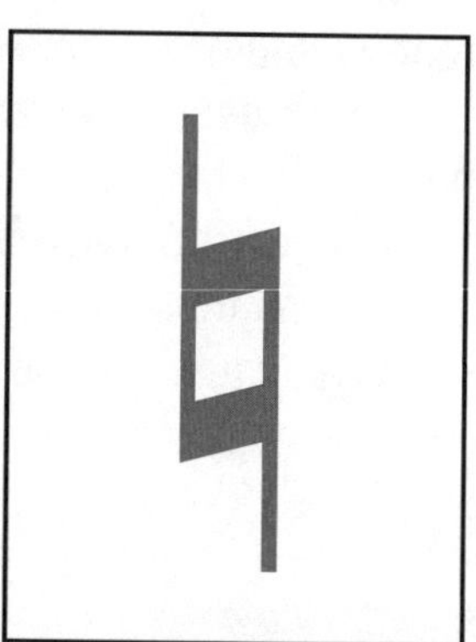

A natural *cancels* a previous sharp or flat.

The Chromatic Scale

The CHROMATIC SCALE is formed exclusively of half steps.
Ascending, this scale uses sharps (♯), but descending, it uses flats (♭).

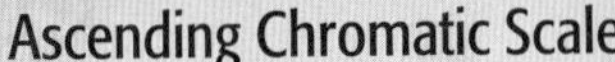

Ascending Chromatic Scale

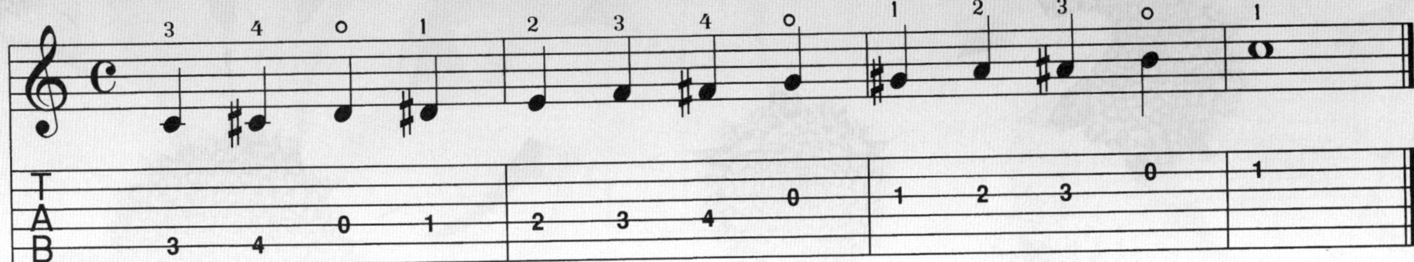

Descending Chromatic Scale

Chromatic Hopscotch

Allegro Moderato

B natural—♭ cancelled

Still B♭*

Still B♭

Still ♭

Still ♭

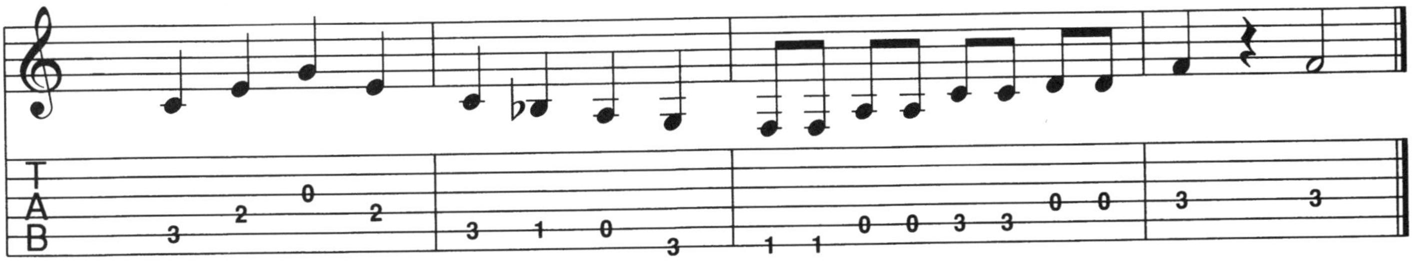

* When a sharped or flatted note appears more than once in the same measure, it is still played as sharped or flatted unless the sharp or flat is cancelled by a natural sign (♮).

The Four-String D7 Chord

*See footnote on page 55.

Strummin' Daisies

D7 C G

Pixies Dancing with Bach

Adapted from a famous minuet by J. S. Bach

Amazing Grace

Learn the solo part and the accompaniment. Use pattern D, E, or F from page 50.

Andante

G C G

mf

D7 G C

G D7 G D7 G

Ani DiFranco

By the age of 9, DiFranco was performing Beatles songs in local Buffalo establishments, and at age 15, began writing her own material. A skilled guitarist who backs her own vocals, she delivers dramatic and unconventional performances with a unique punk-folk style that appeals to conservative folks as well as those on the rock club circuit. Her independent approach to life and unwillingness to conform to popular convention are evident in her creative efforts, which cover the entire range from writing and publishing her own songs, to creating the artwork, producing the recordings and releasing them through her own record label, Righteous Babe Records.

Photo: Albert Sanchez/Courtesy of Righteous Babe Records

Pachelbel's Canon

This 17th-century piece has been widely used, particularly in commercials and as the main theme of the movie *Ordinary People*.

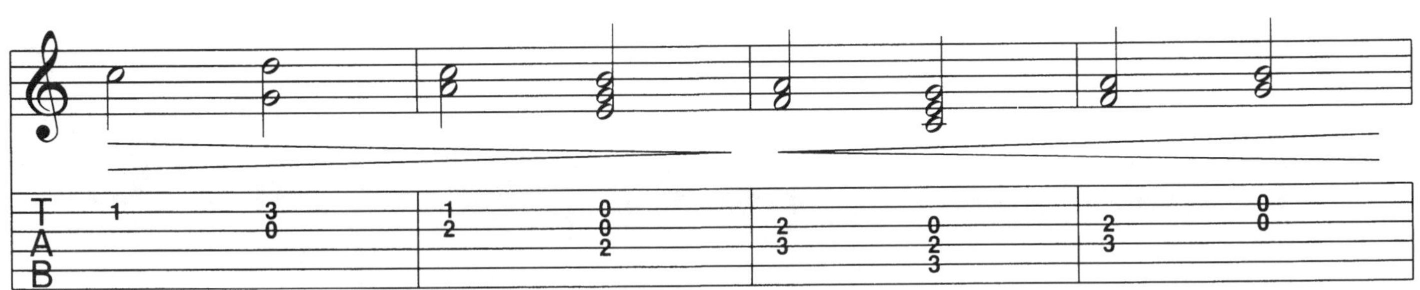

* This sign ——— and the word CRESCENDO both mean to gradually grow louder.
This sign ——— and the word DIMINUENDO both mean to gradually grow softer.

The Major Scale

A SCALE is a series or succession of tones. All major scales are made of eight tones that ascend in alphabetical order following the pattern of whole steps and half steps shown below.

C Major Scale

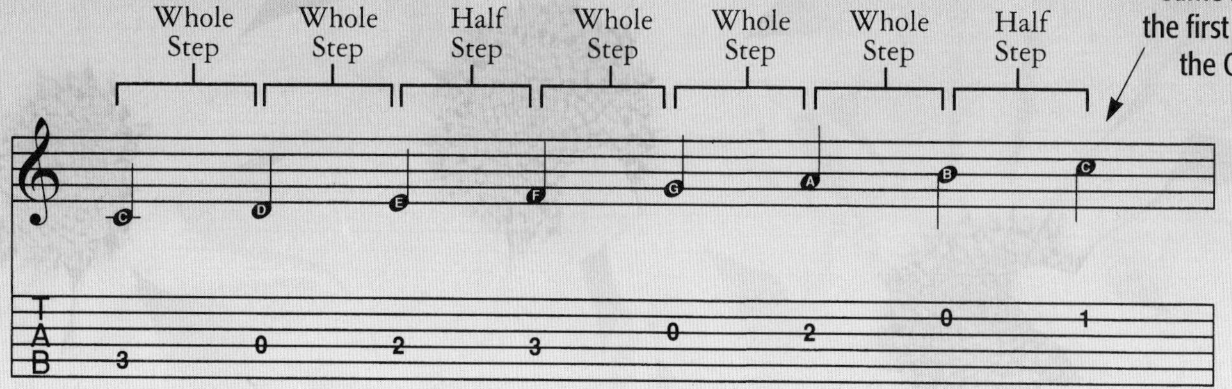

The Octave Note

This scale has eight notes. The highest note, having the same letter name as the first note, is called the OCTAVE NOTE.

It is easier to visualize whole steps and half steps on a piano keyboard. Notice that there is a whole step between every pair of white keys except E–F and B–C.

Whole Steps–One Key Between

Half Steps–No Key Between

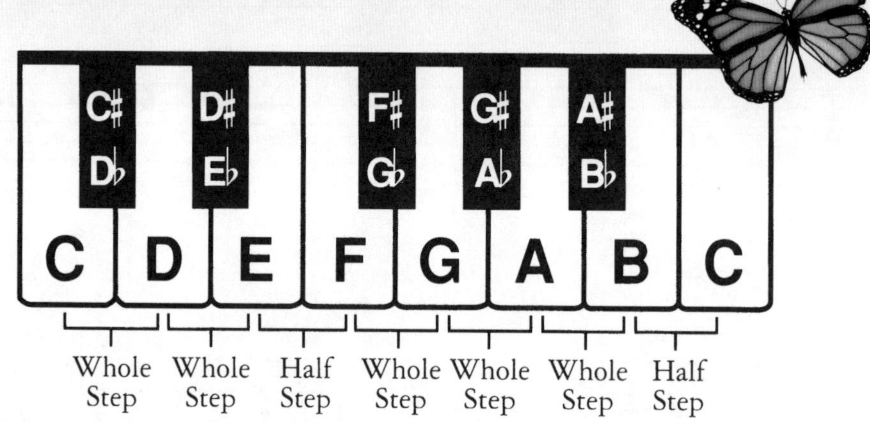

The major scale may be built starting on any note–natural, sharp, or flat. Using the given pattern, write a major scale starting on G.

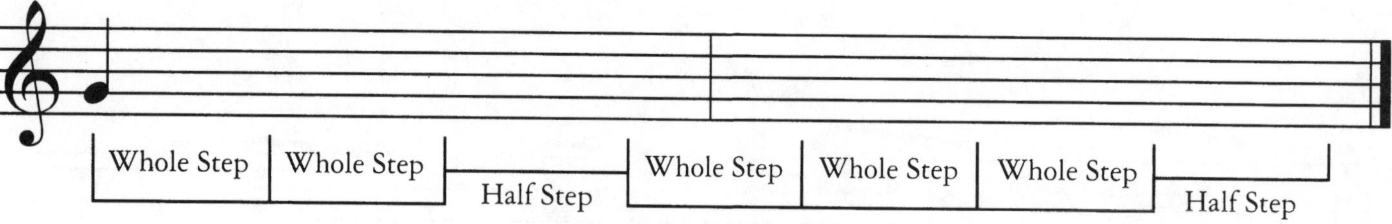

Check: Are the notes in alphabetical order? Did you give the 7th note a sharp?

Write a major scale starting on F.

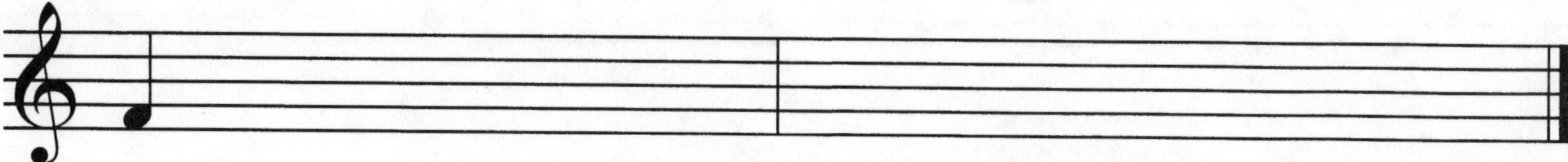

Check: Are the notes in alphabetical order? Did you give the 4th note a flat?

Key Signatures

The Key of C Major

A piece based on the C MAJOR SCALE is in the KEY OF C MAJOR. Since there are no sharps or flats in the C scale, any sharps or flats occurring in a piece in the key of C major are called ACCIDENTALS.

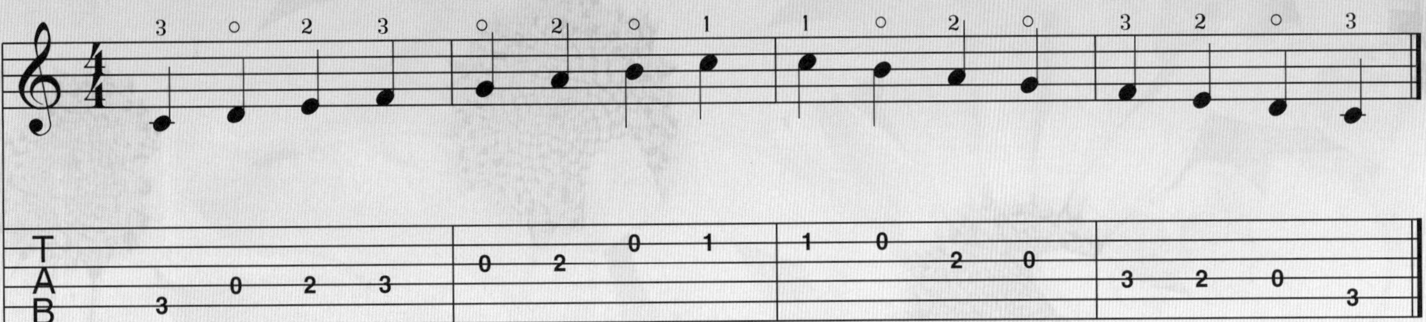

The Key of G Major

A piece based on the G MAJOR SCALE is in the key of G MAJOR. Since F is sharp in the G scale, every F will be sharp in the key of G major. Instead of adding a sharp every time an F appears in a piece, the sharp is indicated at the beginning, in the key signature. Sharps or flats shown in the key signature remain effective throughout the piece.

Key Signature
One Sharp (F♯)

The Key of F Major

A piece based on the F MAJOR SCALE is in the key of F MAJOR, so the B-flat is indicated in the key signature.

Key Signature
One Flat (B♭)

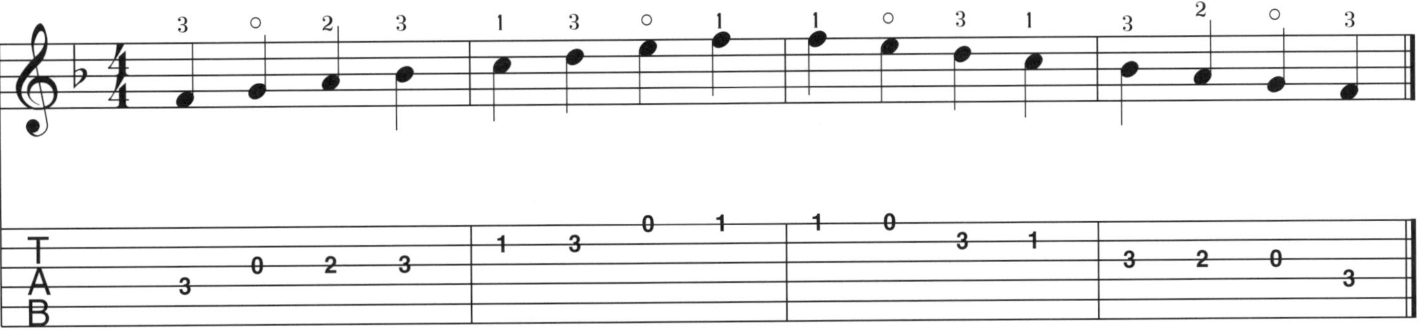

If sharps, flats or naturals not shown in the key signature occur in the piece, they are called ACCIDENTALS. Accidentals are effective only for the measures in which they appear. The three scales shown above should be practiced every day. Students who do this should have little difficulty playing selections written in C major, G major and F major.

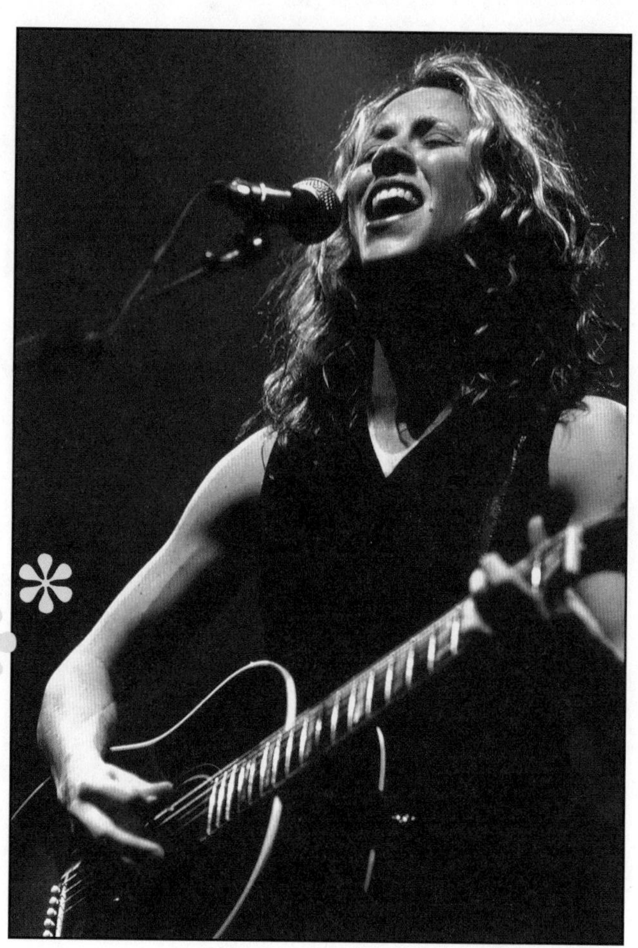

Photo: Ken Settle

Sheryl Crow

The daughter of a trumpeter and a piano teacher, Crow received a degree in music from the University of Missouri at Columbia in 1984. Her unique guitar style is evident in her song "Strong Enough," from her 1993 debut album, "Tuesday Night Music Club." Sheryl has become one of the most prominent guitarists in the music industry.

"The first song I learned how to play was one I wrote myself about my dog. I was six at the time, and I had just learned my first chords: G, D, and A. The toughest chord for me to learn was F, but the more I practiced the easier it got, until eventually I was writing and playing more advanced songs. The main thing to remember-is that you should always-have fun when you're playing guitar. Be encouraged every time you pick it up, because it will get easier and more natural every time you play."

—Anita, Viva Voce

Photo: Ken Settle

Deana Carter

The daughter of guitarist Fred Carter, Jr. (who played on nearly 90 percent of all Nashville recording sessions with artists such as Elvis Presley, Simon and Garfunkel, and Roy Orbison in the 1960s and 1970s), Deana Carter grew up surrounded by musical talent. In 1996, she released her hugely successful debut album, "Did I Shave My Legs for This?," and the record's first of three hit singles, "Strawberry Wine," shot to the top of the charts.

La Bamba

"I was trying to decide whether or not I wanted to take up learning the guitar. Seeing girly looking guitars helped me make up my mind. I'm going to learn as soon as I can, and hopefully I can talk my parents into buying me a guitar." —Sarah

Allegro

8th rest = 1/2 beat of silence

f

Count: 1 & 2 & 3 4 1

8th rest

Count: 1 & 2 & 3 & 4 &

TAB

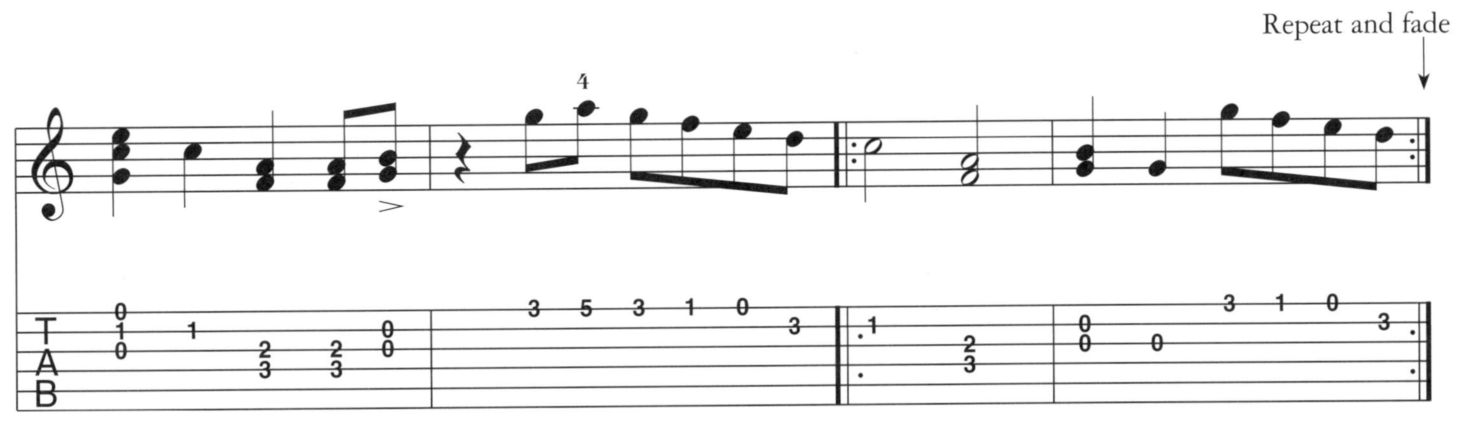

Dotted Quarter Notes

A dot increases the length of a note by one-half.

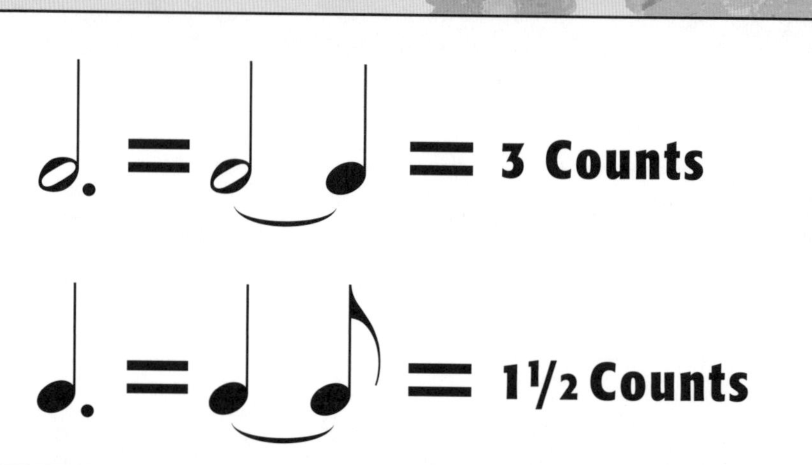

Preparatory Drill

The only difference between the two measures to the right and those directly above them is the way they are written. They should sound the same.

Auld Lang Syne

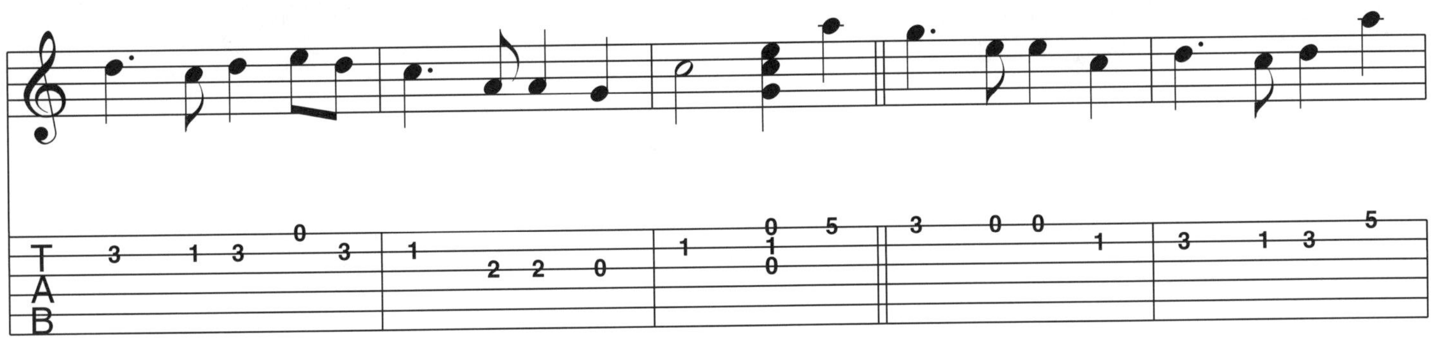

Bass Lines Just Wanna Have Fun!

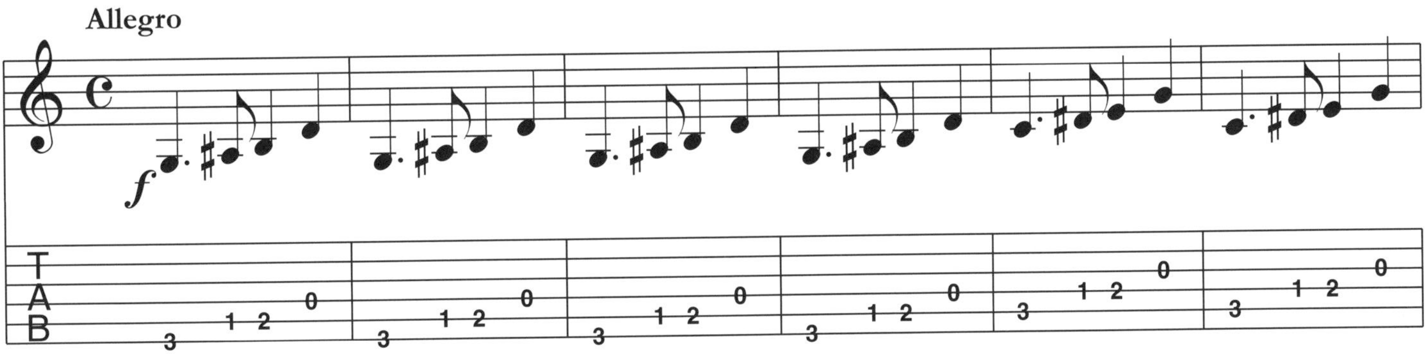

Hava Nagila

Israeli Folk Song

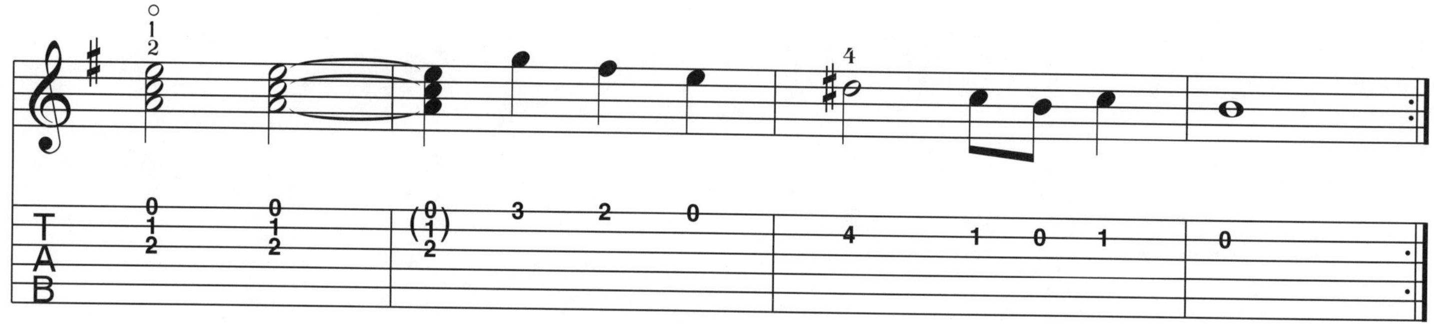

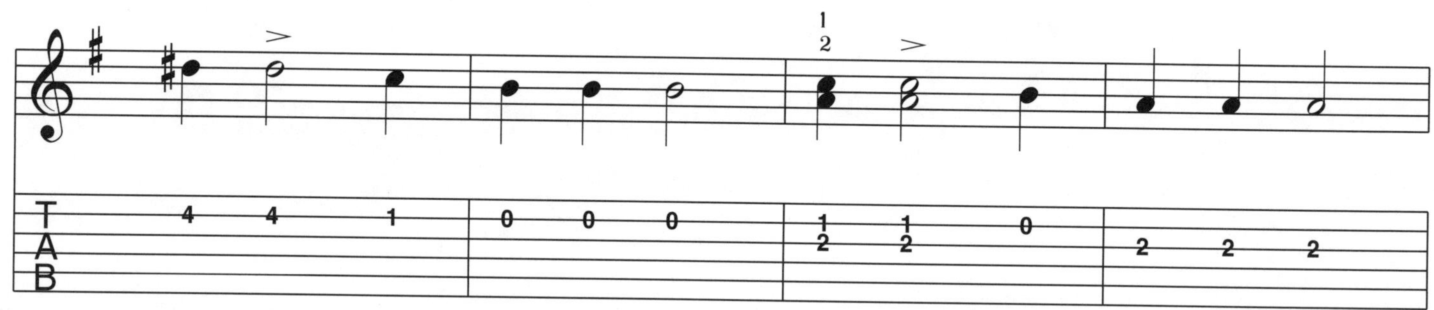

* High B: 1st string, 7th fret.

Photo: Ken Settle

Babes in Toyland

Released in 1990, this hard-core rock trio's debut CD, "Spanking Machine," inspired a new wave of all-girl bands. When the media began a wide-spread movement to classify these female groups, including Babes in Toyland, under a single, over-simplified category, the band revolted. Guitarist Kat Bjelland had this insightful revelation on the differences between the sexes: "Men and women play their instruments to a completely different beat. Women are a lot more rhythmic–naturally–than men. It doesn't even have anything to do with music, it all has to do with timing."

Patty Griffin

The youngest of seven children, Griffin grew up listening to her mother sing while doing housework and to her grandmother's family as they would sing on the front porch at night. In addition to listening to the Beatles, Griffin was fascinated by the music of Bruce Springsteen and Rickie Lee Jones. Even though she got a 50-dollar guitar and began writing songs at the age of 16, she gave little thought to a career as a musician. Griffin's debut album, "Living with Ghosts," was released in 1996 and inspired comparisons with recordings by Tori Amos and Alanis Morissette.

Photo: Ken Settle

Advanced Tablature Techniques

Used in Rock, Heavy Metal, Blues, Country, Jazz and Fusion

One of the problems with traditional music notation in relation to the guitar is that it doesn't show how the music is to be played or where the notes should be fingered on the neck. Tablature enables the guitarist to play more precisely by the use of special symbols we will introduce to you now. Through these symbols, you will be able to see when a note should be bent up, when to slide from one note to another, when to hammer-on or pull-off and much more. Tablature gives the guitarist a graphic representation of the exact technique that the music requires.

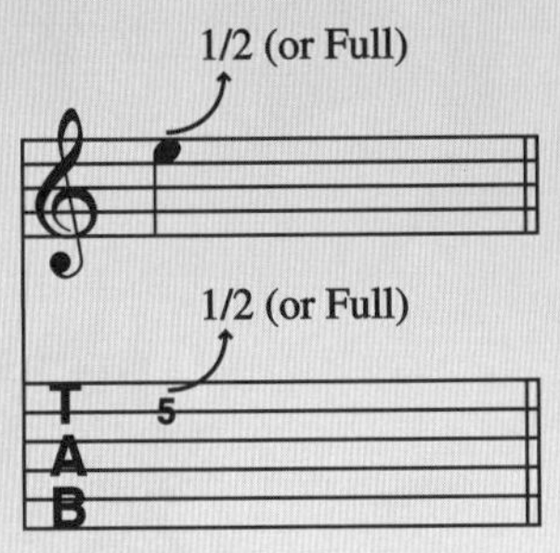

Bend

When you see this symbol, pick the note shown and then bend the string by pushing it up until the desired pitch is reached. We will start with a 1/2 bend. This means to bend the note up one half step—the same sound as the note one fret up. At first it may be somewhat difficult to bend the string, but the more you practice, the stronger your fingers will become. The farther up the neck you play, the easier it is to bend the strings.

Bend Exercise No. 1

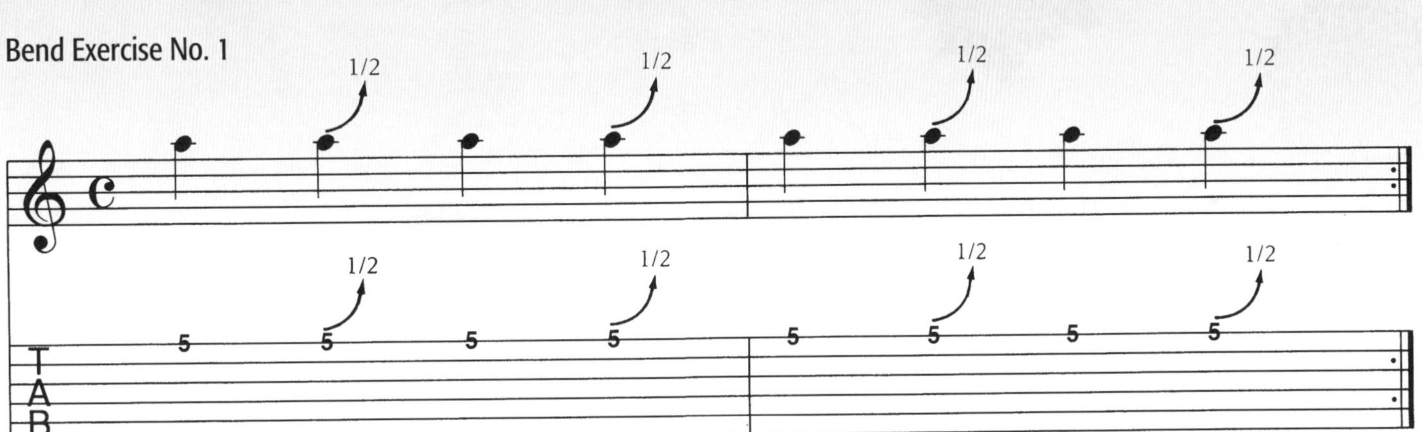

Bend Exercise No. 2

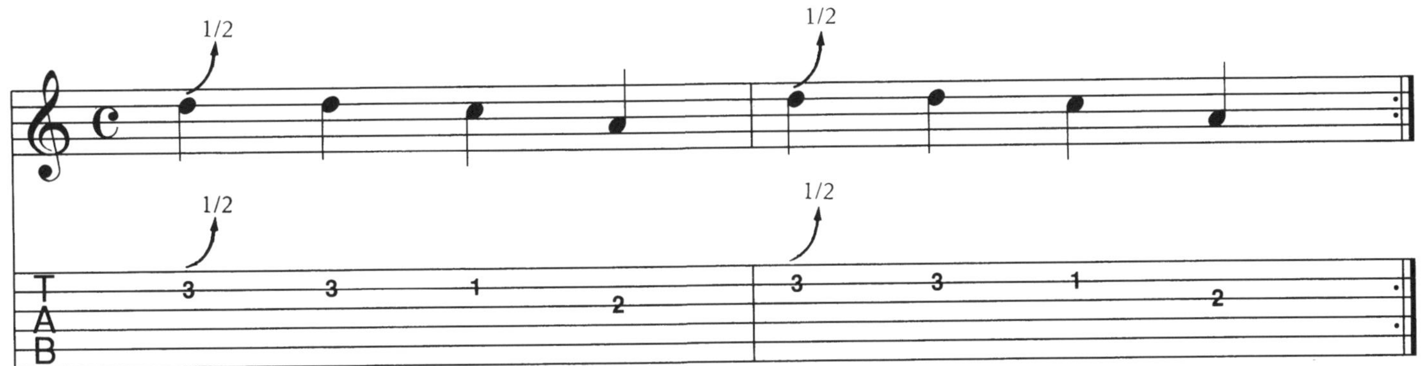

Pick Bend & Release

Pick the first note (the lower note), bend the string up one half step to sound the higher second note, then straighten the string to sound the original lower note again. Pick only the first note.

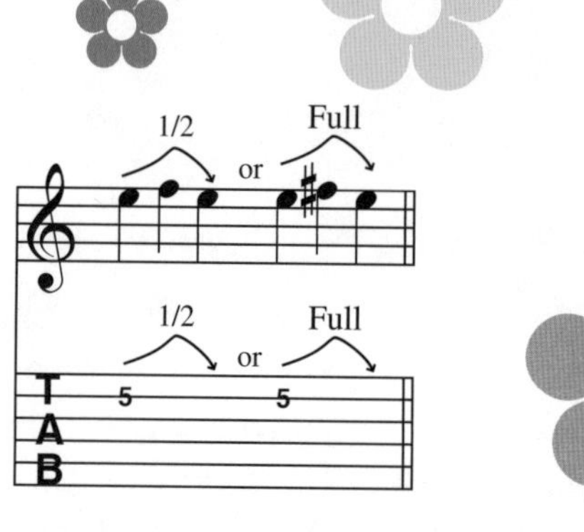

Pick Bend & Release Exercise No. 1

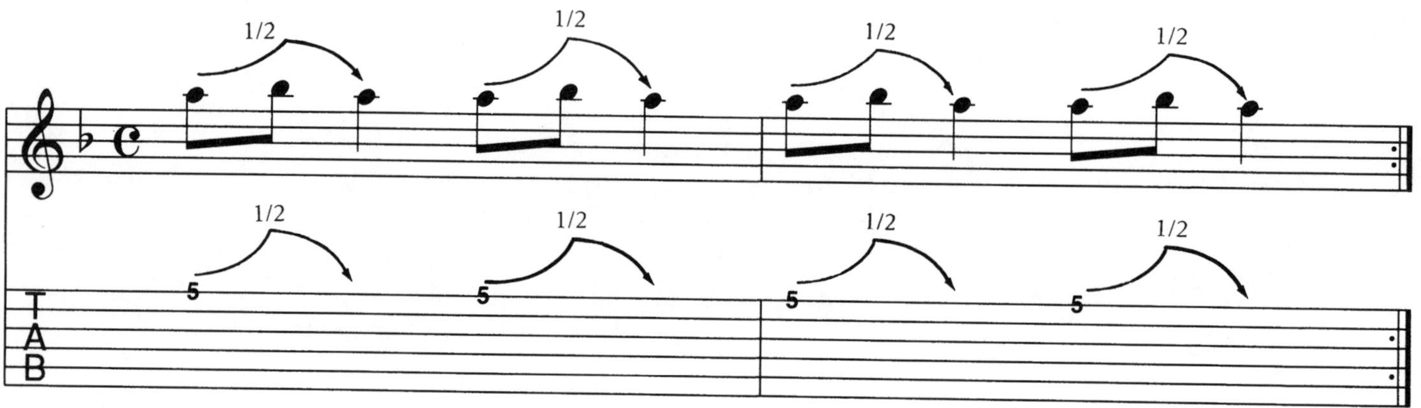

Pick Bend & Release Exercise No. 2

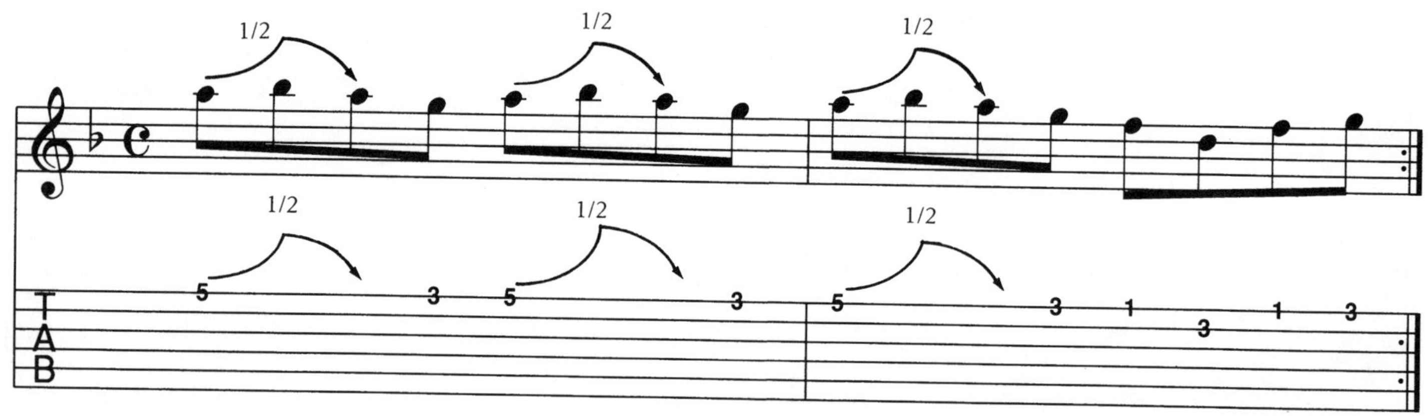

Bend and Pick Bend & Release Exercise

Hammer-on

Pick the first note (the lower note), then hammer-on the second note by tapping down firmly on the fretboard with another finger of your left hand. Pick only the first note—the sound of the second note is made by the hammer-on. These notes are always played on the same string.

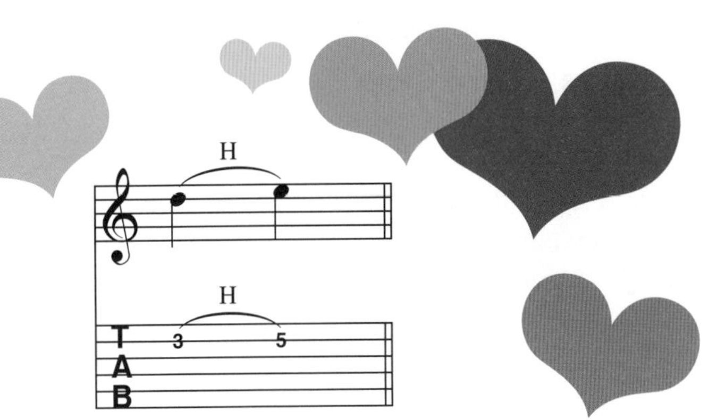

Hammer-on Exercise No. 1

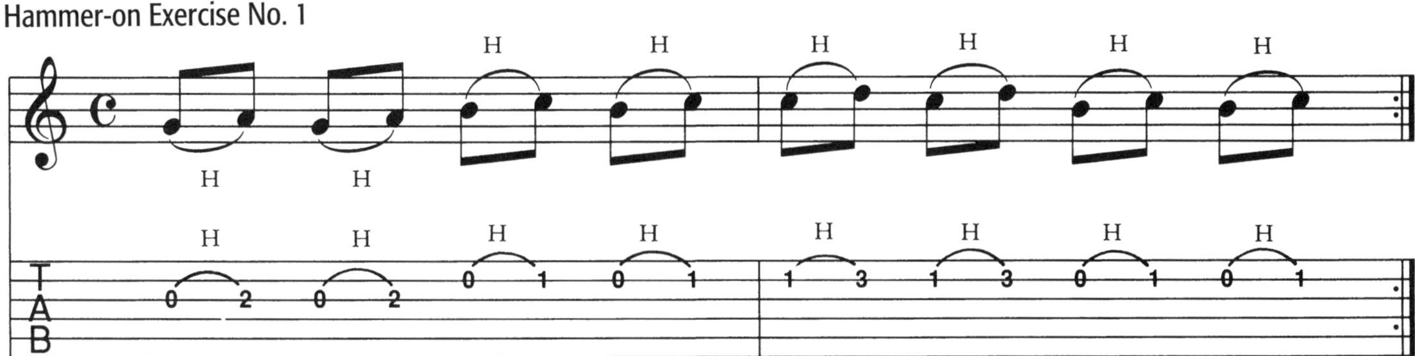

Hammer-on Exercise No. 2

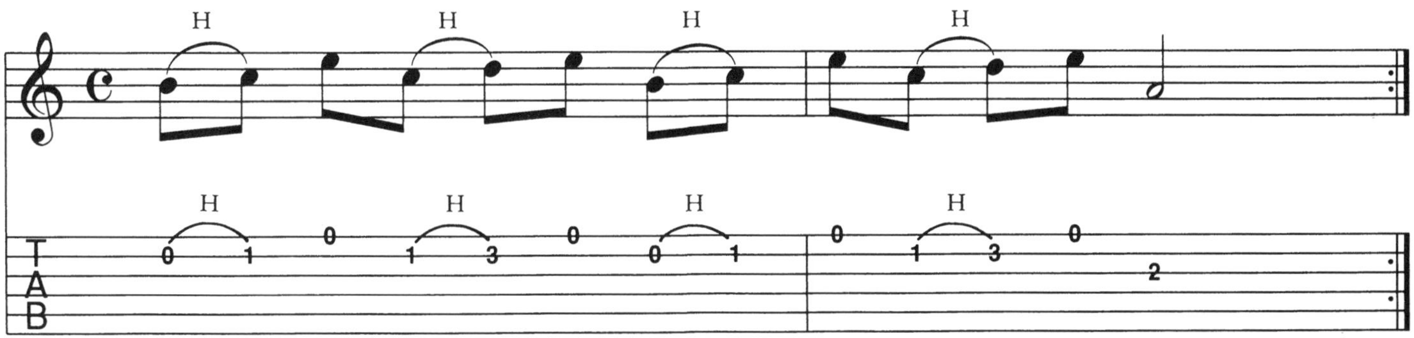

Hammer-on Exercise No. 3

Pull-off

To perform a pull-off to an *open string note*, pick only the first note (the higher note), then pull the finger off the string. The sound of the open string is made by the pull-off from the first note.

Pull-off Exercise No. 1

To perform a pull-off to a *fingered note*, first finger both notes to be played. Pick only the first note (the higher note), then pull the finger off the string while keeping the lower note fretted. The sound of the second note is made by the pull-off from the first note.

Pull-off Exercise No. 2

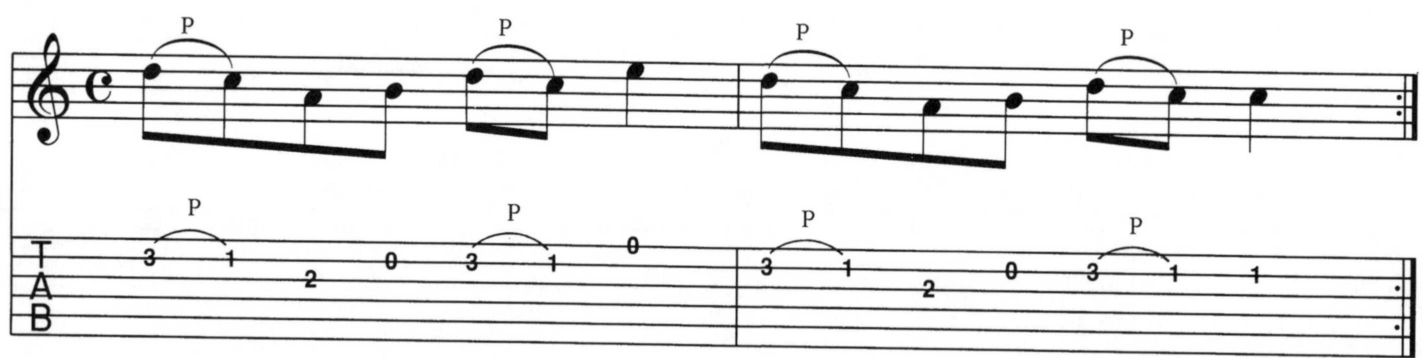

Hammer-on & Pull-off Exercise

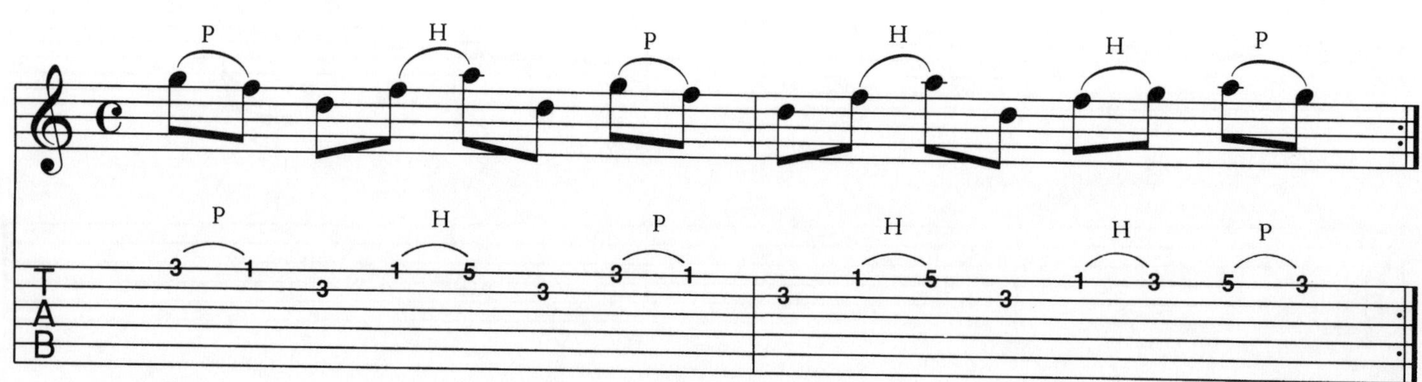

Slide

Pick the first note (the lower note), then slide the finger up the string until you are sounding the second note. The second note is not picked.

Slide Exercise No. 1

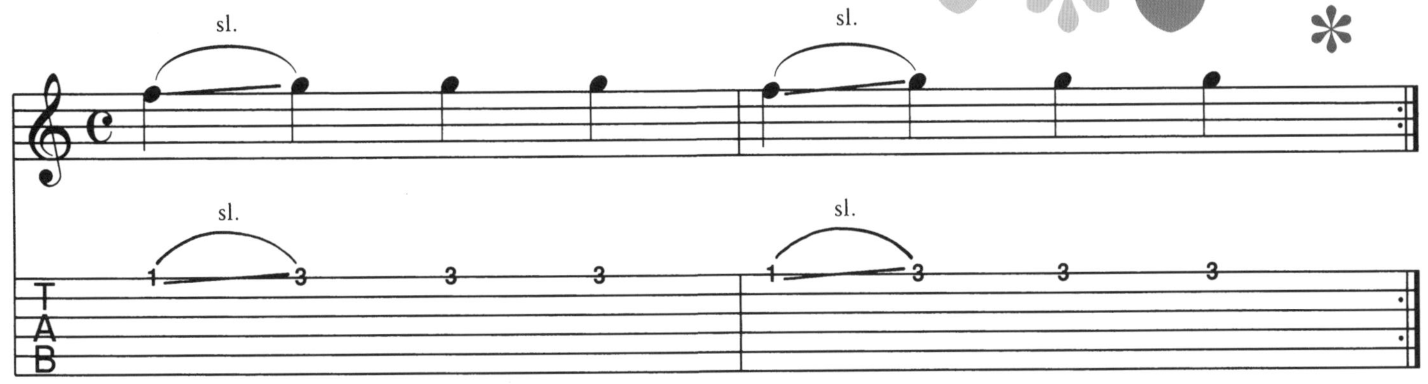

Slide Exercise No. 2

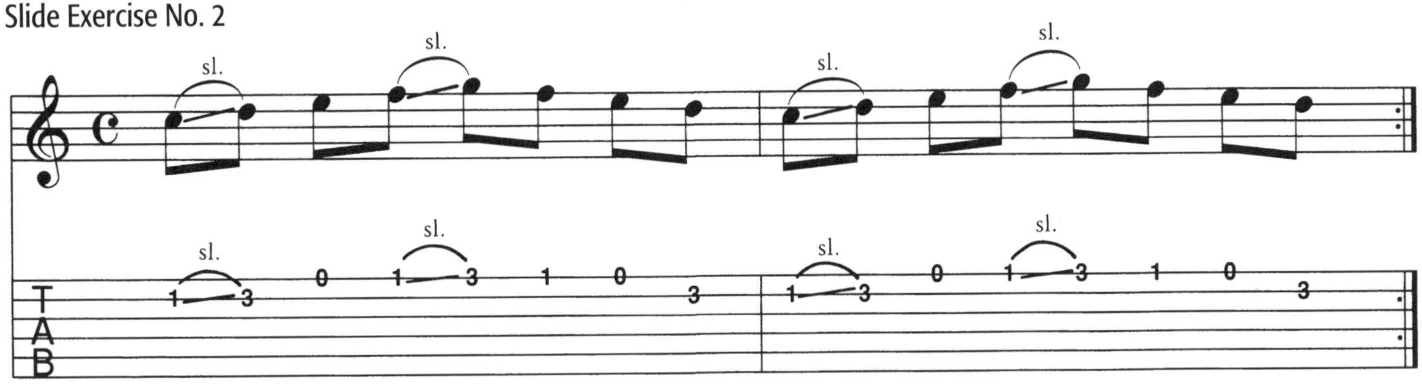

Hammer-on, Pull-off and Slide Exercise

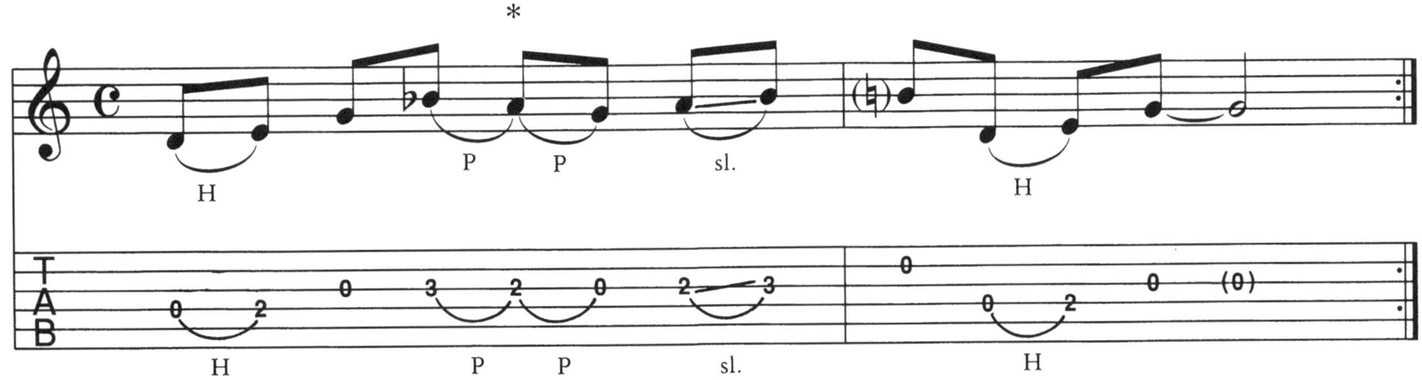

* When playing two consecutive pull-offs, pick the first note, then pull-off to sound the second note, then pull-off to sound the third note. Pick the string only once.

Palm Mute

The note is partially muted by lightly touching the string just before the bridge with the heel of the right hand. When the note is then picked, it has a muffled sound. The key is not to press too hard with the right hand as this will overly silence the note.

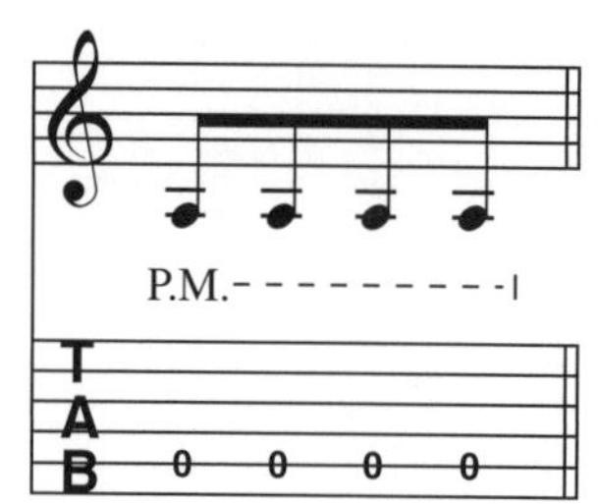

Palm Mute Exercise No. 1

Palm Mute Exercise No. 2

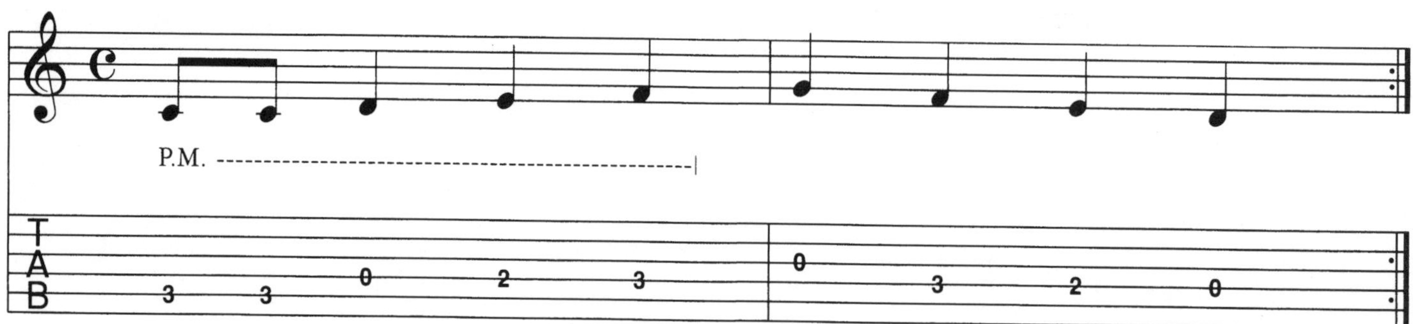

Hammer-on, Pull-off, Slide and Palm Mute Exercise

* Pick only the first note.

Tablature Licks

A lick is a pattern or series of notes that is commonly used as a basis for soloing. On the next few pages, we will introduce you to different styles of music through the use of licks. These licks should help you understand how tablature and the new special techniques you've learned can affect the sounds you can get out of your guitar.

Rock

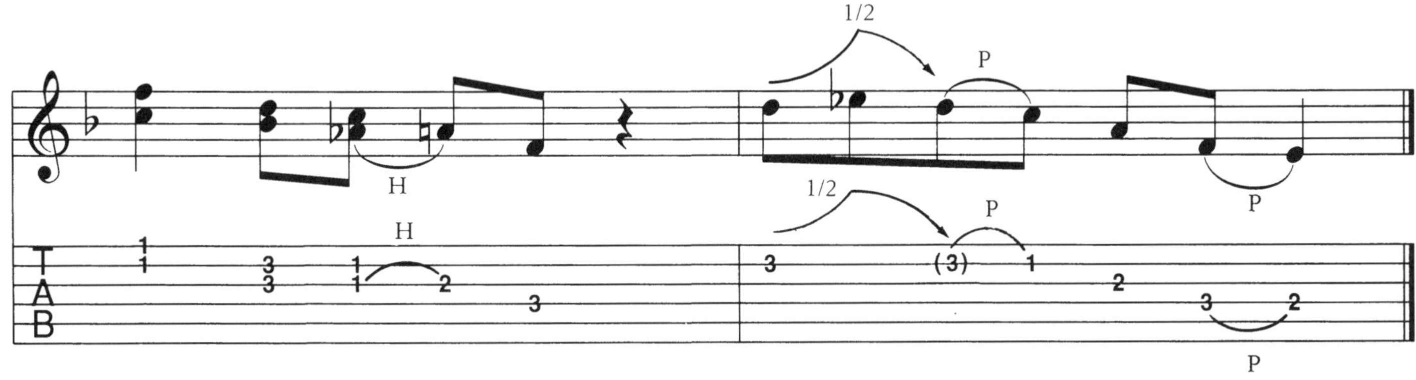

Heavy Metal

Bonnie Raitt

An outstanding slide guitarist and highly original songwriter, Raitt has embraced many styles of music including country and rock, but most prominently draws from the blues. She was one of the most interesting performers of the 1980s and 1990s.

Blues

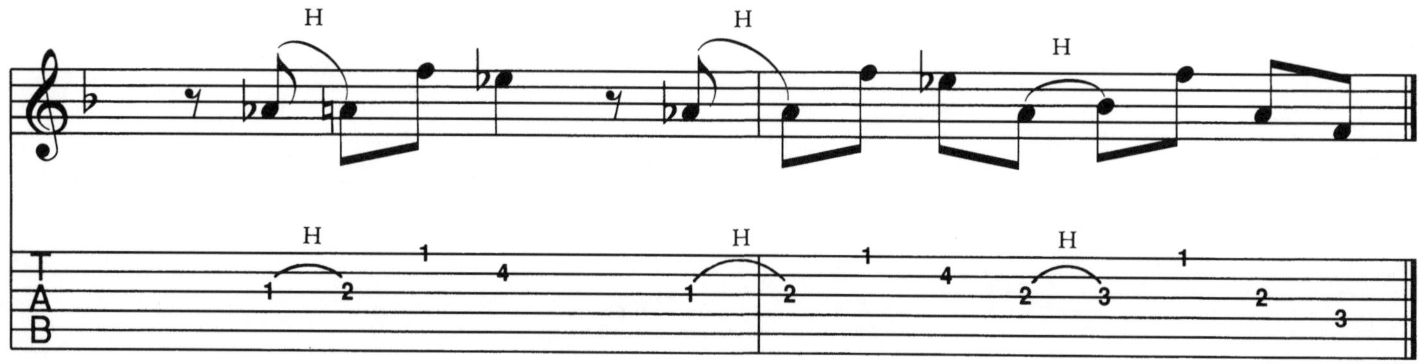

Country

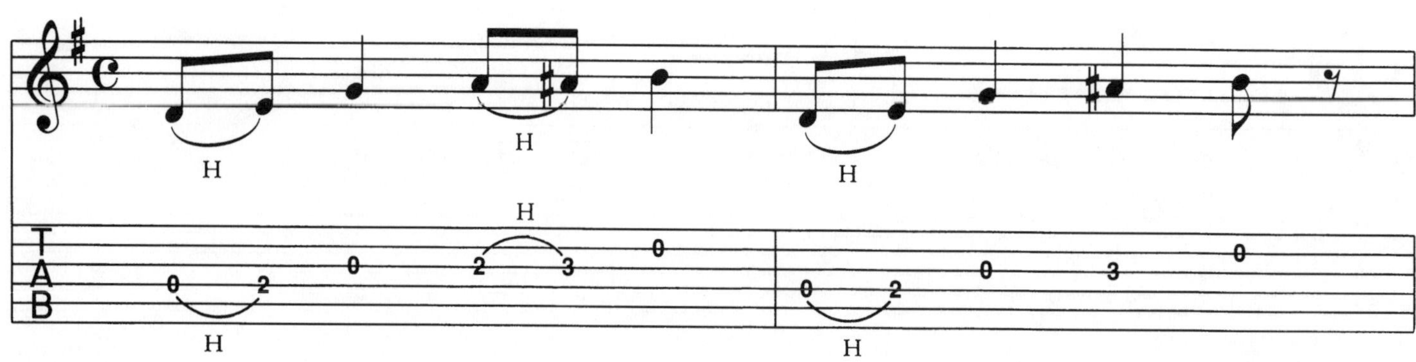

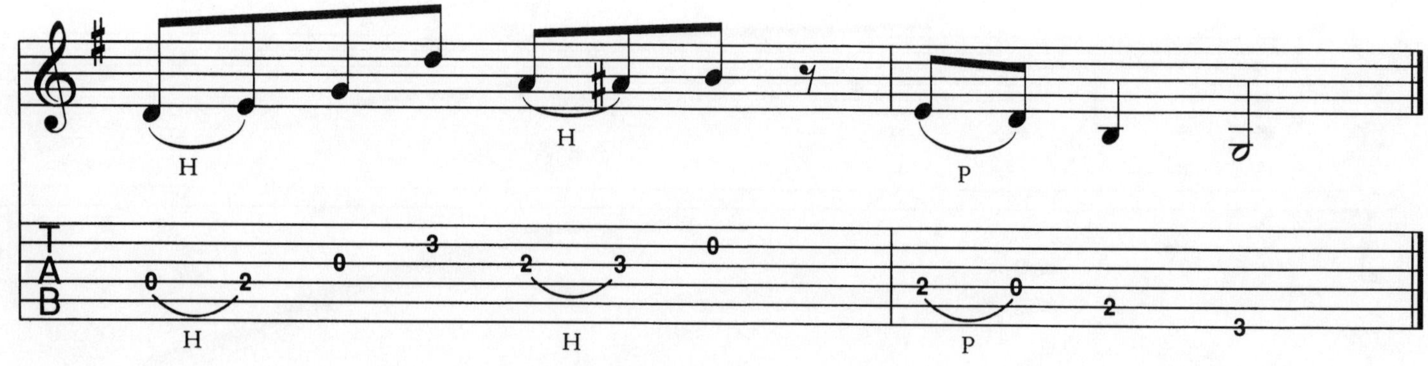

Jazz

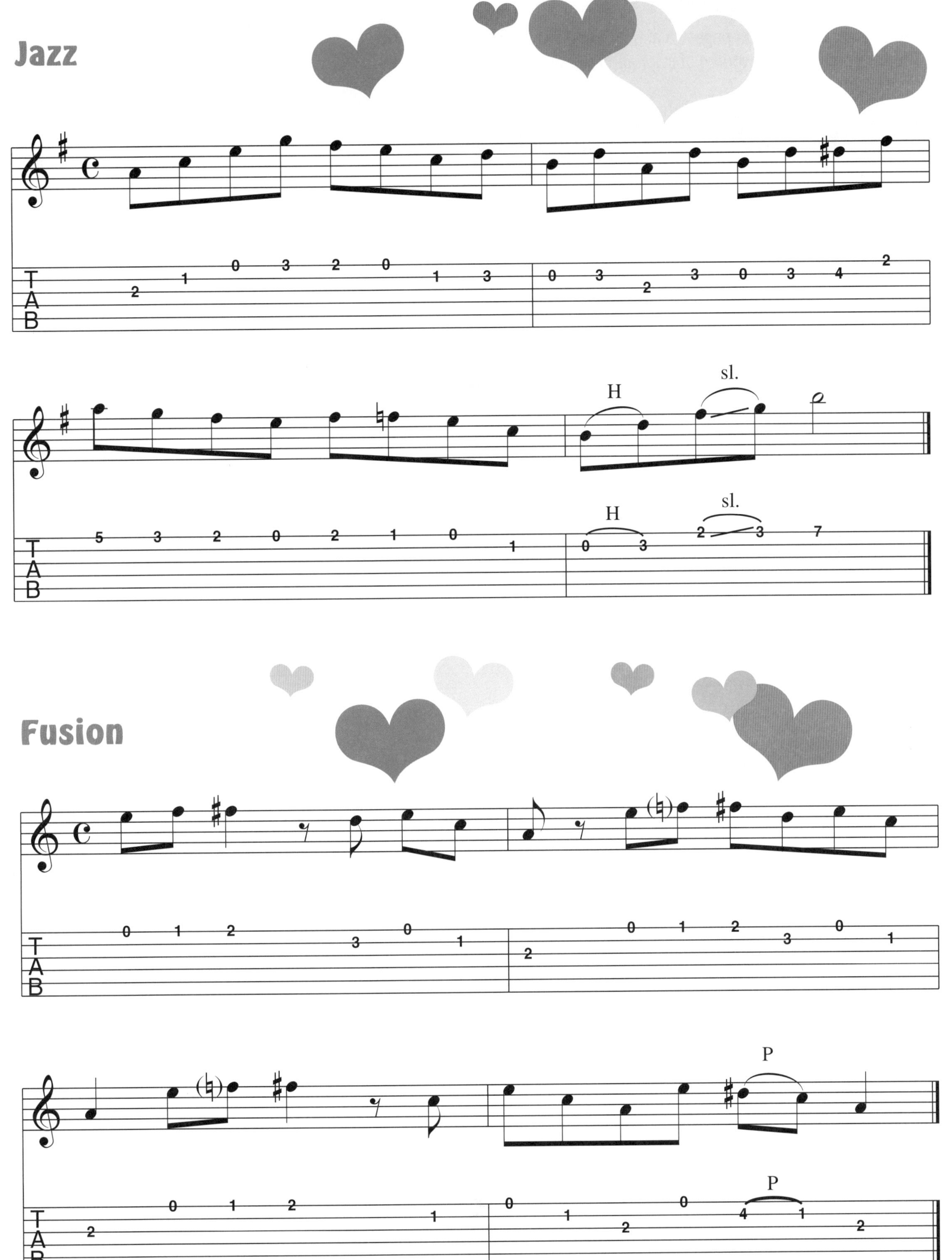

Country Grooves

The musical examples on pages 78 and 79 explore different styles. They are provided as a source of inspiration for further experimentation.

Sunflower Shower

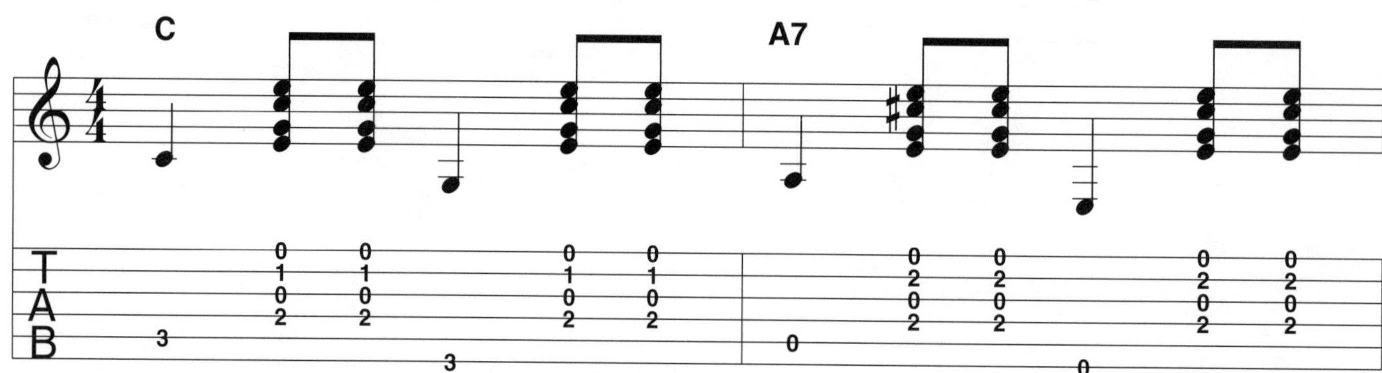

Ladybug Jitterbug

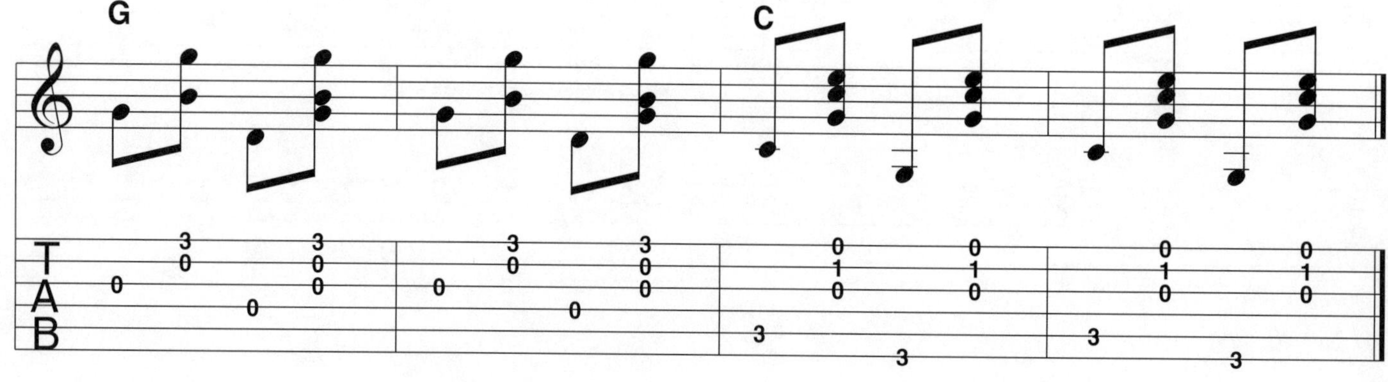

Rock Grooves

Rollerskate Date

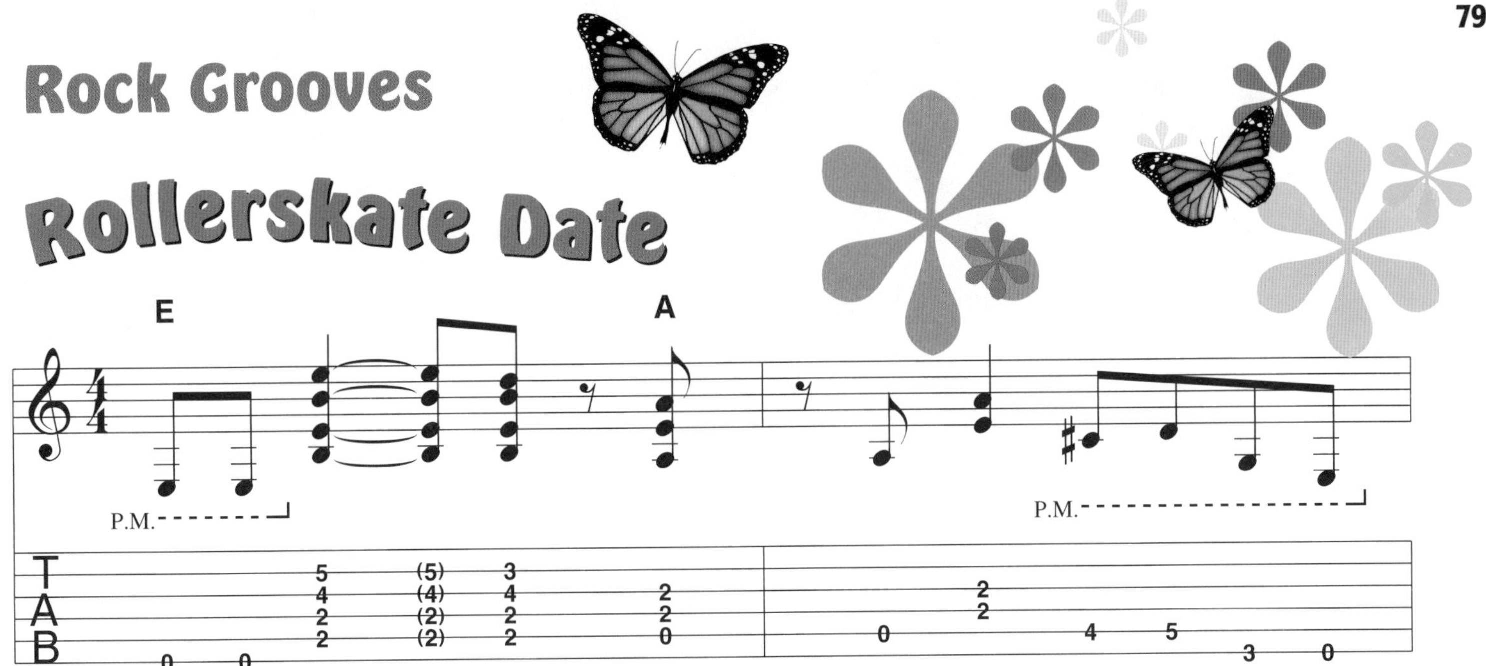

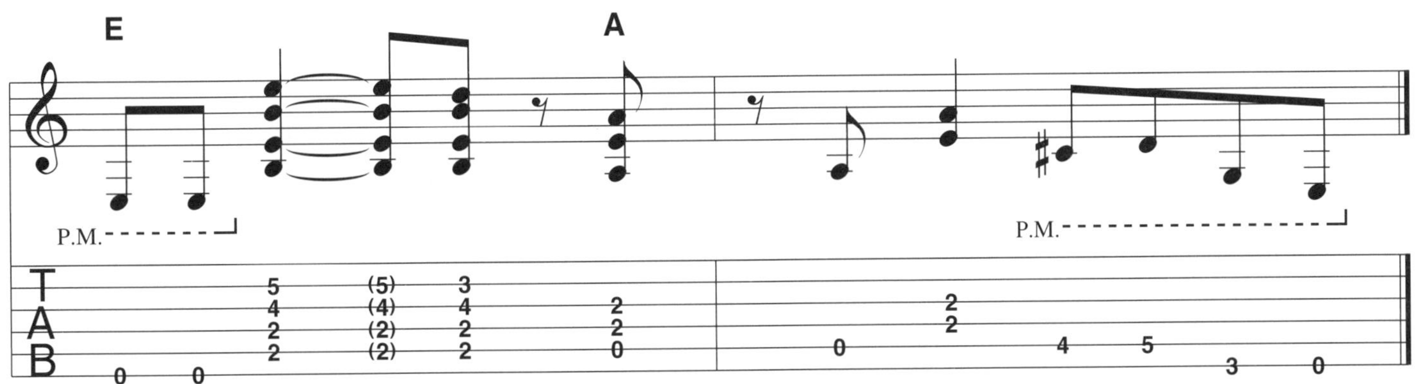

Petals to the Metal

Dictionary of Guitar Notation

Arpeggio

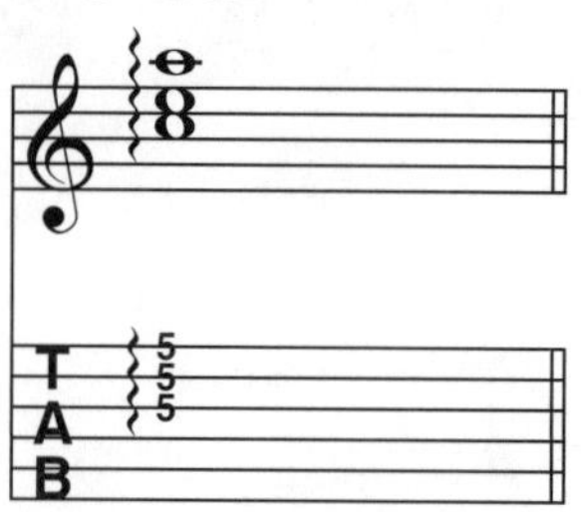

Strike the notes of the chord shown from the bottom up. Quickly release each note after striking.

Bends

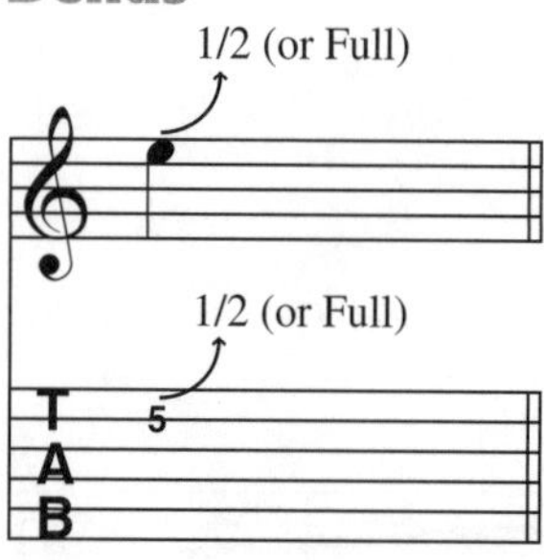

One- or Two-Note Up Bend: Pick the first note, then bend the string to sound up either one or two frets.

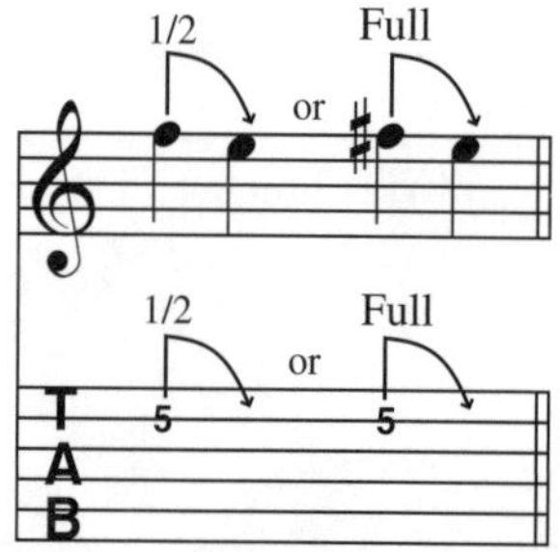

One- or Two-Note Down Bend: Pick the first (bent) note, then straighten the string to sound the lower (second) note.

1/2 or Full

1/2 or Full

Pick Bend and Release: Pick the first note, bend the string up one or two frets to sound the higher (second) note, then straighten the string to sound the original (first) note again. Pick only the first note.

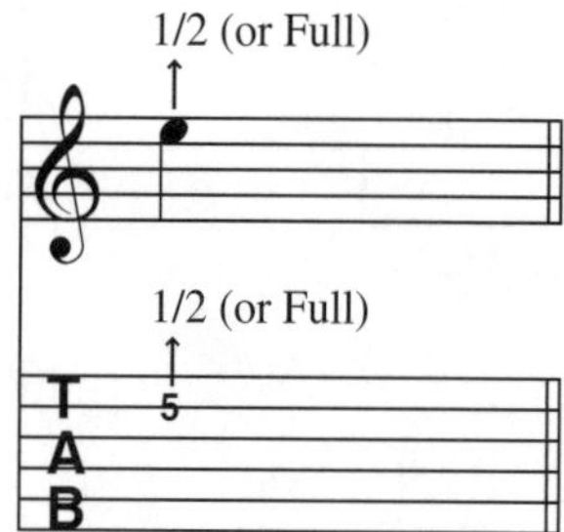

Bend and then Pick: Bend the first note up one or two frets before picking it. This is usually followed by a down bend.

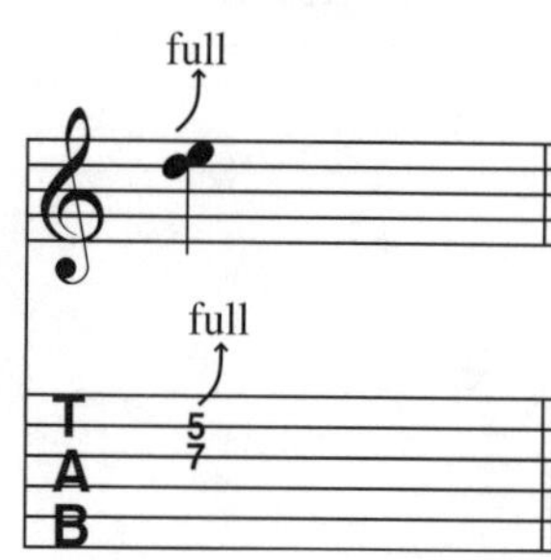

Unison Bend: Pick the lower (first) note slightly before picking the higher (second) note, but before picking the higher note, bend the string of the lower note so it matches the pitch of the higher note. These notes are always picked on adjacent strings.

Harmonics

Natural Harmonic: The fret finger lightly touches the string over the fret, and then the string is picked. A chimelike sound is produced.

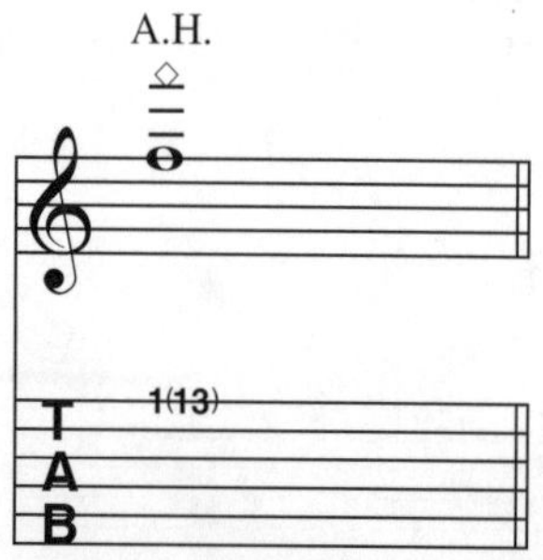

Artificial Harmonic: After the note is fretted normally, the pick hand lightly touches the string at the fret (in parentheses) with one finger while plucking with another.

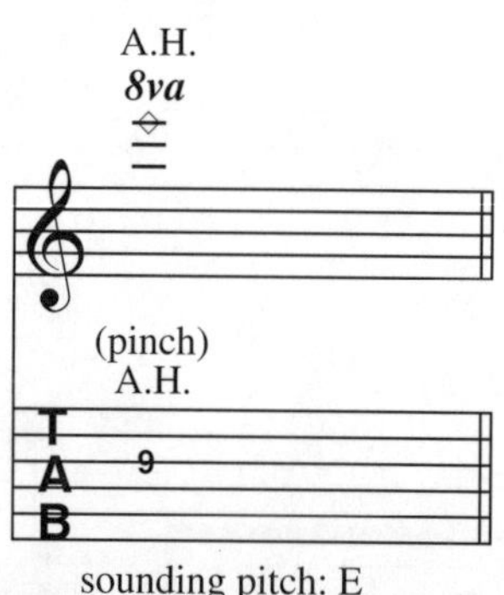

Artificial "Pinch" Harmonic: After the note is fretted normally, add the edge of the thumb or the tip of the index finger to the normal pick attack to produce the harmonic. High volume or distortion will allow for a greater variety of harmonics.

Mutes

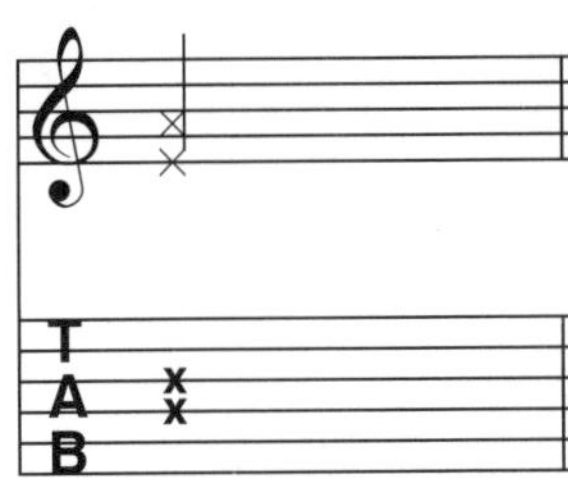

Muffled Strings: A percussive sound is produced by laying the fret hand across the strings without depressing them to the fretboard, and then striking the strings with the pick hand.

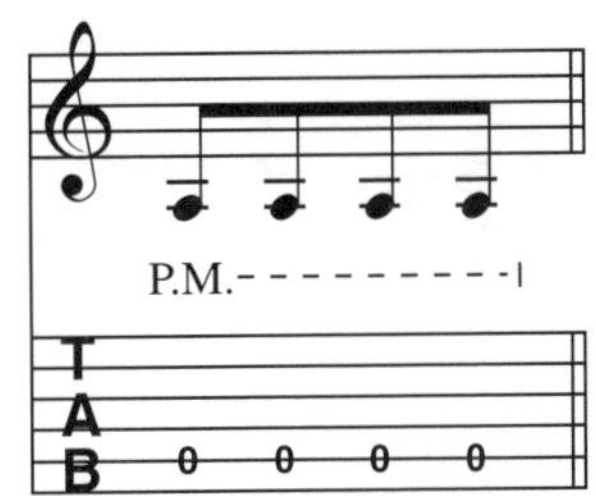

Palm Mute (P.M.): The note is partially muted by the pick hand by lightly touching the string or strings just before the bridge.

Slides

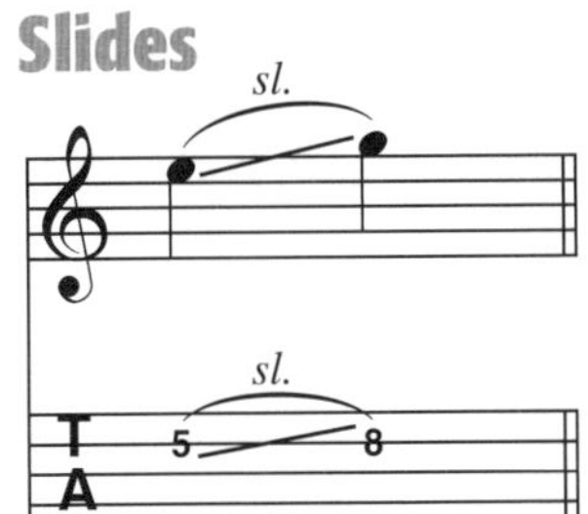

Slide: Pick the lower (first) note, then slide the fret finger up to sound the higher (second) note. The higher note is not picked again.

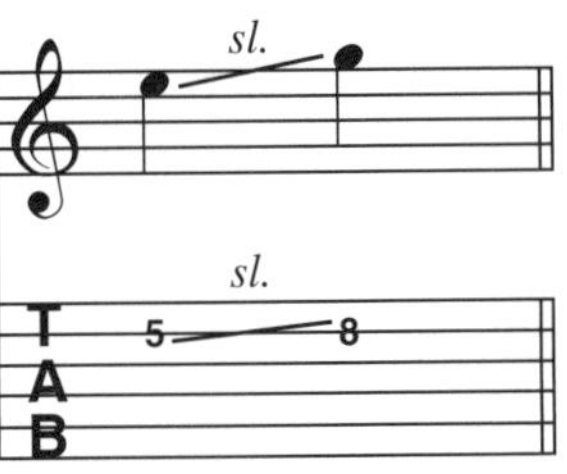

Slide and Pick: Same as the slide except the higher note is also picked.

Long Slide: Strike the note during the slide up to the desired note.

Slide Off: Same as the slide except the fret finger slides up or down an indefinite number of frets, removing the finger tension at the end of the slide.

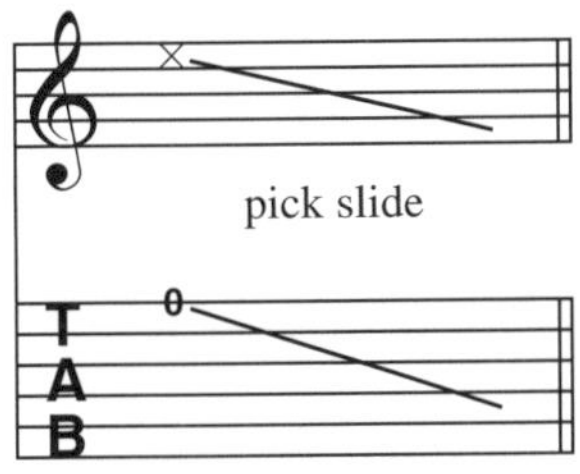

Pick Slide: The edge of the pick slides down the entire string. A sctratchy downward sound is produced.

Tapping

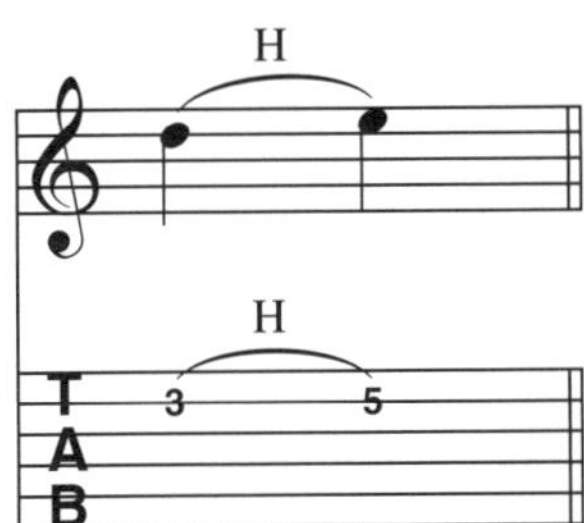

Hammer-on: Pick the lower (first) note, then hammer-on (tap down) the higher (second) note with another finger. Pick only the first note. These notes are always played on the same string.

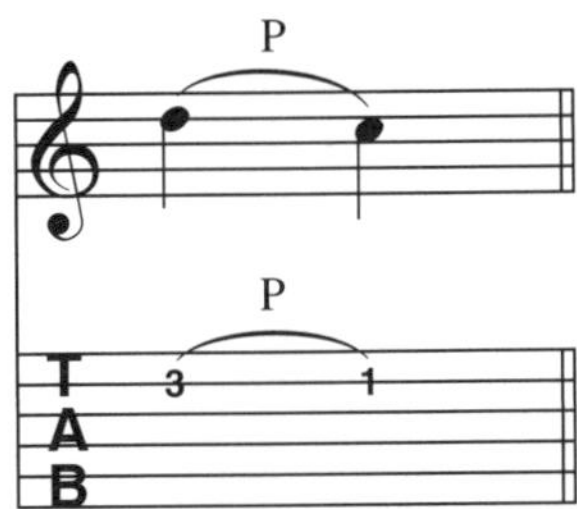

Pull-off: Place both fret fingers on the two notes to be played. Pick the higher (first) note, then pull-off (raise up) the finger of the higher note while keeping the lower note fretted. Pick only the first note.

Tapping: Tap down on the fretted string with the index or middle finger of the pick hand. This is usually followed by a pull-off to sound the lower note.

Tremolos

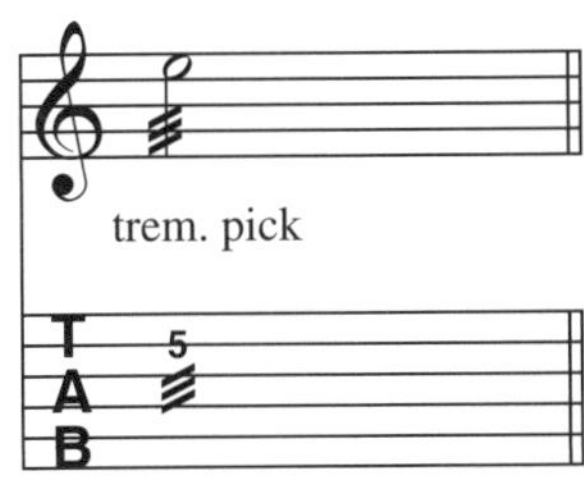

Tremolo Picking: The string is picked down-and-up as rapidly as possible.

Tremolo Bar: A note or chord is raised or lowered a specified number of frets by pushing down or pulling up on the tremolo bar, and then returning to the original note or chord.

Vibrato

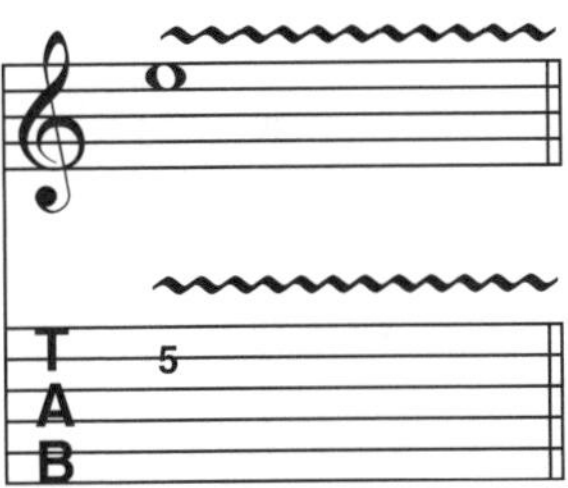

Pick the string as the fret finger or a tremolo bar rapidly rolls back and forth or bends up and down, making the note sound slightly higher and lower. An exaggerated vibrato can be achieved by rolling the fret finger a greater distance.

CHORD THEORY

Intervals

Play any note on the guitar, then play a note one fret above it. The distance between these two notes is a *half step.* Play another note followed by a note two frets above it. The distance between these two notes is a *whole step* (two half steps). The distance between any two notes is referred to as an *interval.*

In the example of the C major scale below, the letter names are shown above the notes and the *scale degrees* (numbers) of the notes are written below. Notice that C is the first degree of the scale, D is the second, etc.

The name of an interval is determined by counting the number of scale degrees from one note to the next. For example, an interval of a 3rd, starting on C, would be determined by counting up three scale degrees, or C-D-E (1-2-3). C to E is a 3rd. An interval of a 4th, starting on C, would be determined by counting up four scale degrees, or C-D-E-F (1-2-3-4). C to F is a 4th.

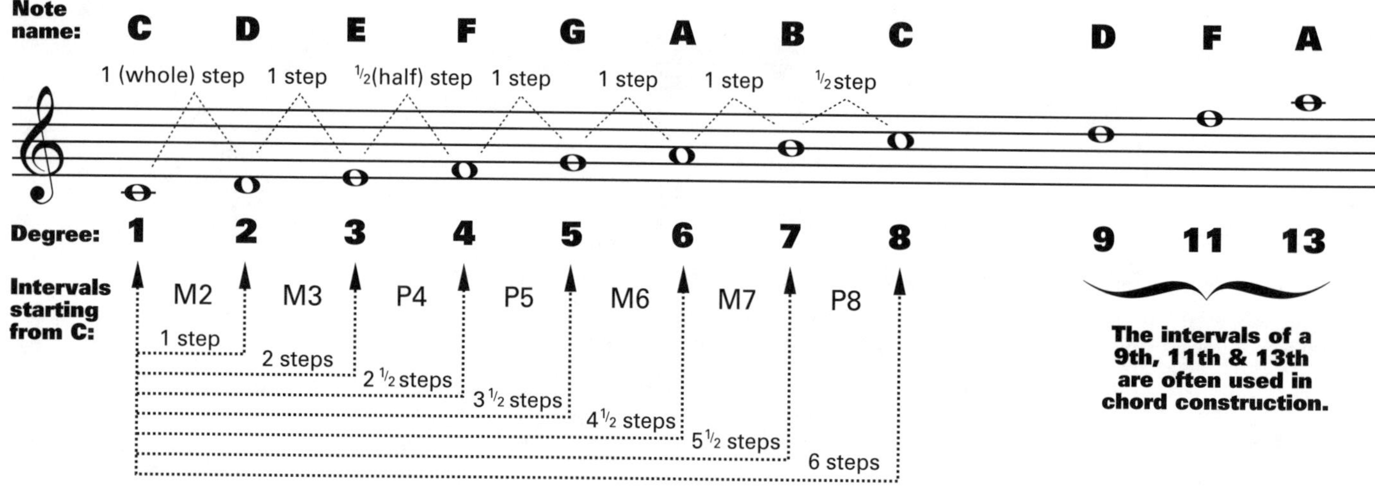

Intervals are not only labeled by the distance between scale degrees, but by the *quality* of the interval. An interval's quality is determined by counting the number of whole steps and half steps between the two notes of an interval. For example, C to E is a 3rd. C to E is also a major third because there are 2 whole steps between C and E. Likewise, C to E♭ is a 3rd. C to E♭ is also a minor third because there are 1½ steps between C and E♭. There are five qualities used to describe intervals: *major, minor, perfect, diminished,* and *augmented.*

M = Major
m = Minor
P = Perfect

o = Diminished (dim)
+ = Augmented (aug)

Particular intervals are associated with certain qualities:

2nds, 9ths	**=**	**Major, Minor & Augmented**
3rds, 6ths, 13ths	**=**	**Major, Minor, Augmented & Diminished**
4ths, 5ths, 11ths	**=**	**Perfect, Augmented & Diminished**
7ths	**=**	**Major, Minor & Diminished**

When a *major* interval is made ***smaller*** by a half step it becomes a *minor* interval.

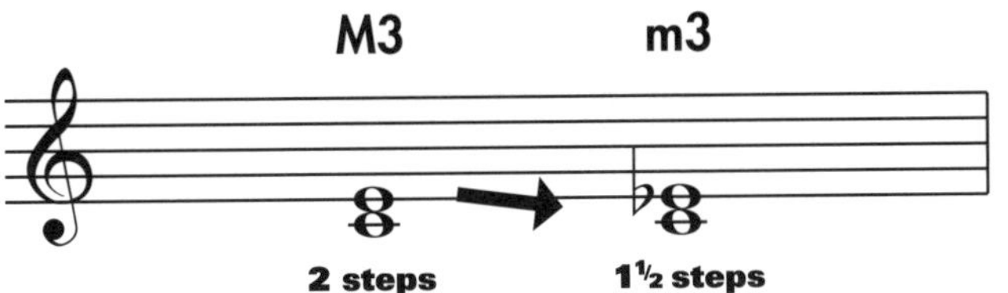

When a *minor* interval is made ***larger*** by a half step it becomes a *major* interval.

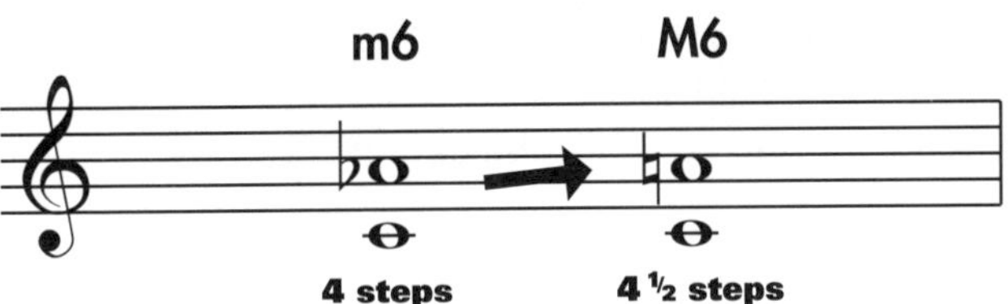

When a *minor* or *perfect* interval is made ***smaller*** by a half step it becomes a *diminished* interval.

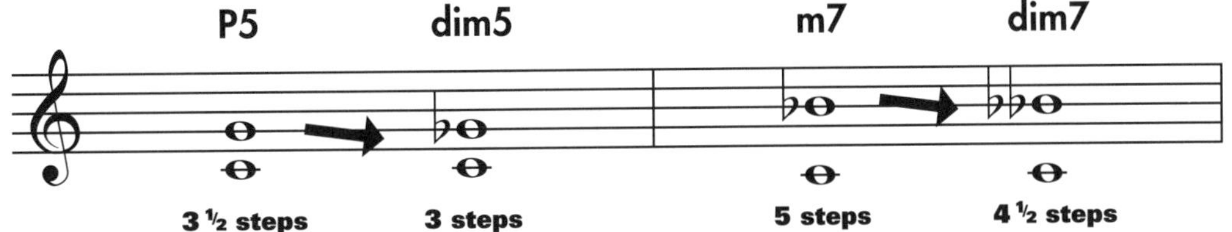

When a *major* or *perfect* interval is made ***larger*** by a half step it becomes an *augmented* interval.

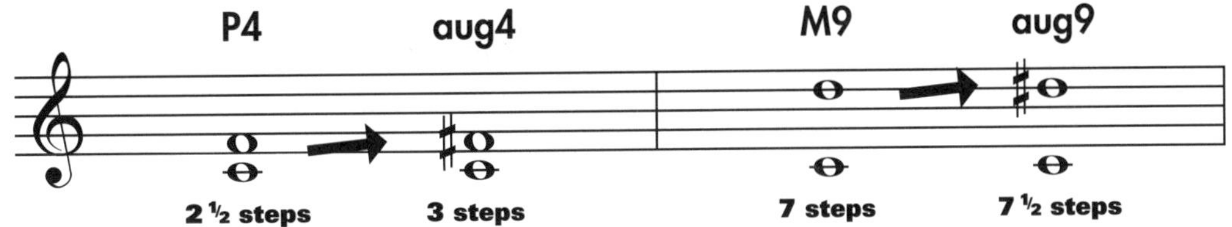

Below is a table of intervals starting on the note C. Notice that some intervals are labeled enharmonic, which means that they are written differently but sound the same (see **aug2** & **m3**).

TABLE OF INTERVALS

Basic Triads

Two or more notes played together is called a *chord*. Most commonly, a chord will consist of three or more notes. A three-note chord is called a *triad*. The *root* of a triad (or any other chord) is the note from which a chord is constructed. The relationship of the intervals from the root to the other notes of a chord determines the chord *type*. Triads are most frequently identified as one of four chord types: *major, minor, diminished* and *augmented.*

All chord types can be identified by the intervals used to create the chord. For example, the C major triad is built beginning with C as the root, adding a major 3rd (E) and adding a perfect 5th (G). All major triads contain a root, M3 and P5.

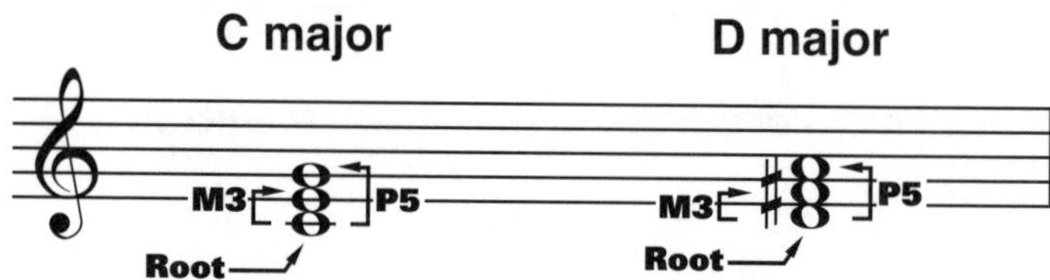

Minor triads contain a root, minor 3rd and perfect 5th. (An easier way to build a minor triad is to simply lower the 3rd of a major triad.) All minor triads contain a root, m3 and P5.

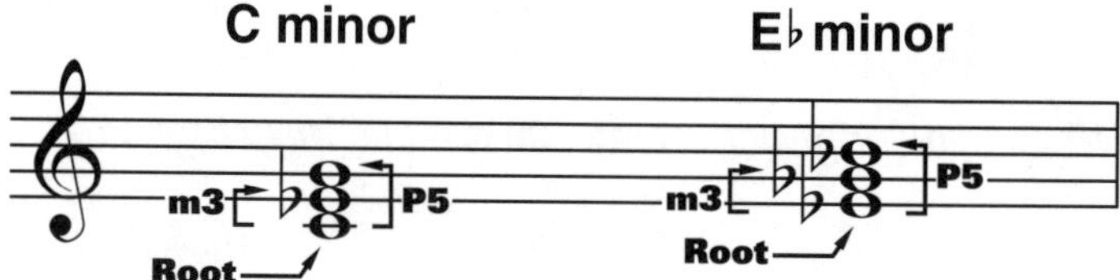

Diminished triads contain a root, minor 3rd and diminished 5th. If the perfect 5th of a minor triad is made smaller by a half step (to become a diminished 5th), the result is a diminished triad. All diminished triads contain a root, m3 and dim5.

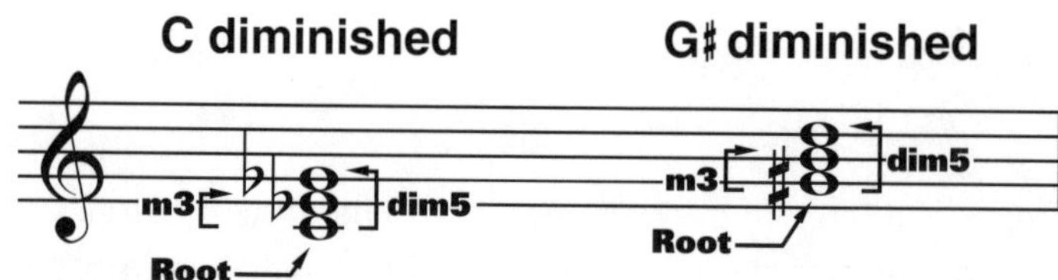

Augmented triads contain a root, major 3rd and augmented 5th. If the perfect 5th of a major triad is made larger by a half step (to become an augmented 5th), the result is an augmented triad. All augmented triads contain a root, M3 and aug5.

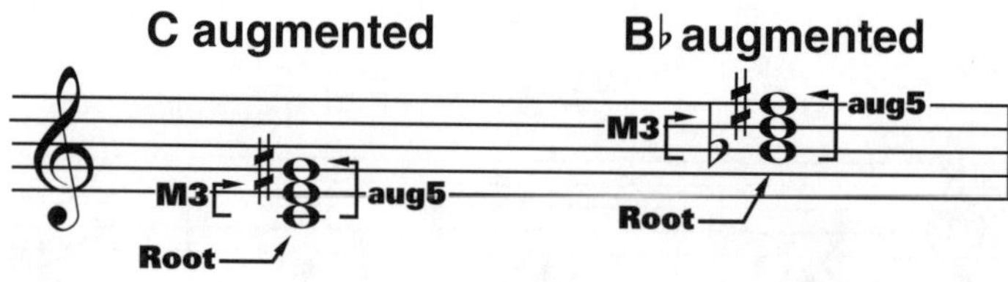

An important concept to remember about chords is that the bottom note of a chord will not always be the root. If the root of a triad, for instance, is moved above the 5th so that the 3rd is the bottom note of the chord, it is said to be in the *first inversion*. If the root and 3rd are moved above the 5th, the chord is in the *second inversion*. The number of inversions that a chord can have is related to the number of notes in the chord: a three-note chord can have two inversions, a four-note chord can have three inversions, etc.

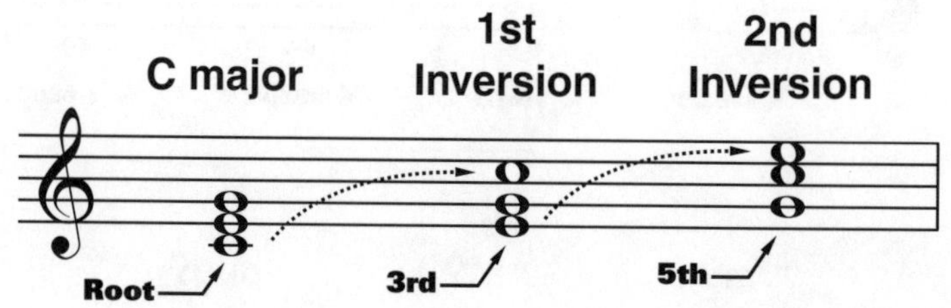

Building Chords

By using the four chord types as basic building blocks, it is possible to create a variety of chords by adding 6ths, 7ths, 9ths, 11ths, etc. The following are e xamples of some of the many variations.

* The *suspended fourth* chord does not contain a third. An assumption is made that the 4th degree of the chord will harmonically be inclined to *resolve* to the 3rd degree. In other words, the 4th is *suspended* until it moves to the 3rd.

Thus far, the examples provided to illustrate intervals and chord construction have been based on C. Until familiarity with chords is achieved, the C chord examples on the previous page can serve as a reference guide when building chords based on other notes: For instance, locate C7(♭9). To construct a G7(♭9) chord, first determine what intervals are contained in C7(♭9), then follow the steps outlined below.

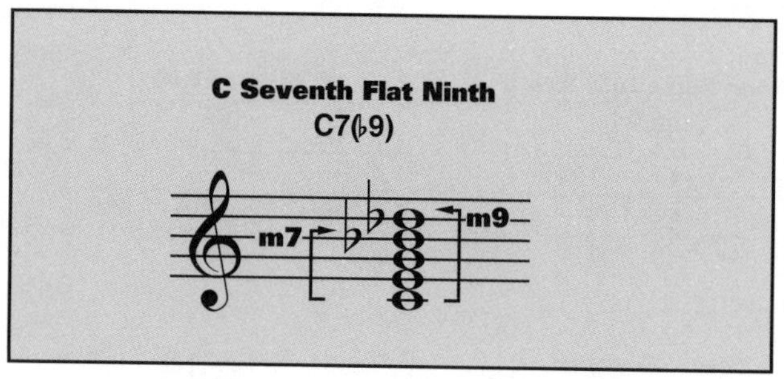

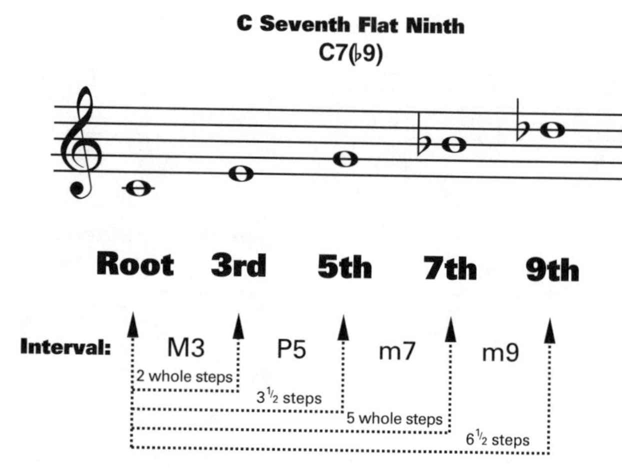

- Determine the *root* of the chord. A chord is always named for its root–in this instance, G is the root of G7(♭9).

- Count *letter names* up from the *letter name of the root* (G), as was done when building intervals on page 96, to determine the intervals of the chord. Therefore, counting three letter names up from G to B (G-A-B, 1-2-3) is a 3rd, G to D (G-A-B-C-D) is a 5th, G to F is a 7th, and G to A is a 9th.

- Determine the *quality* of the intervals by counting whole steps and half steps up from the root; G to B (2 whole steps) is a major 3rd, G to D (3½ steps) is a perfect 5th, G to F (5 whole steps) is a minor 7th, and G to A♭ (6½ steps) is a minor 9th.

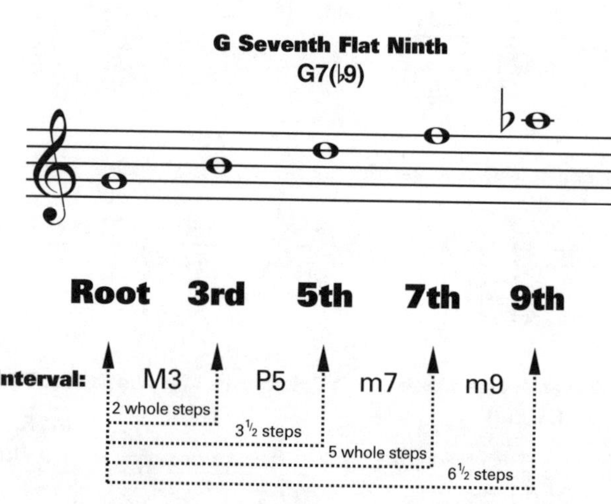

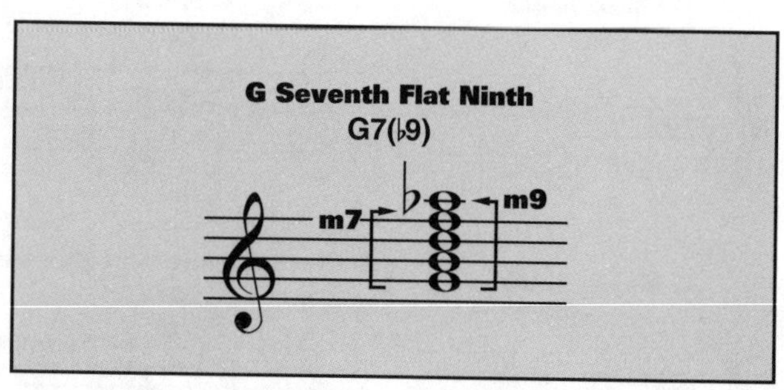

Follow this general guideline for determining the notes of any chord. As interval and chord construction become more familiar to the beginning guitarist, it will become possible to create original fingerings on the guitar. Experimentation is suggested.

The Circle of Fifths

The *circle of fifths* will help to clarify which chords are enharmonic equivalents (notice that *chords* can be written enharmonically as well as *notes*). The circle of fifths also serves as a quick reference guide to the relationship of the keys and how key signatures can be figured out in a logical manner. Clockwise movement (up a P5) provides all of the sharp keys by adding one sharp to the key signature progressively. Counter-clockwise (down a P5) provides the flat keys by adding one flat similarly.

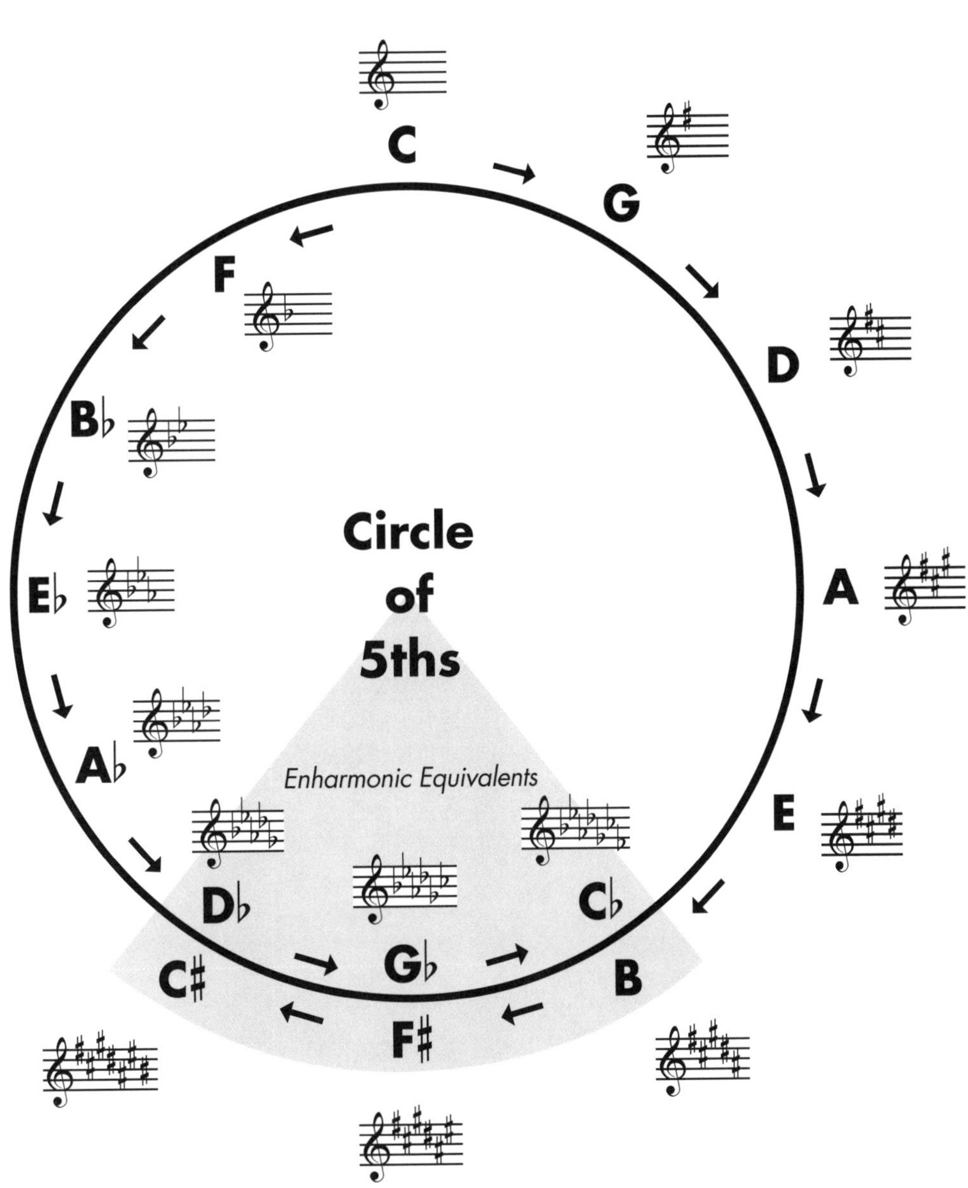

Chord Symbol Variations

Chord symbols are a form of musical shorthand providing the guitarist with as much information about a chord as quickly as possible. The intent of using chord symbols is to convey enough information to recognize the chord yet not so much as to confuse the meaning of the symbol. Since chord symbols are not universally standardized, they are often written in many different ways–some are understandable, others are confusing. To illustrate this point, below is a listing of some of the ways copyists, composers and arrangers have created variations on the more common chord symbols.

C	**Csus**	**C(♭5)**	**C(add9)**	**C5**	**Cm**
C major	Csus4	C-5	C(9)	C(no3)	Cmin
Cmaj	C(addF)	C(5-)	C(add2)	C(omit3)	Cmi
CM	C4	C(♯4)	C(+9)		C-
			C(+D)		

C+	**C°**	**C6**	**C6/9**	**Cm6/9**	**Cm6**
C+5	Cdim	Cmaj6	C6(add9)	C-6/9	C-6
Caug	Cdim7	C(addA)	C6(addD)	Cm6(+9)	Cm(addA)
Caug5	C7dim	C(A)	C9(no7)	Cm6(add9)	Cm(+6)
C(♯5)			C9/6	Cm6(+D)	

C7	**C7sus**	**Cm7**	**Cm7(♭5)**	**C7+**	**C7(♭5)**
C(addB♭)	C7sus4	Cmi7	Cmi7-5	C7+5	C7-5
C7̸	Csus7	Cmin7	C-7(5-)	C7aug	C7(5-)
C(-7)	C7(+4)	C-7	Cø	C7aug5	C7̸-5
C(+7)		C7mi	C ½dim	C7(♯5)	C7(♯4)

Cmaj7	**Cmaj7(♭5)**	**Cm(maj7)**	**C7(♭9)**	**C7(♯9)**	**C7+(♭9)**
Cma7	Cmaj7(-5)	C-maj7	C7(-9)	C7(+9)	Caug7-9
C7	C7̸(-5)	C-7̸	C9♭	C9♯	C+7(♭9)
C△	C△(♭5)	Cmi7̸	C9-	C9+	C+9♭
C△7					C7+(-9)

Cm9	**C9**	**C9+**	**C9(♭5)**	**Cmaj9**	**C9(♯11)**
Cm7(9)	C^{9}_{7}	C9(+5)	C9(-5)	C7̸(9)	C9(+11)
Cm7(+9)	C7add9	Caug9	$C7^{9}_{-5}$	C7̸(+9)	C(♯11)
C-9	C7(addD)	C(♯9♯5)	C9(5♭)	C9(maj7)	C11+
Cmi7(9+)	C7(+9)	C+9		C9̸	C11♯

Cm9(maj7)	**C11**	**Cm11**	**C13**	**C13(♭9)**	**C13($^{♭9}_{♭5}$)**
C-9(♯7)	C9(11)	C-11	C9addA	C13(-9)	C13(-9-5)
C(-9)7̸	C9addF	Cm(♭11)	C9(6)	$C^{13}_{♭9}$	C(♭9♭5)addA
Cmi9(♯7)	C9+11	$Cmi7^{11}_{9}$	C7addA	C(♭9)addA	
	$C7^{9}_{11}$	C-7($^{9}_{11}$)	C7+A		

Reading Chords

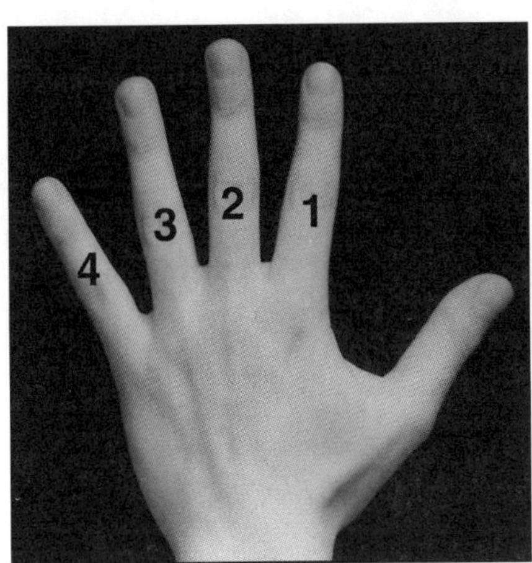

Guitar chord frames are diagrams that contain all the information necessary to play a particular chord. The fingerings, note names and position of the chord on the neck are all provided on the chord frame (see below). The photograph at left shows which finger number corresponds to which finger.

Choose chord positions that require the least motion from one chord to the next; select fingerings that are in approximately the same location on the guitar neck. This will provide smoother and more comfortable transitions between chords in a progression.

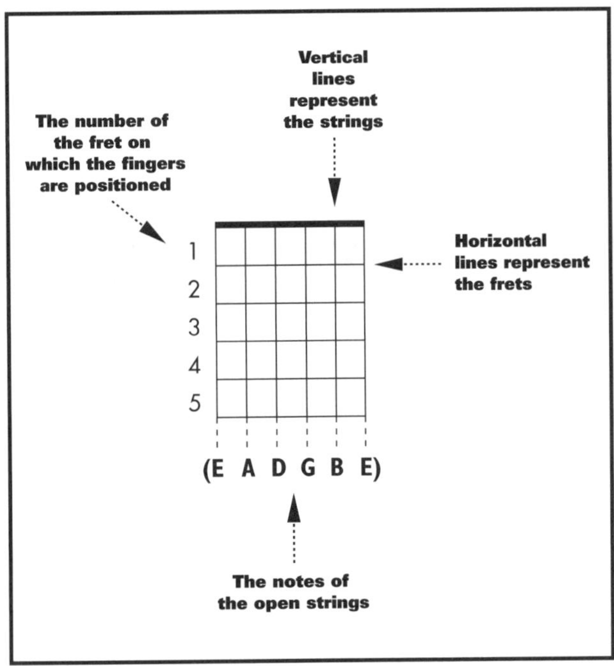

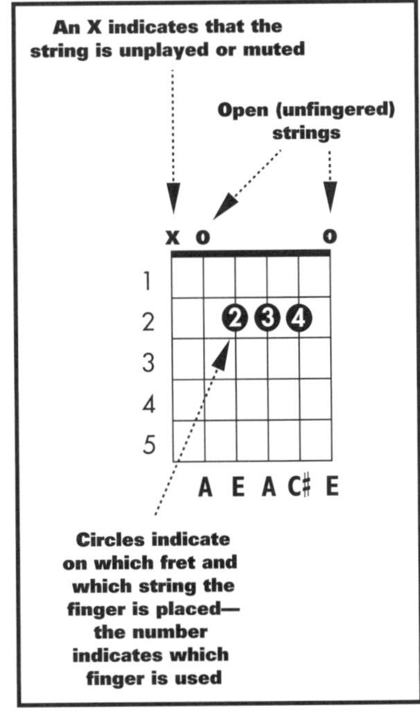

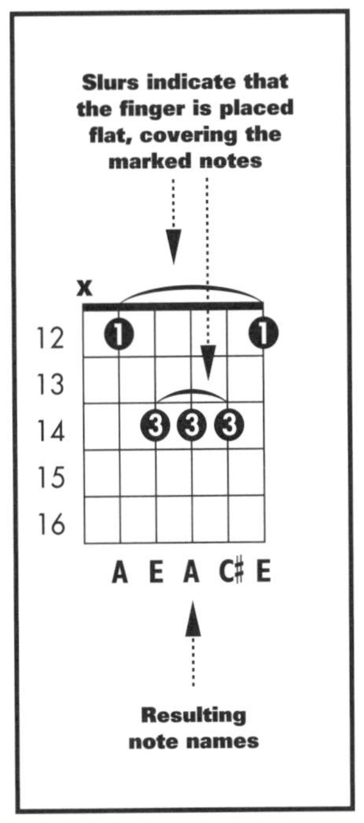

A

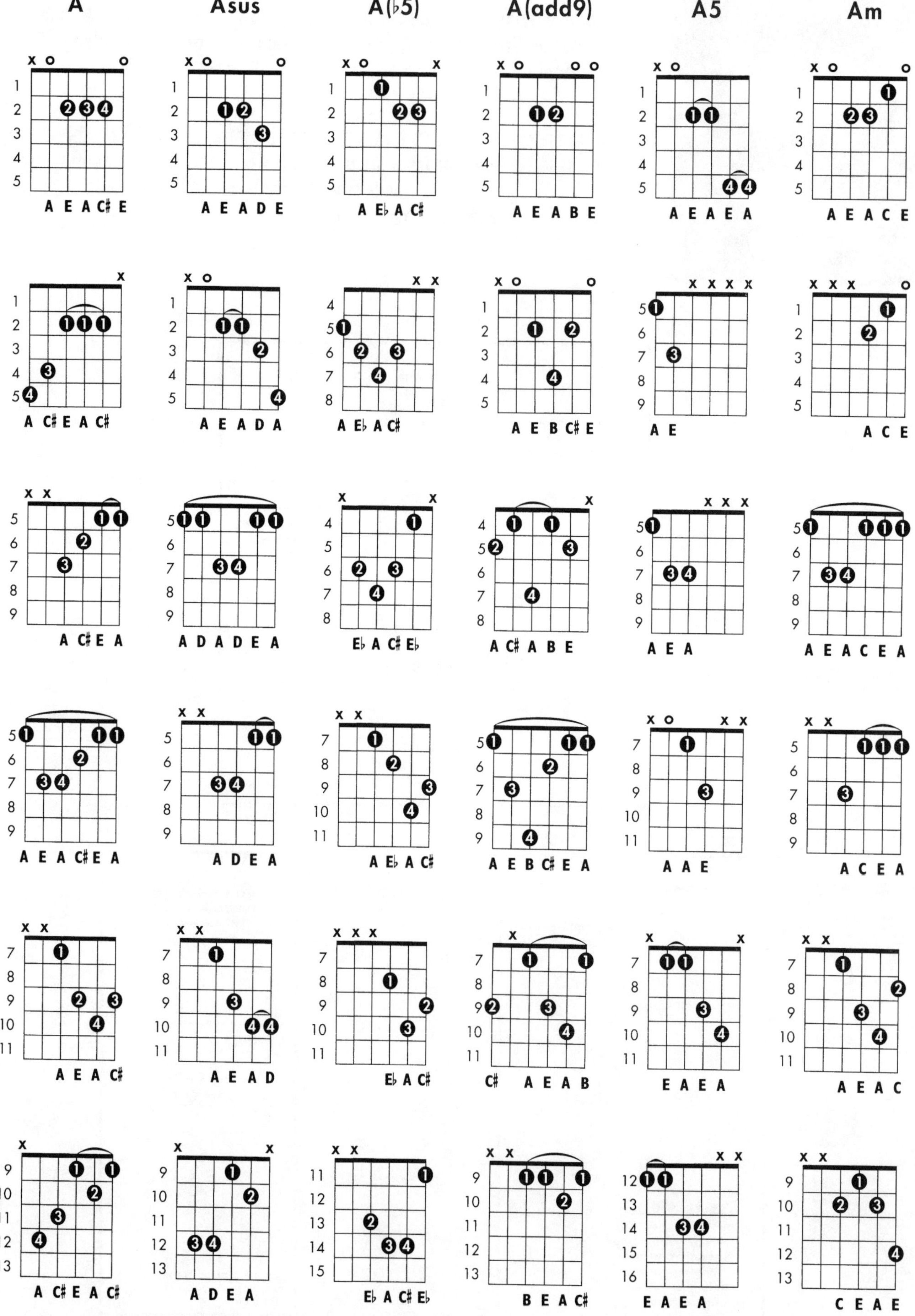

A

A+	A°	A6	A6/9	Am6/9	Am6

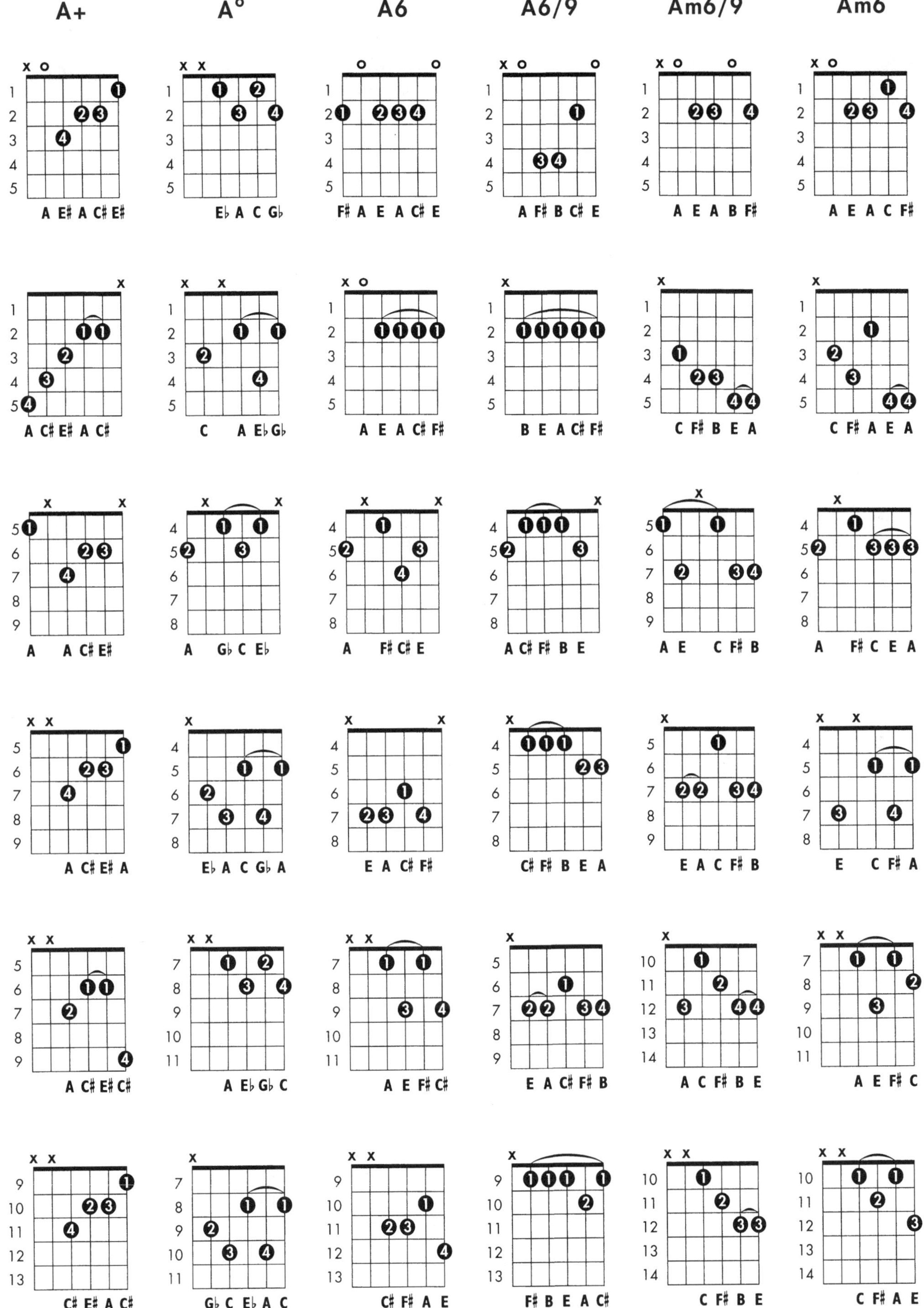

A

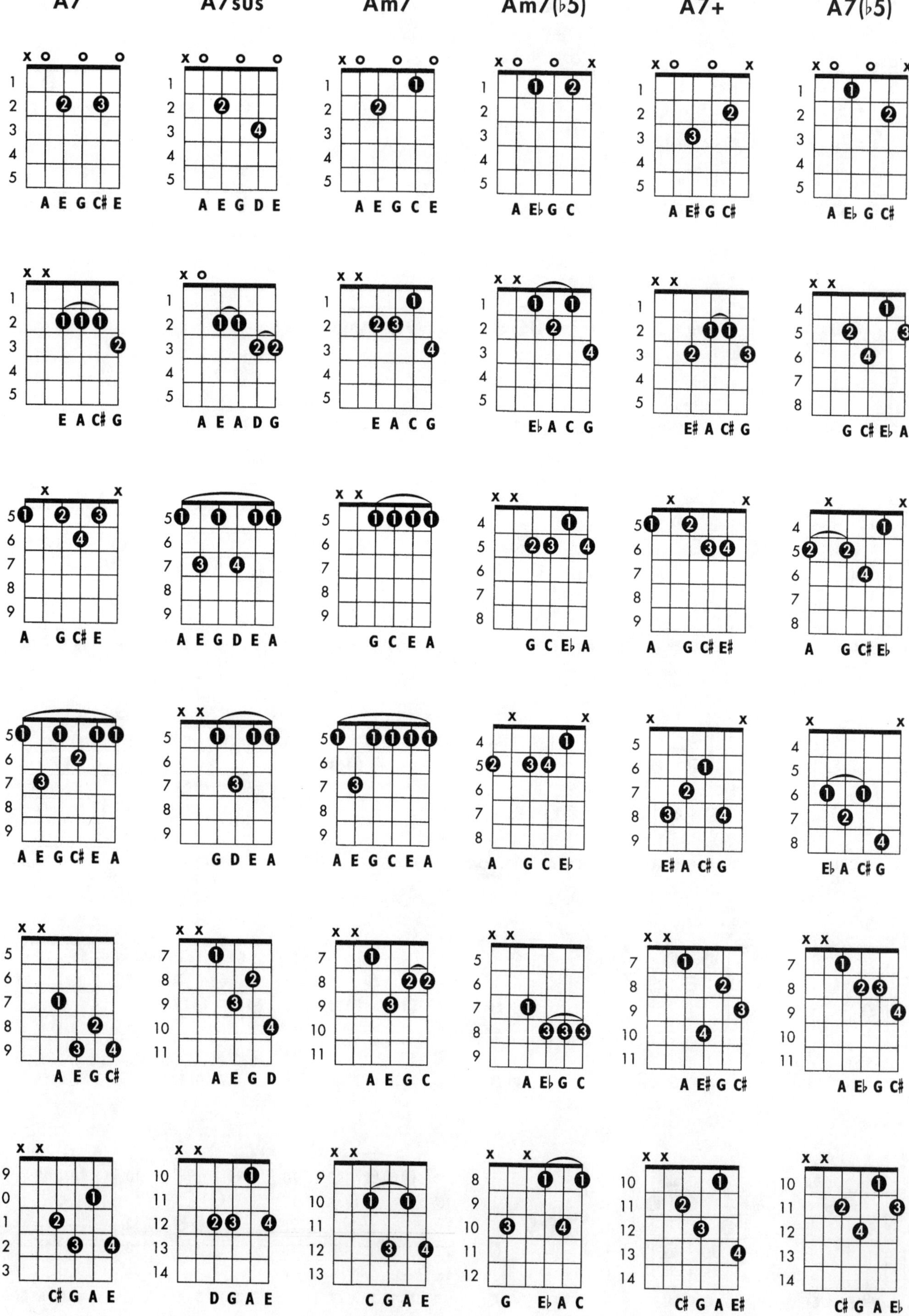
A7
A7sus
Am7
Am7(♭5)
A7+
A7(♭5)
A E G C♯ E
A E G D E
A E G C E
A E♭ G C
A E♯ G C♯
A E♭ G C♯
E A C♯ G
A E A D G
E A C G
E♭ A C G
E♯ A C♯ G
G C♯ E♭ A
A G C♯ E
A E G D E A
G C E A
G C E♭ A
A G C♯ E♯
A G C♯ E♭
A E G C♯ E A
G D E A
A E G C E A
A G C E♭
E♯ A C♯ G
E♭ A C♯ G
A E G C♯
A E G D
A E G C
A E♭ G C
A E♯ G C♯
A E♭ G C♯
C♯ G A E
D G A E
C G A E
G E♭ A C
C♯ G A E♯
C♯ G A E♭

A

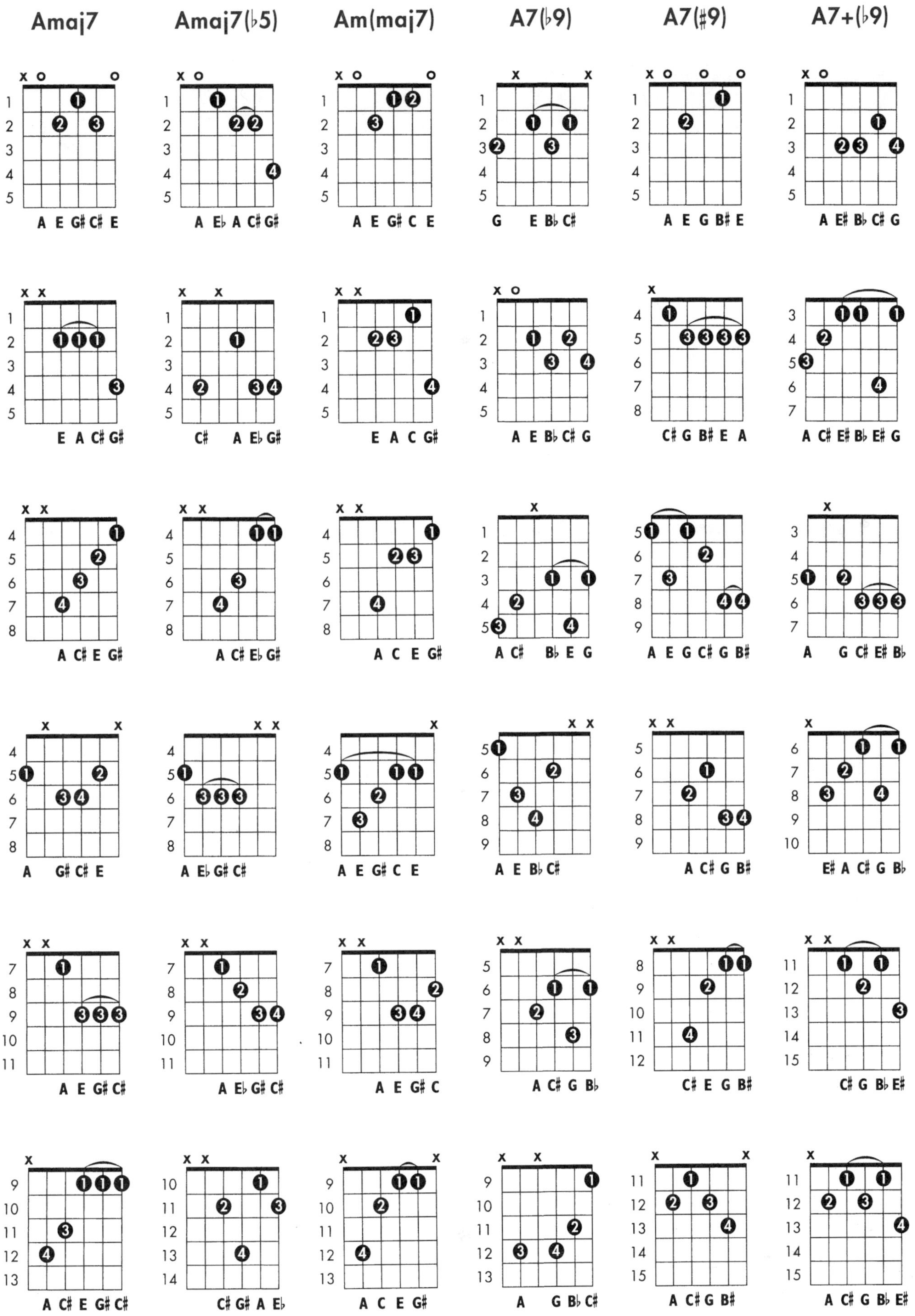
Amaj7
Amaj7(♭5)
Am(maj7)
A7(♭9)
A7(♯9)
A7+(♭9)
A E G♯ C♯ E
A E♭ A C♯ G♯
A E G♯ C E
G E B♭ C♯
A E G B♯ E
A E♯ B♭ C♯ G
E A C♯ G♯
C♯ A E♭ G♯
E A C G♯
A E B♭ C♯ G
C♯ G B♯ E A
A C♯ E♯ B♭ E♯ G
A C♯ E G♯
A C♯ E♭ G♯
A C E G♯
A C♯ B♭ E G
A E G C♯ G B♯
A G C♯ E♯ B♭
A G♯ C♯ E
A E♭ G♯ C♯
A E G♯ C E
A E B♭ C♯
A C♯ G B♯
E♯ A C♯ G B♭
A E G♯ C♯
A E♭ G♯ C♯
A E G♯ C
A C♯ G B♭
C♯ E G B♯
C♯ G B♭ E♯
A C♯ E G♯ C♯
C♯ G♯ A E♭
A C E G♯
A G B♭ C♯
A C♯ G B♯
A C♯ G B♭ E♯

B♭

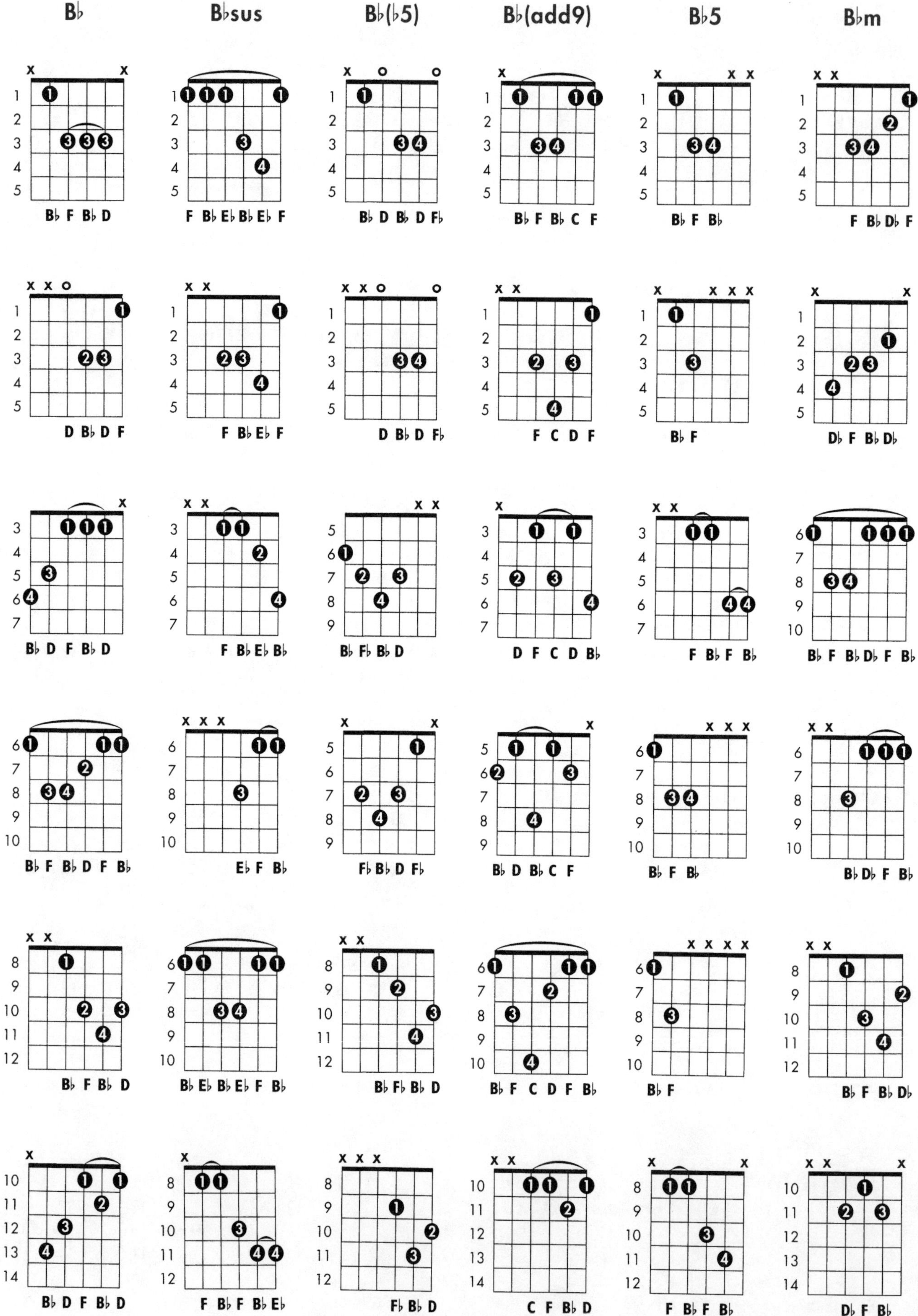
B♭
B♭sus
B♭(♭5)
B♭(add9)
B♭5
B♭m
B♭ F B♭ D
F B♭ E♭ B♭ E♭ F
B♭ D B♭ D F♭
B♭ F B♭ C F
B♭ F B♭
F B♭ D♭ F
D B♭ D F
F B♭ E♭ F
D B♭ D F♭
F C D F
B♭ F
D♭ F B♭ D♭
B♭ D F B♭ D
F B♭ E♭ B♭
B♭ F♭ B♭ D
D F C D B♭
F B♭ F B♭
B♭ F B♭ D♭ F B♭
B♭ F B♭ D F B♭
E♭ F B♭
F♭ B♭ D F♭
B♭ D B♭ C F
B♭ F B♭
B♭ D♭ F B♭
B♭ F B♭ D
B♭ E♭ B♭ E♭ F B♭
B♭ F♭ B♭ D
B♭ F C D F B♭
B♭ F
B♭ F B♭ D♭
B♭ D F B♭ D
F B♭ F B♭ E♭
F♭ B♭ D
C F B♭ D
F B♭ F B♭
D♭ F B♭

B♭

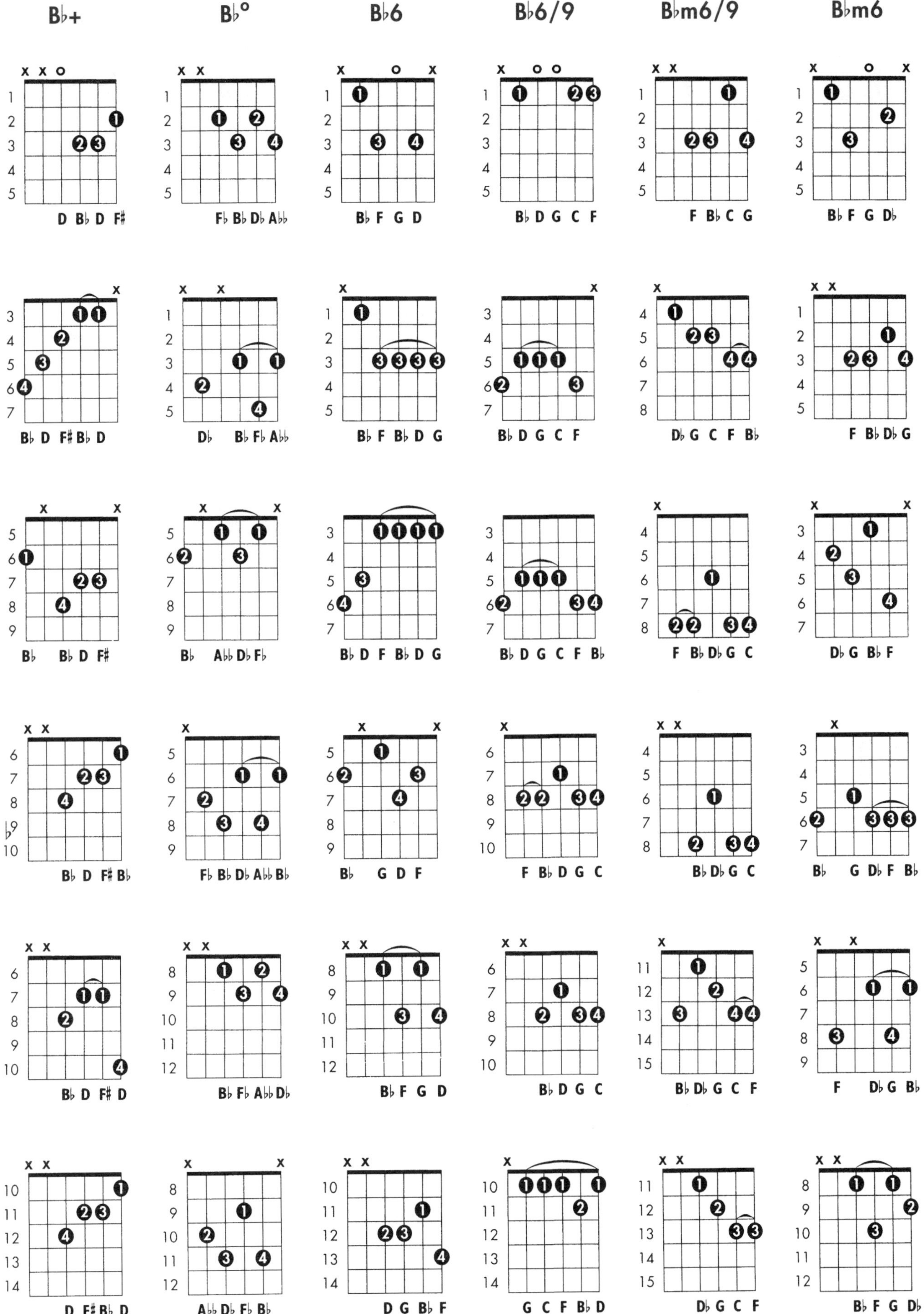
B♭+
B♭°
B♭6
B♭6/9
B♭m6/9
B♭m6
D B♭ D F♯
F♭ B♭ D♭ A♭♭
B♭ F G D
B♭ D G C F
F B♭ C G
B♭ F G D♭
B♭ D F♯ B♭ D
D♭ B♭ F♭ A♭♭
B♭ F B♭ D G
B♭ D G C F
D♭ G C F B♭
F B♭ D♭ G
B♭ B♭ D F♯
B♭ A♭♭ D♭ F♭
B♭ D F B♭ D G
B♭ D G C F B♭
F B♭ D♭ G C
D♭ G B♭ F
B♭ D F♯ B♭
F♭ B♭ D♭ A♭♭ B♭
B♭ G D F
F B♭ D G C
B♭ D♭ G C
B♭ G D♭ F B♭
B♭ D F♯ D
B♭ F♭ A♭♭ D♭
B♭ F G D
B♭ D G C
B♭ D♭ G C F
F D♭ G B♭
D F♯ B♭ D
A♭♭ D♭ F♭ B♭
D G B♭ F
G C F B♭ D
D♭ G C F
B♭ F G D♭

B♭

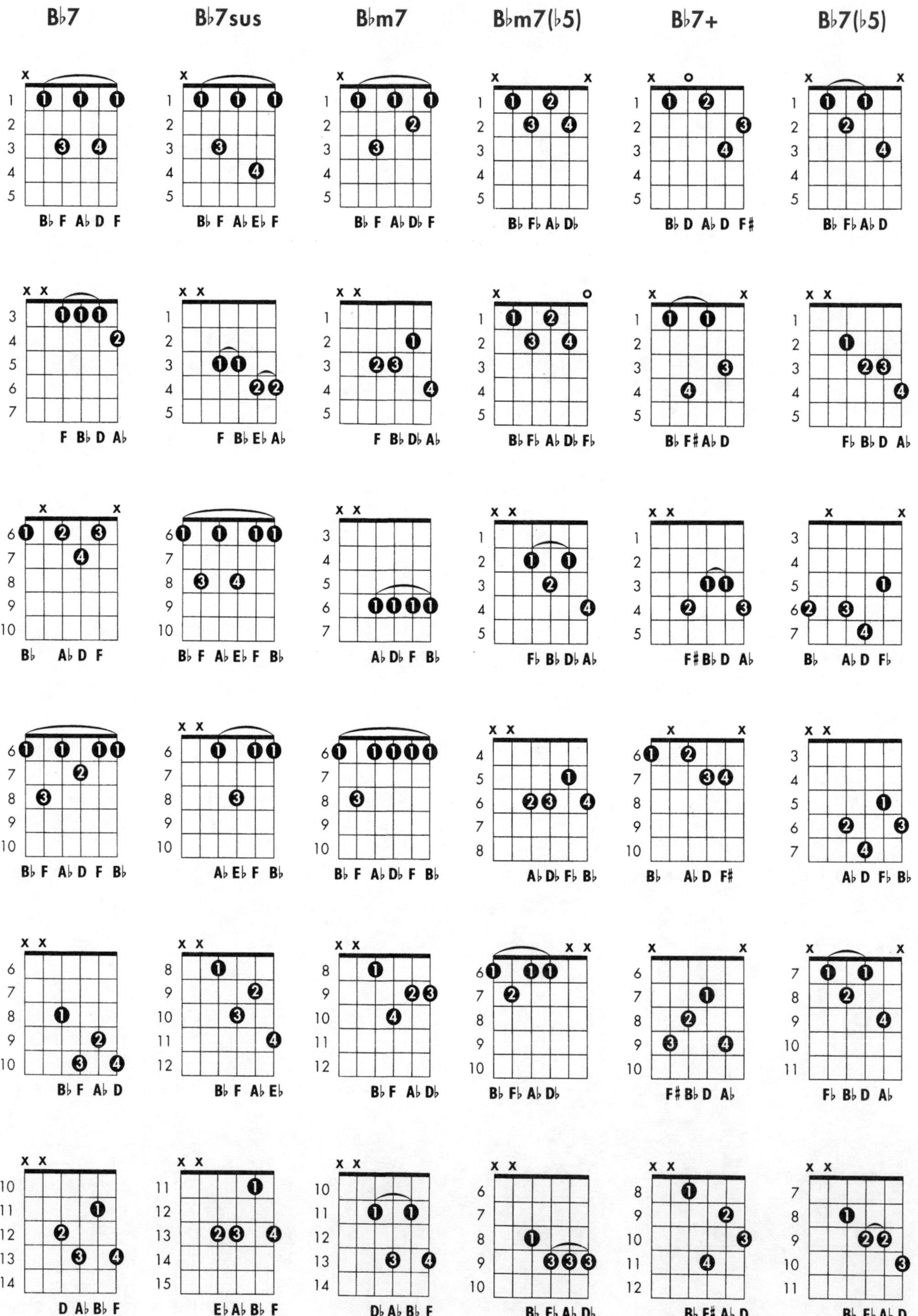
B♭7
B♭7sus
B♭m7
B♭m7(♭5)
B♭7+
B♭7(♭5)
B♭ F A♭ D F
B♭ F A♭ E♭ F
B♭ F A♭ D♭ F
B♭ F♭ A♭ D♭
B♭ D A♭ D F♯
B♭ F♭ A♭ D
F B♭ D A♭
F B♭ E♭ A♭
F B♭ D♭ A♭
B♭ F♭ A♭ D♭ F♭
B♭ F♯ A♭ D
F♭ B♭ D A♭
B♭ A♭ D F
B♭ F A♭ E♭ F B♭
A♭ D♭ F B♭
F♭ B♭ D♭ A♭
F♯ B♭ D A♭
B♭ A♭ D F♭
B♭ F A♭ D F B♭
A♭ E♭ F B♭
B♭ F A♭ D♭ F B♭
A♭ D♭ F♭ B♭
B♭ A♭ D F♯
A♭ D F♭ B♭
B♭ F A♭ D
B♭ F A♭ E♭
B♭ F A♭ D♭
B♭ F♭ A♭ D♭
F♯ B♭ D A♭
F♭ B♭ D A♭
D A♭ B♭ F
E♭ A♭ B♭ F
D♭ A♭ B♭ F
B♭ F♭ A♭ D♭
B♭ F♯ A♭ D
B♭ F♭ A♭ D

B♭

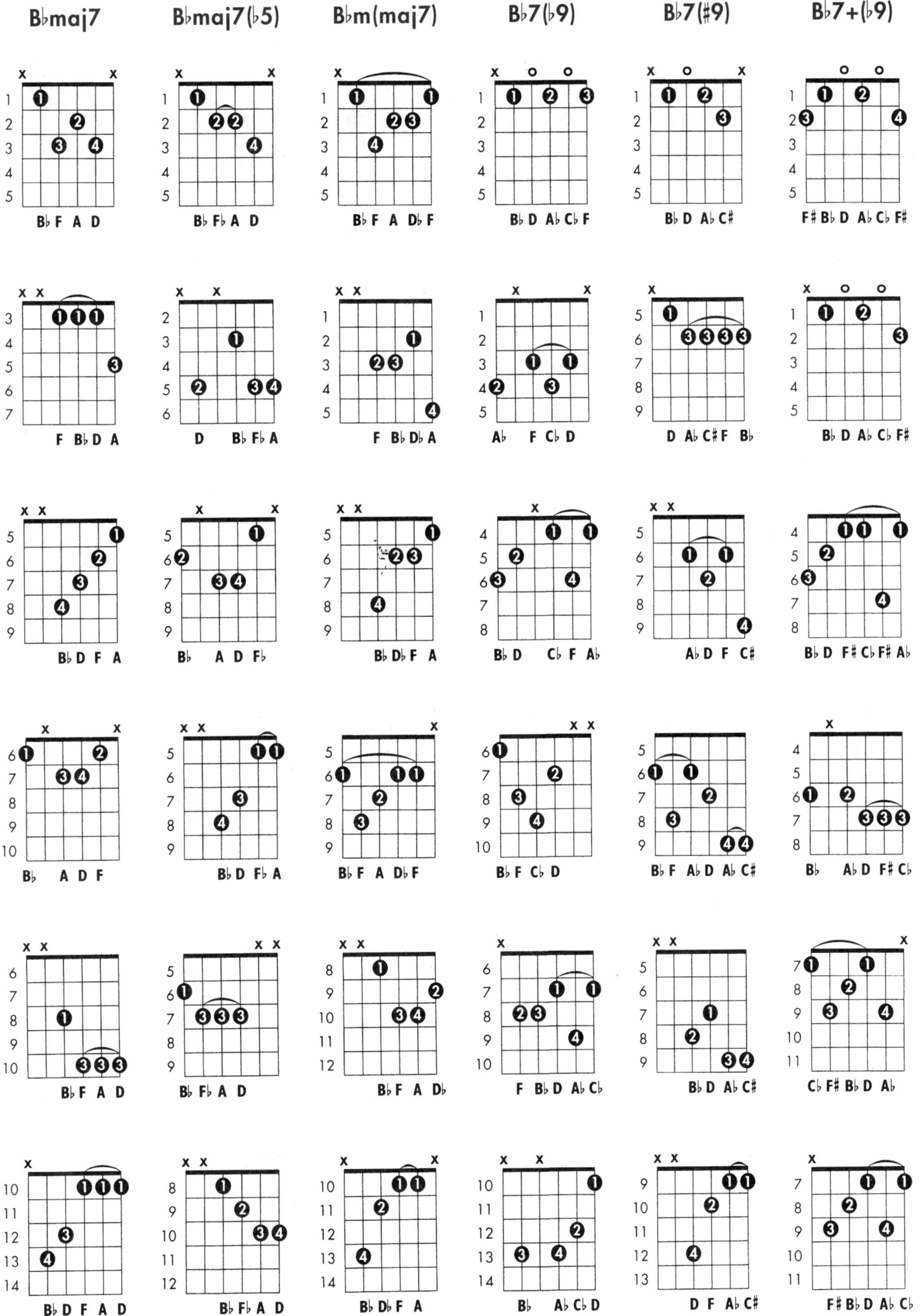

B♭maj7
B♭maj7(♭5)
B♭m(maj7)
B♭7(♭9)
B♭7(♯9)
B♭7+(♭9)
B♭ F A D
B♭ F♭ A D
B♭ F A D♭ F
B♭ D A♭ C♭ F
B♭ D A♭ C♯
F♯ B♭ D A♭ C♭ F♯
F B♭ D A
D B♭ F♭ A
F B♭ D♭ A
A♭ F C♭ D
D A♭ C♯ F B♭
B♭ D A♭ C♭ F♯
B♭ D F A
B♭ A D F♭
B♭ D♭ F A
B♭ D C♭ F A♭
A♭ D F C♯
B♭ D F♯ C♭ F♯ A♭
B♭ A D F
B♭ D F♭ A
B♭ F A D♭ F
B♭ F C♭ D
B♭ F A♭ D A♭ C♯
B♭ A♭ D F♯ C♭
B♭ F A D
B♭ F♭ A D
B♭ F A D♭
F B♭ D A♭ C♭
B♭ D A♭ C♯
C♭ F♯ B♭ D A♭
B♭ D F A D
B♭ F♭ A D
B♭ D♭ F A
B♭ A♭ C♭ D
D F A♭ C♯
F♯ B♭ D A♭ C♭

B

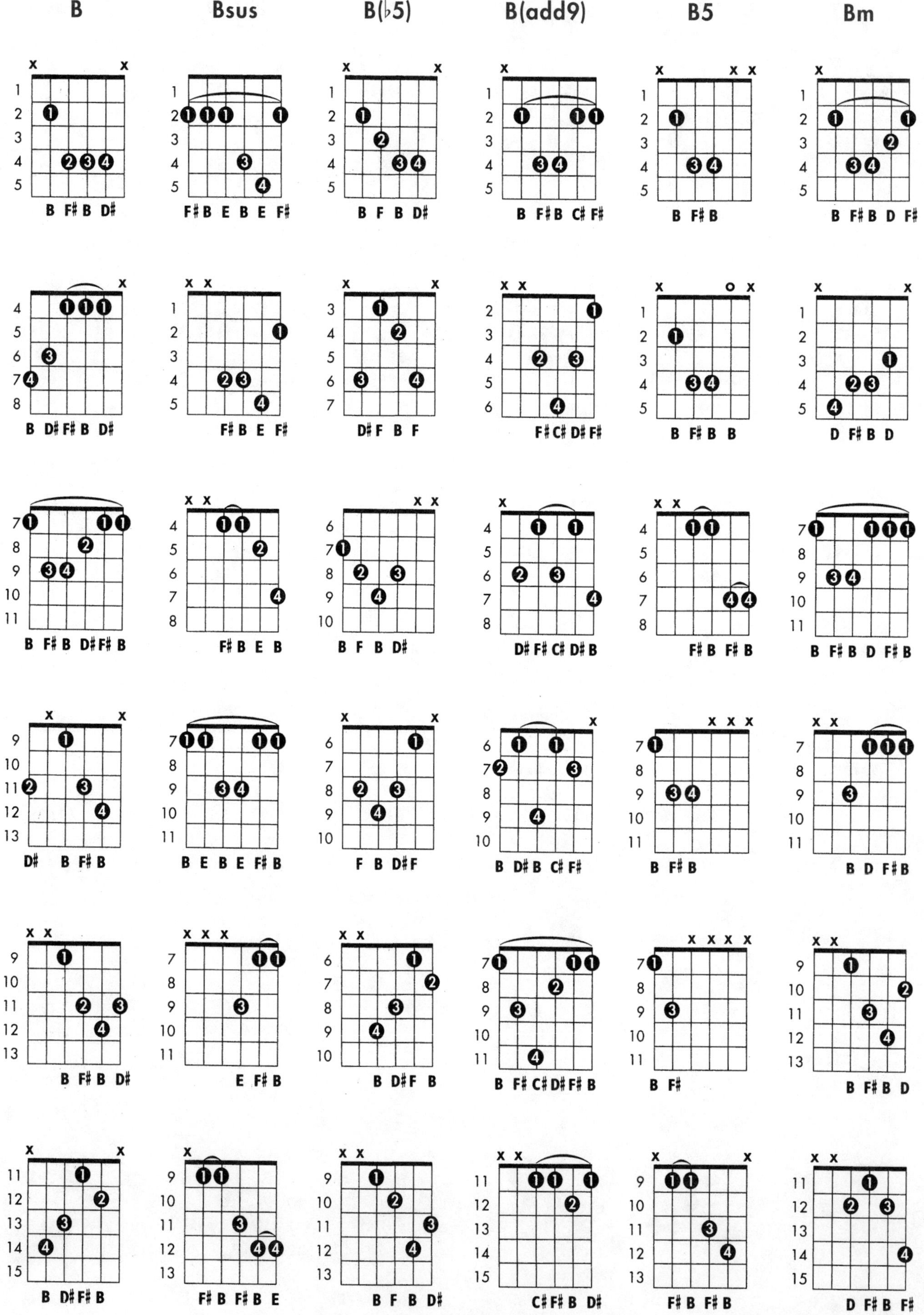

B

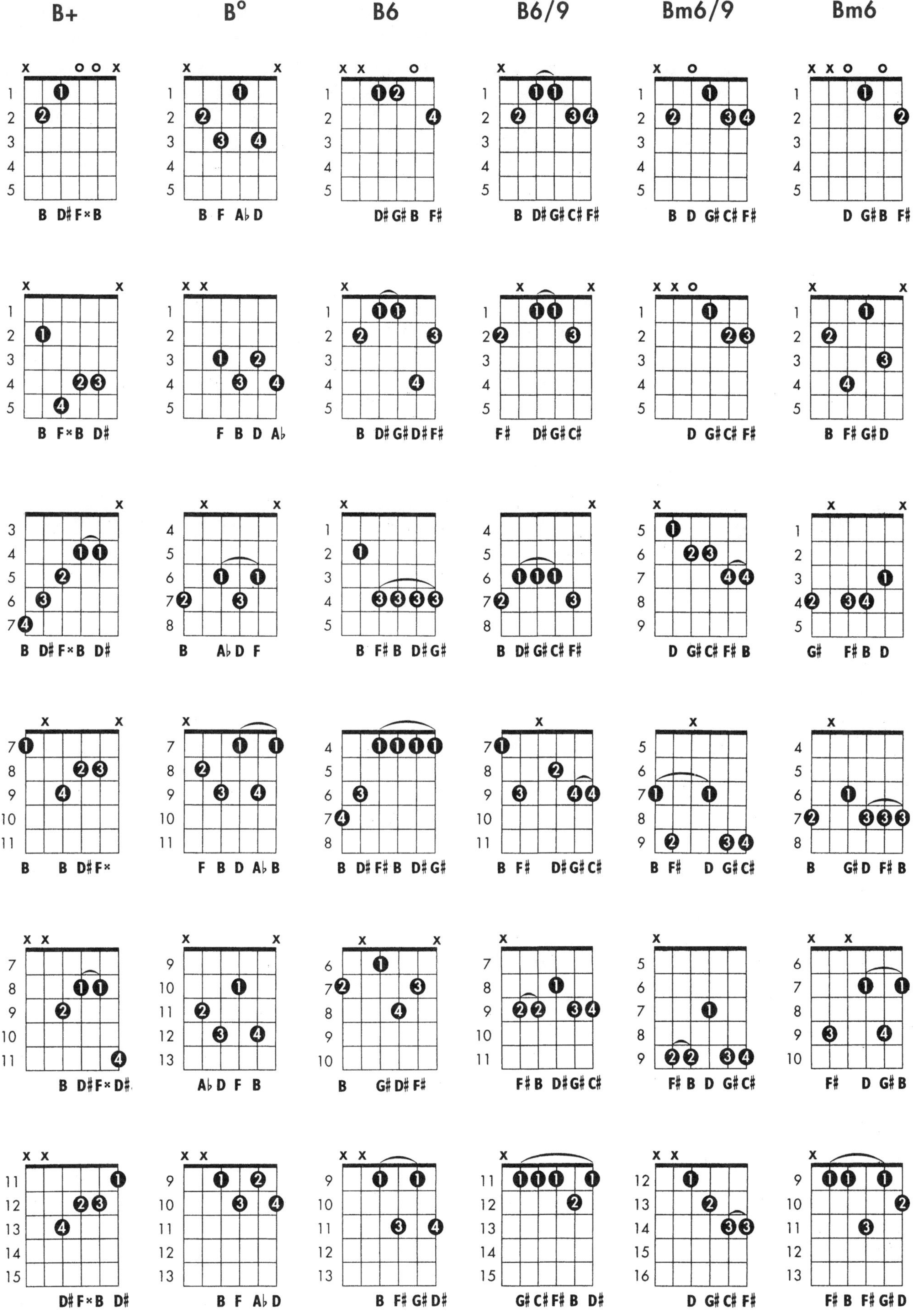

B

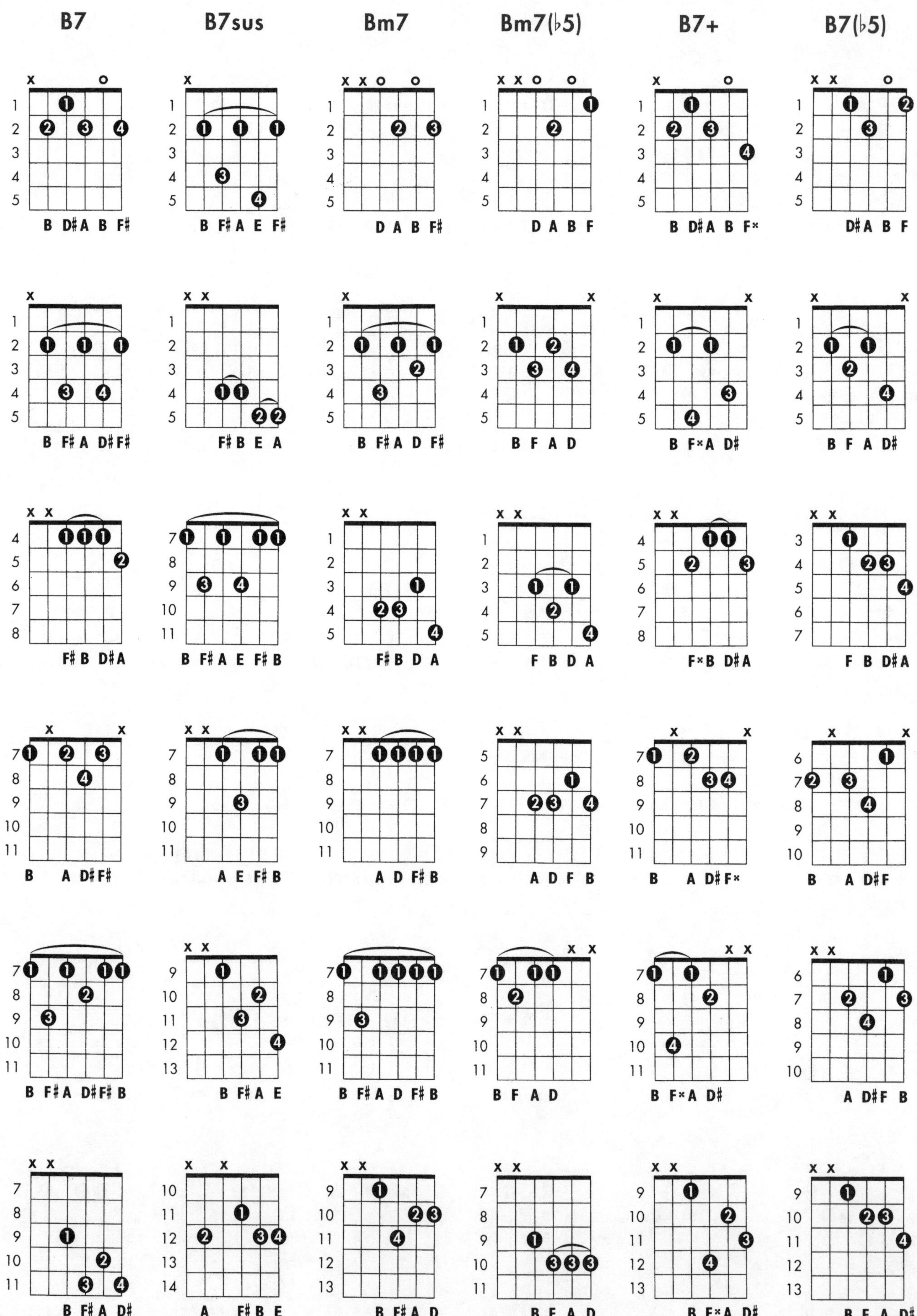

B

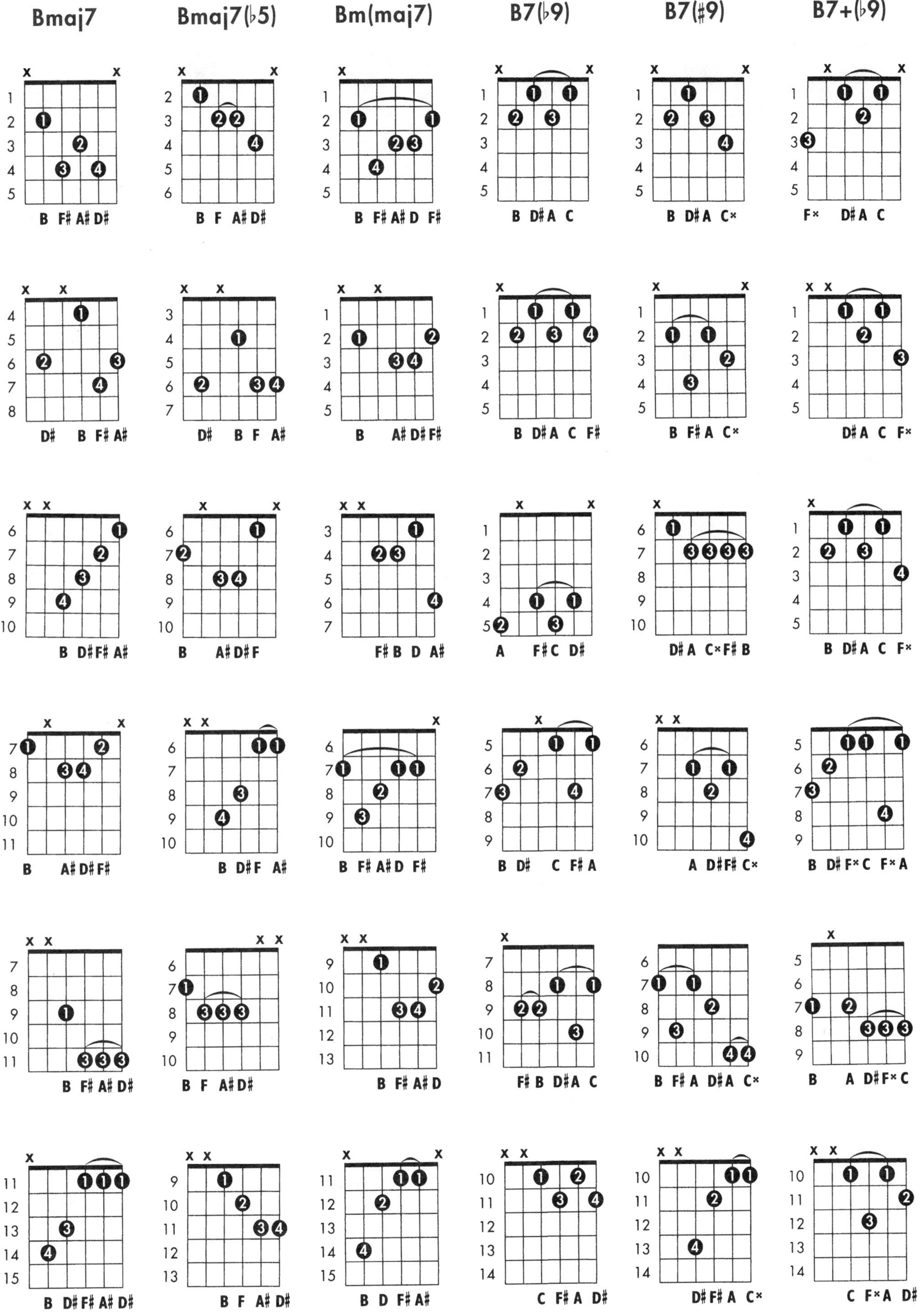

Bmaj7
Bmaj7(♭5)
Bm(maj7)
B7(♭9)
B7(♯9)
B7+(♭9)
B F♯ A♯ D♯
B F A♯ D♯
B F♯ A♯ D F♯
B D♯ A C
B D♯ A C×
F× D♯ A C
D♯ B F♯ A♯
D♯ B F A♯
B A♯ D♯ F♯
B D♯ A C F♯
B F♯ A C×
D♯ A C F×
B D♯ F♯ A♯
B A♯ D♯ F
F♯ B D A♯
A F♯ C D♯
D♯ A C× F♯ B
B D♯ A C F×
B A♯ D♯ F♯
B D♯ F A♯
B F♯ A♯ D F♯
B D♯ C F♯ A
A D♯ F♯ C×
B D♯ F× C F× A
B F♯ A♯ D♯
B F A♯ D♯
B F♯ A♯ D
F♯ B D♯ A C
B F♯ A D♯ A C×
B A D♯ F× C
B D♯ F♯ A♯ D♯
B F A♯ D♯
B D F♯ A♯
C F♯ A D♯
D♯ F♯ A C×
C F× A D♯

C

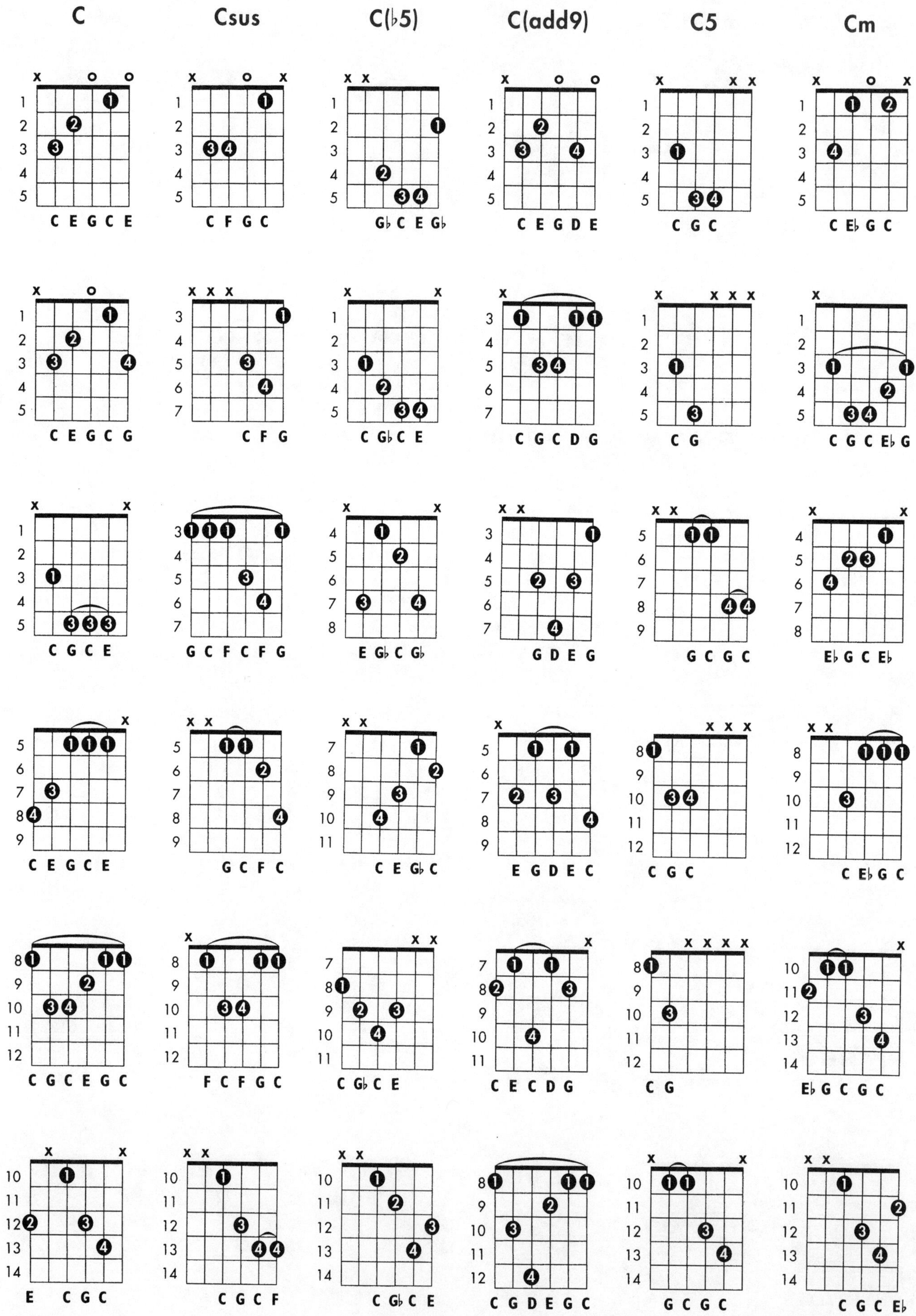

C
Csus
C(♭5)
C(add9)
C5
Cm
C E G C E
C F G C
G♭ C E G♭
C E G D E
C G C
C E♭ G C
C E G C G
C F G
C G♭ C E
C G C D G
C G
C G C E♭ G
C G C E
G C F C F G
E G♭ C G♭
G D E G
G C G C
E♭ G C E♭
C E G C E
G C F C
C E G♭ C
E G D E C
C G C
C E♭ G C
C G C E G C
F C F G C
C G♭ C E
C E C D G
C G
E♭ G C G C
E C G C
C G C F
C G♭ C E
C G D E G C
G C G C
C G C E♭

C

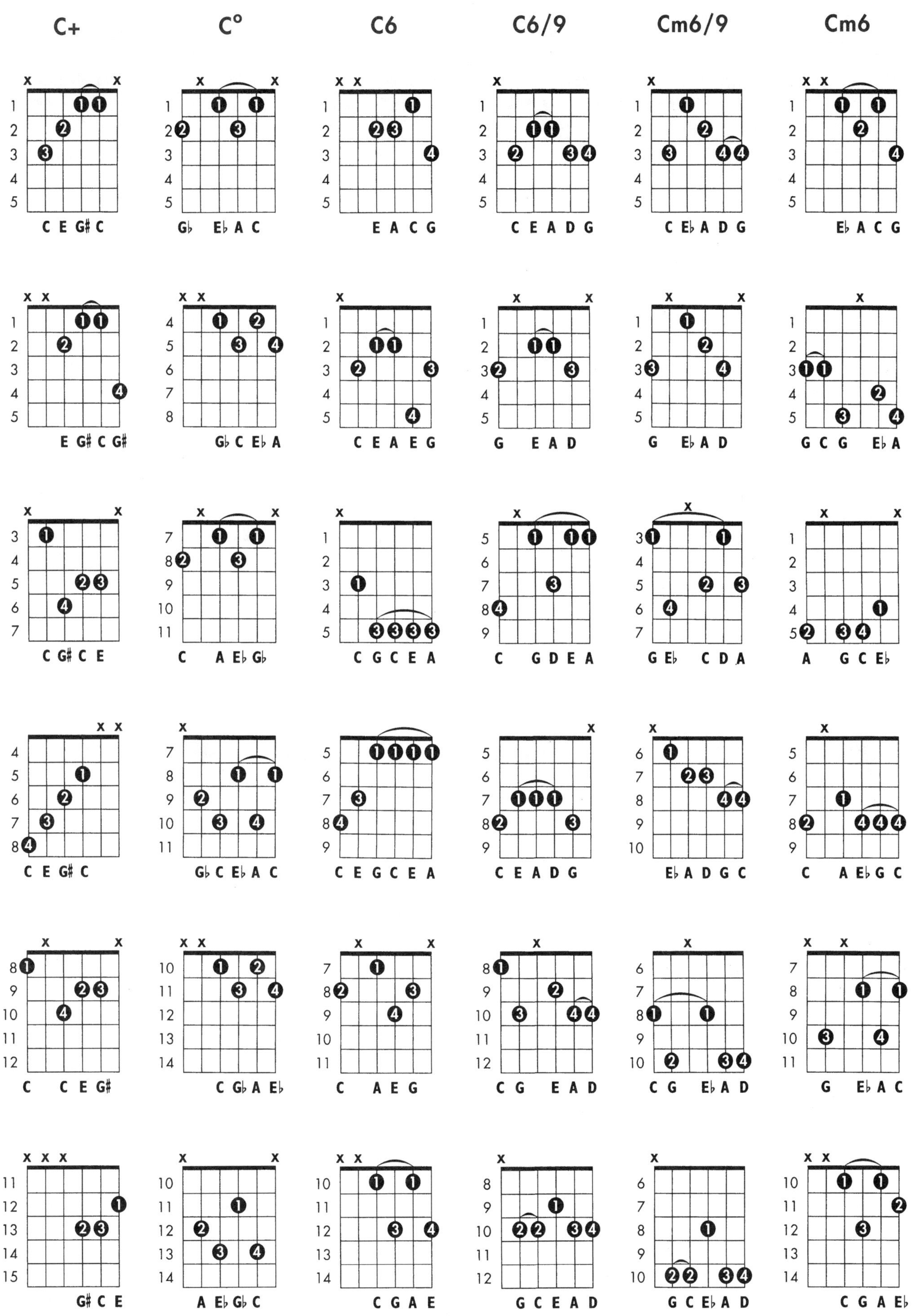
C+
C°
C6
C6/9
Cm6/9
Cm6
C E G♯ C
G♭ E♭ A C
E A C G
C E A D G
C E♭ A D G
E♭ A C G
E G♯ C G♯
G♭ C E♭ A
C E A E G
G E A D
G E♭ A D
G C G E♭ A
C G♯ C E
C A E♭ G♭
C G C E A
C G D E A
G E♭ C D A
A G C E♭
C E G♯ C
G♭ C E♭ A C
C E G C E A
C E A D G
E♭ A D G C
C A E♭ G C
C C E G♯
C G♭ A E♭
C A E G
C G E A D
C G E♭ A D
G E♭ A C
G♯ C E
A E♭ G♭ C
C G A E
G C E A D
G C E♭ A D
C G A E♭

C

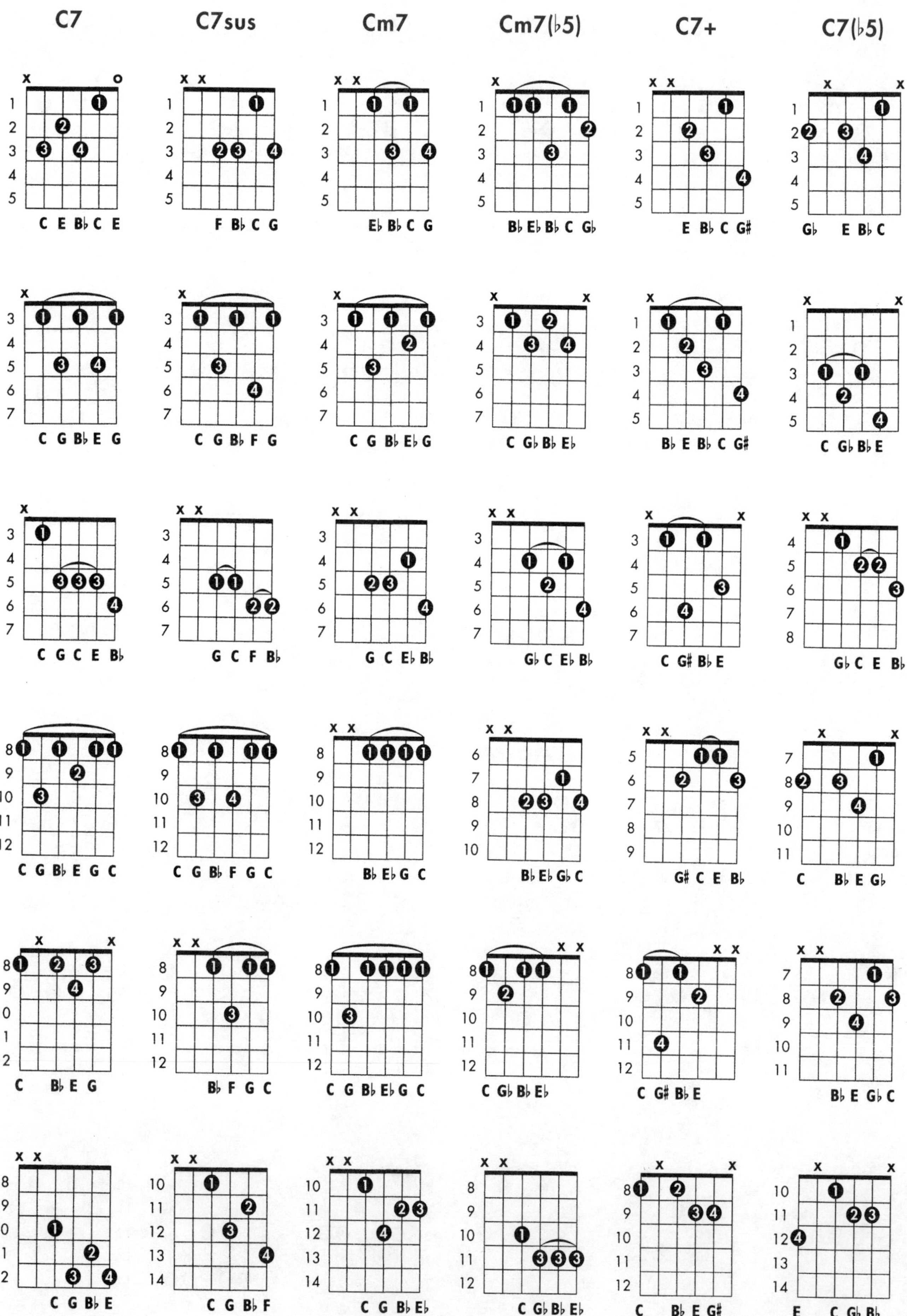
C7
C7sus
Cm7
Cm7(♭5)
C7+
C7(♭5)
C E B♭ C E
F B♭ C G
E♭ B♭ C G
B♭ E♭ B♭ C G♭
E B♭ C G♯
G♭ E B♭ C
C G B♭ E G
C G B♭ F G
C G B♭ E♭ G
C G♭ B♭ E♭
B♭ E B♭ C G♯
C G♭ B♭ E
C G C E B♭
G C F B♭
G C E♭ B♭
G♭ C E♭ B♭
C G♯ B♭ E
G♭ C E B♭
C G B♭ E G C
C G B♭ F G C
B♭ E♭ G C
B♭ E♭ G♭ C
G♯ C E B♭
C B♭ E G♭
C B♭ E G
B♭ F G C
C G B♭ E♭ G C
C G♭ B♭ E♭
C G♯ B♭ E
B♭ E G♭ C
C G B♭ E
C G B♭ F
C G B♭ E♭
C G♭ B♭ E♭
C B♭ E G♯
E C G♭ B♭

C

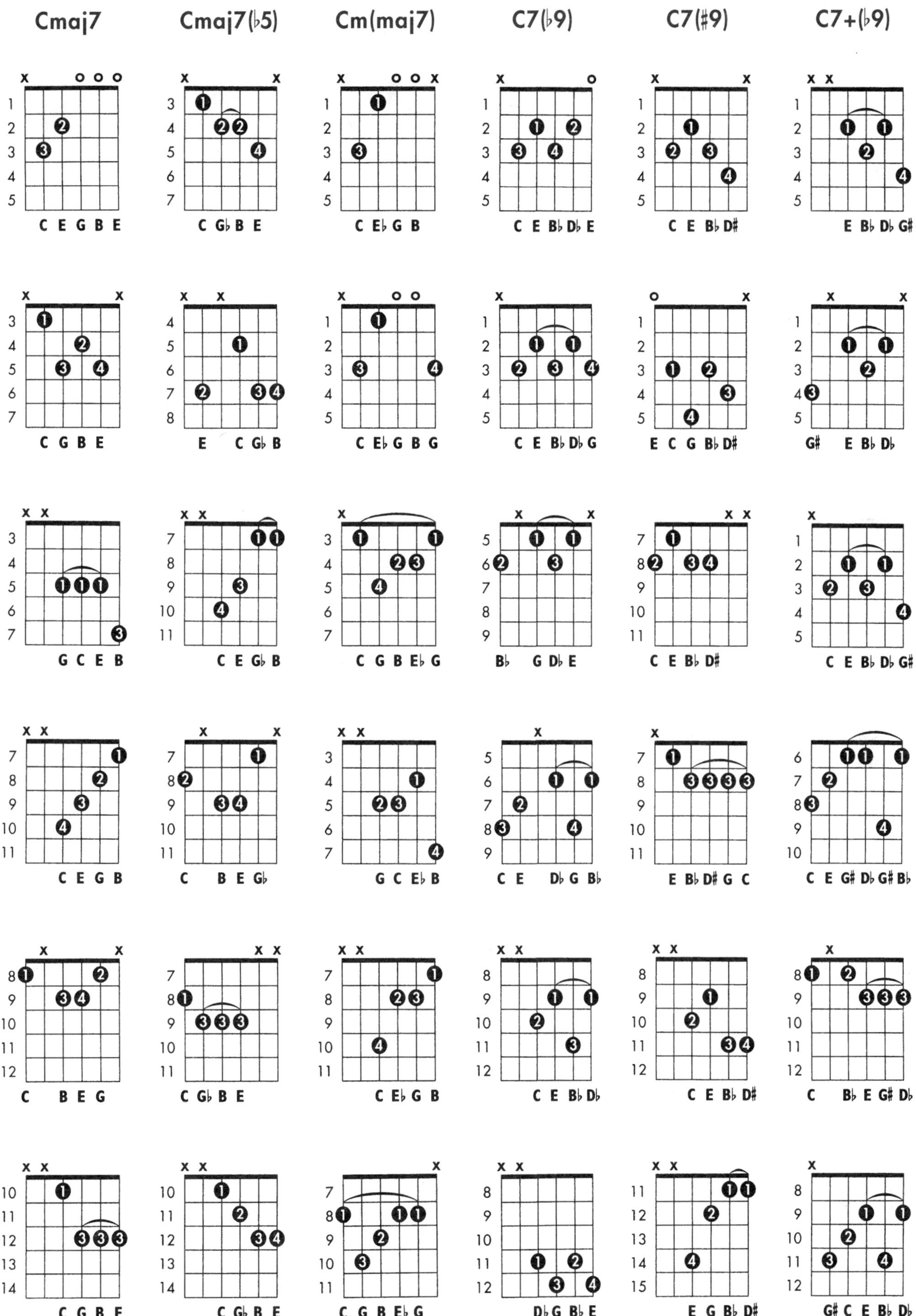

D♭

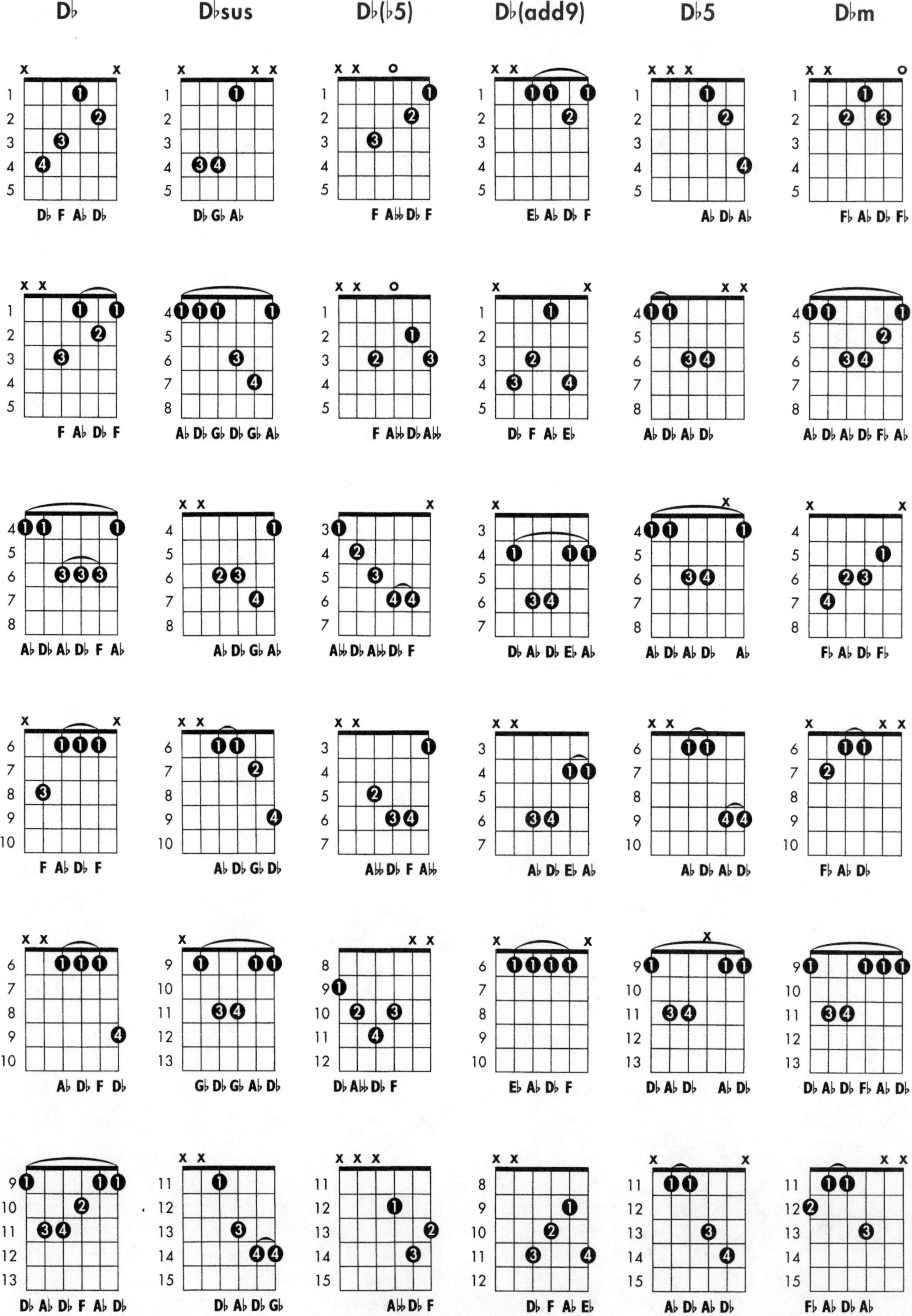
D♭
D♭sus
D♭(♭5)
D♭(add9)
D♭5
D♭m
D♭ F A♭ D♭
D♭ G♭ A♭
F A♭♭ D♭ F
E♭ A♭ D♭ F
A♭ D♭ A♭
F♭ A♭ D♭ F♭
F A♭ D♭ F
A♭ D♭ G♭ D♭ G♭ A♭
F A♭♭ D♭ A♭♭
D♭ F A♭ E♭
A♭ D♭ A♭ D♭
A♭ D♭ A♭ D♭ F♭ A♭
A♭ D♭ A♭ D♭ F A♭
A♭ D♭ G♭ A♭
A♭♭ D♭ A♭♭ D♭ F
D♭ A♭ D♭ E♭ A♭
A♭ D♭ A♭ D♭ A♭
F♭ A♭ D♭ F♭
F A♭ D♭ F
A♭ D♭ G♭ D♭
A♭♭ D♭ F A♭♭
A♭ D♭ E♭ A♭
A♭ D♭ A♭ D♭
F♭ A♭ D♭
A♭ D♭ F D♭
G♭ D♭ G♭ A♭ D♭
D♭ A♭♭ D♭ F
E♭ A♭ D♭ F
D♭ A♭ D♭ A♭ D♭
D♭ A♭ D♭ F♭ A♭ D♭
D♭ A♭ D♭ F A♭ D♭
D♭ A♭ D♭ G♭
A♭♭ D♭ F
D♭ F A♭ E♭
A♭ D♭ A♭ D♭
F♭ A♭ D♭ A♭

D♭

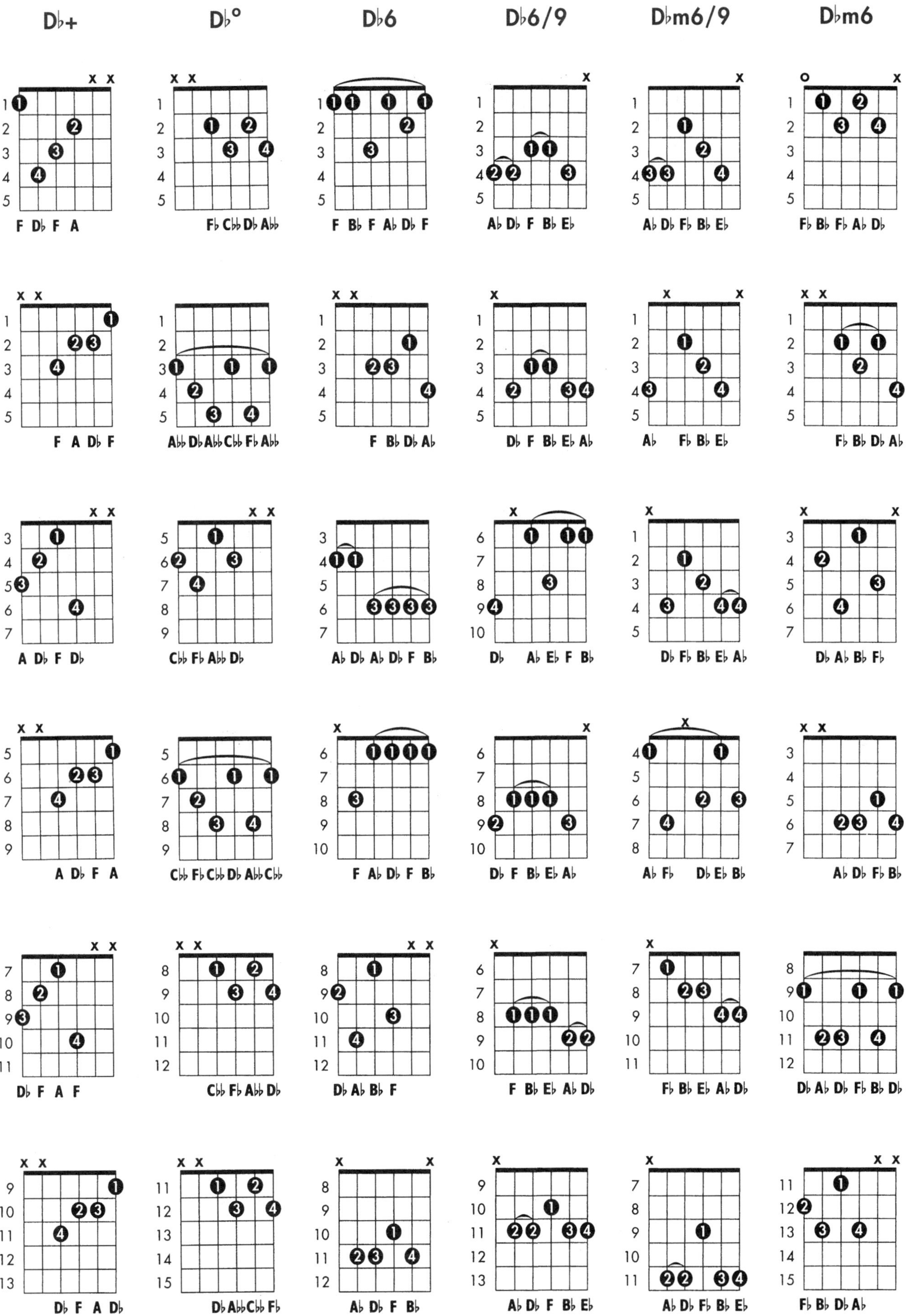

D♭

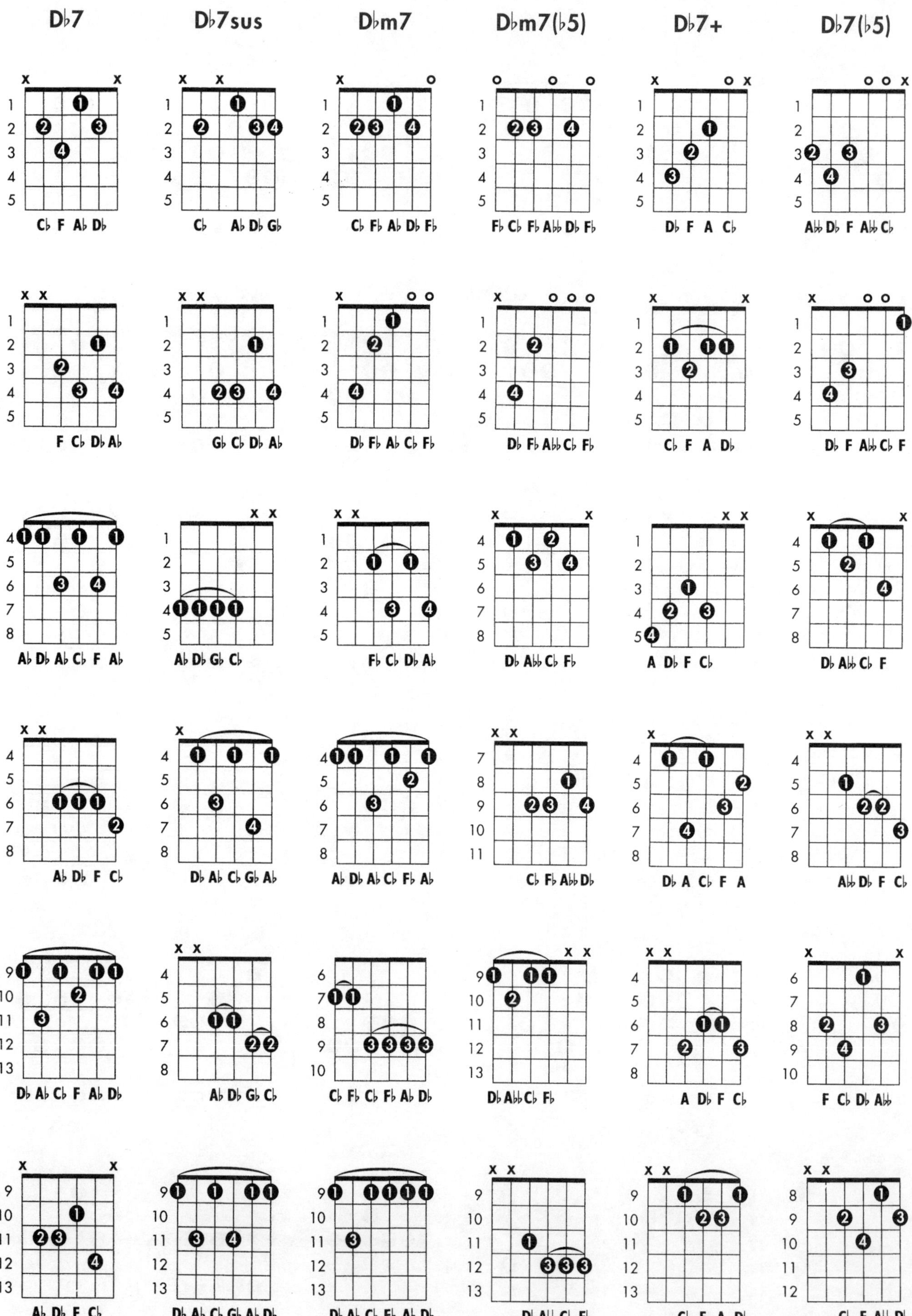
D♭7
D♭7sus
D♭m7
D♭m7(♭5)
D♭7+
D♭7(♭5)
C♭ F A♭ D♭
C♭ A♭ D♭ G♭
C♭ F♭ A♭ D♭ F♭
F♭ C♭ F♭ A♭♭ D♭ F♭
D♭ F A C♭
A♭♭ D♭ F A♭♭ C♭
F C♭ D♭ A♭
G♭ C♭ D♭ A♭
D♭ F♭ A♭ C♭ F♭
D♭ F♭ A♭♭ C♭ F♭
C♭ F A D♭
D♭ F A♭♭ C♭ F
A♭ D♭ A♭ C♭ F A♭
A♭ D♭ G♭ C♭
F♭ C♭ D♭ A♭
D♭ A♭♭ C♭ F♭
A D♭ F C♭
D♭ A♭♭ C♭ F
A♭ D♭ F C♭
D♭ A♭ C♭ G♭ A♭
A♭ D♭ A♭ C♭ F♭ A♭
C♭ F♭ A♭♭ D♭
D♭ A C♭ F A
A♭♭ D♭ F C♭
D♭ A♭ C♭ F A♭ D♭
A♭ D♭ G♭ C♭
C♭ F♭ C♭ F♭ A♭ D♭
D♭ A♭♭ C♭ F♭
A D♭ F C♭
F C♭ D♭ A♭♭
A♭ D♭ F C♭
D♭ A♭ C♭ G♭ A♭ D♭
D♭ A♭ C♭ F♭ A♭ D♭
D♭ A♭♭ C♭ F♭
C♭ F A D♭
C♭ F A♭♭ D♭

D♭

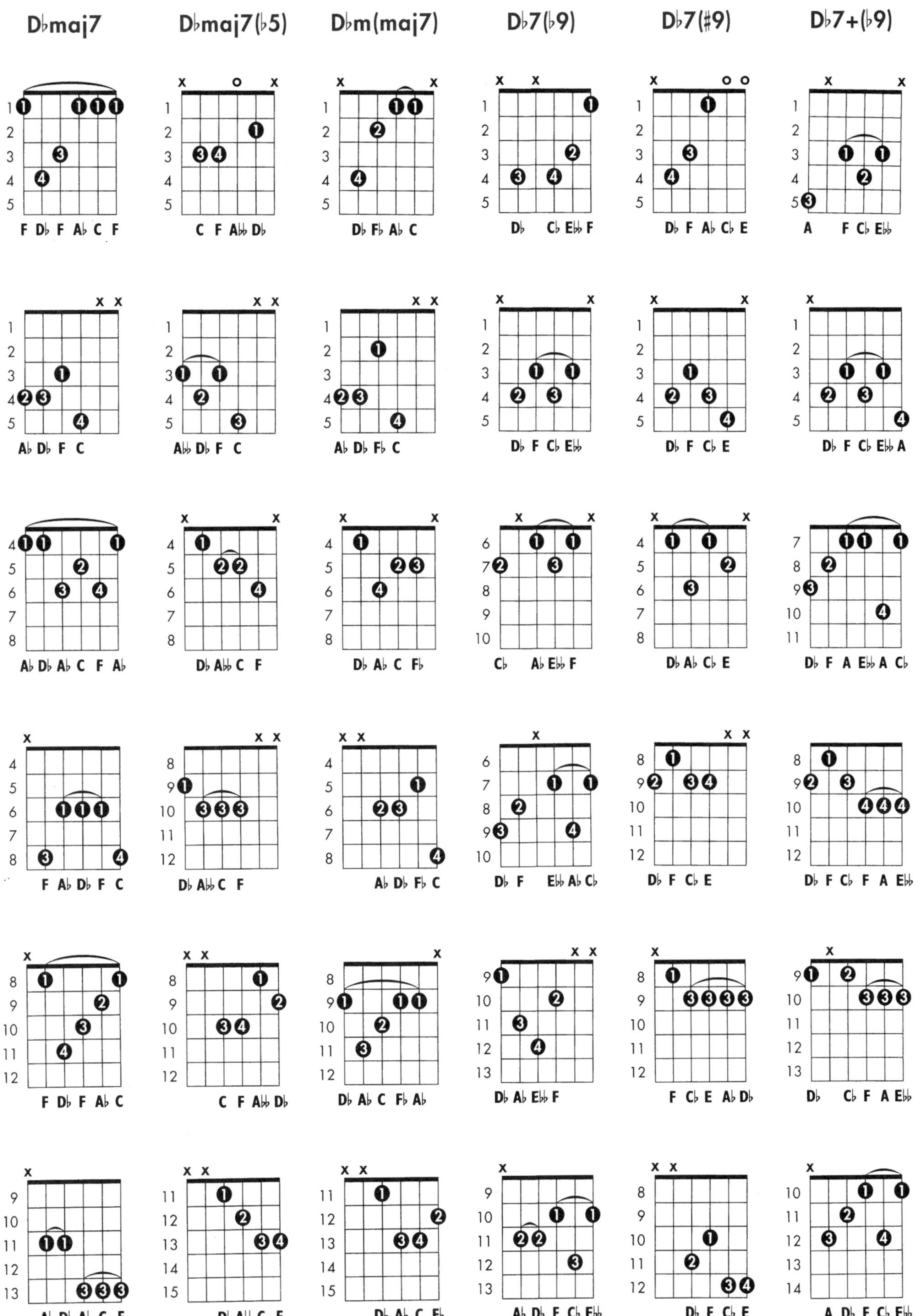

D♭maj7
D♭maj7(♭5)
D♭m(maj7)
D♭7(♭9)
D♭7(♯9)
D♭7+(♭9)
F D♭ F A♭ C F
C F A♭♭ D♭
D♭ F♭ A♭ C
D♭ C♭ E♭♭ F
D♭ F A♭ C♭ E
A F C♭ E♭♭
A♭ D♭ F C
A♭♭ D♭ F C
A♭ D♭ F♭ C
D♭ F C♭ E♭♭
D♭ F C♭ E
D♭ F C♭ E♭♭ A
A♭ D♭ A♭ C F A♭
D♭ A♭♭ C F
D♭ A♭ C F♭
C♭ A♭ E♭♭ F
D♭ A♭ C♭ E
D♭ F A E♭♭ A C♭
F A♭ D♭ F C
D♭ A♭♭ C F
A♭ D♭ F♭ C
D♭ F E♭♭ A♭ C♭
D♭ F C♭ E
D♭ F C♭ F A E♭♭
F D♭ F A♭ C
C F A♭♭ D♭
D♭ A♭ C F♭ A♭
D♭ A♭ E♭♭ F
F C♭ E A♭ D♭
D♭ C♭ F A E♭♭
A♭ D♭ A♭ C F
D♭ A♭♭ C F
D♭ A♭ C F♭
A♭ D♭ F C♭ E♭♭
D♭ F C♭ E
A D♭ F C♭ E♭♭

D

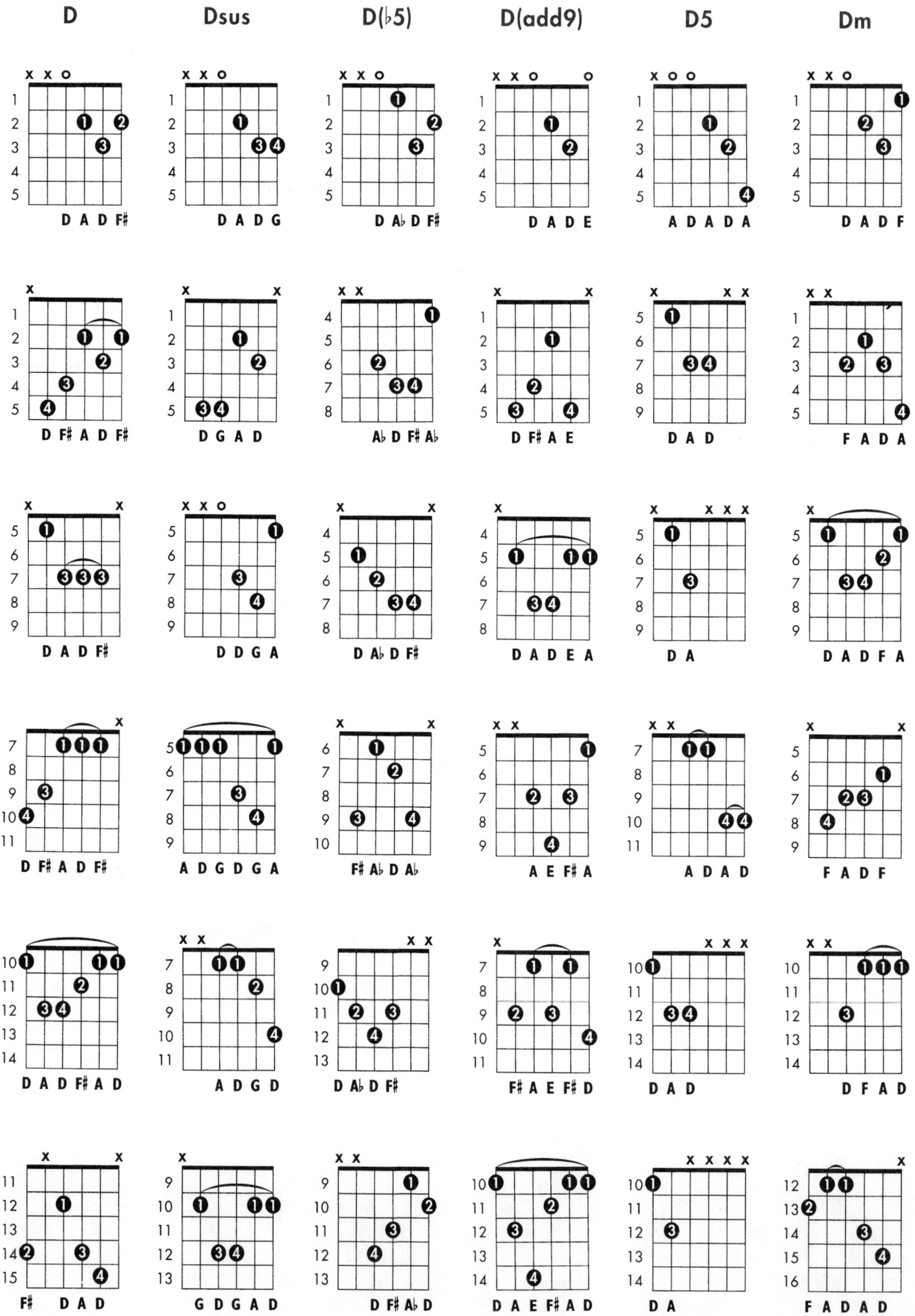
D
Dsus
D(♭5)
D(add9)
D5
Dm
D A D F♯
D A D G
D A♭ D F♯
D A D E
A D A D A
D A D F
D F♯ A D F♯
D G A D
A♭ D F♯ A♭
D F♯ A E
D A D
F A D A
D A D F♯
D D G A
D A♭ D F♯
D A D E A
D A
D A D F A
D F♯ A D F♯
A D G D G A
F♯ A♭ D A♭
A E F♯ A
A D A D
F A D F
D A D F♯ A D
A D G D
D A♭ D F♯
F♯ A E F♯ D
D A D
D F A D
F♯ D A D
G D G A D
D F♯ A♭ D
D A E F♯ A D
D A
F A D A D

D

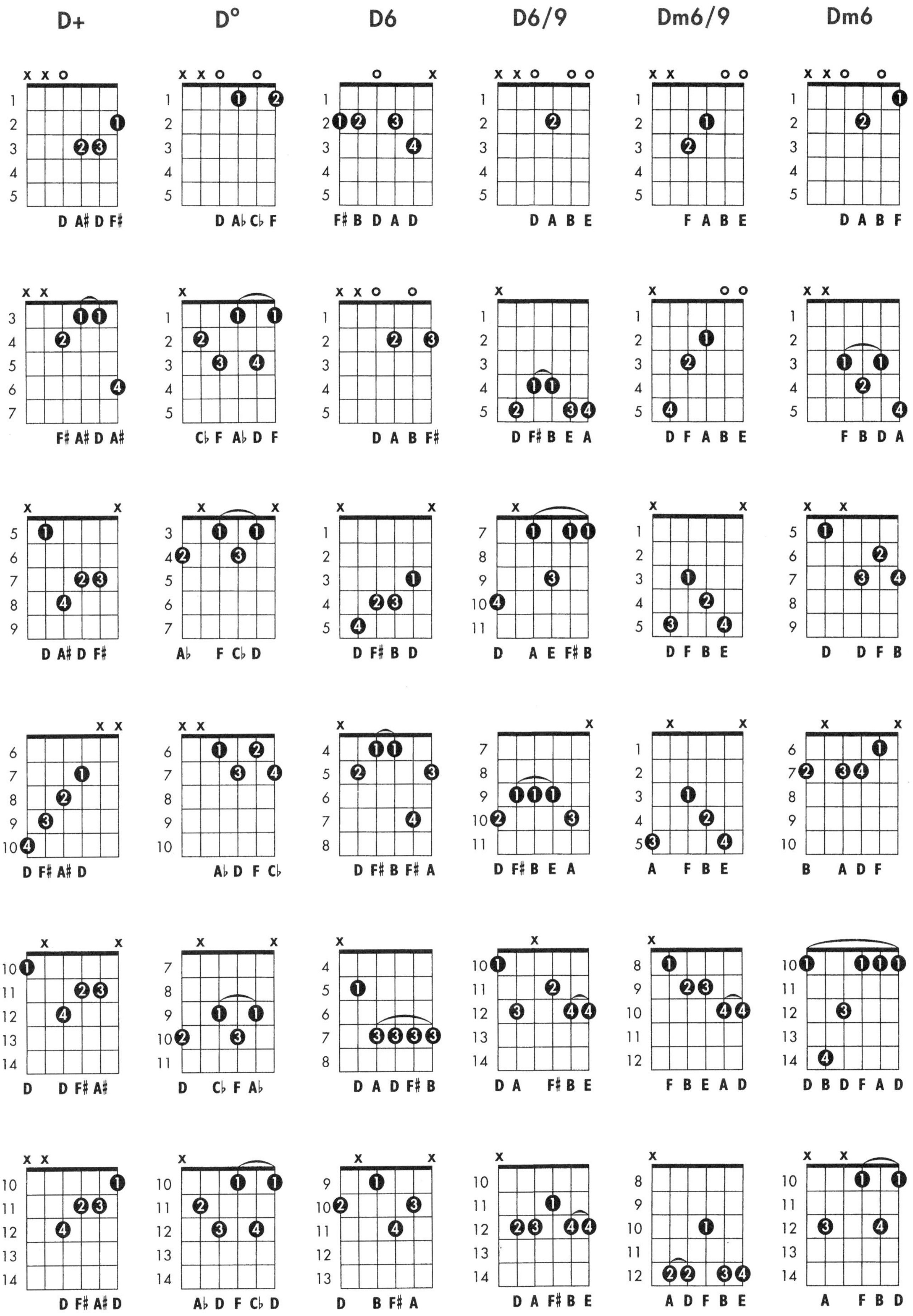
D+
D°
D6
D6/9
Dm6/9
Dm6
D A♯ D F♯
D A♭ C♭ F
F♯ B D A D
D A B E
F A B E
D A B F
F♯ A♯ D A♯
C♭ F A♭ D F
D A B F♯
D F♯ B E A
D F A B E
F B D A
D A♯ D F♯
A♭ F C♭ D
D F♯ B D
D A E F♯ B
D F B E
D D F B
D F♯ A♯ D
A♭ D F C♭
D F♯ B F♯ A
D F♯ B E A
A F B E
B A D F
D D F♯ A♯
D C♭ F A♭
D A D F♯ B
D A F♯ B E
F B E A D
D B D F A D
D F♯ A♯ D
A♭ D F C♭ D
D B F♯ A
D A F♯ B E
A D F B E
A F B D

D

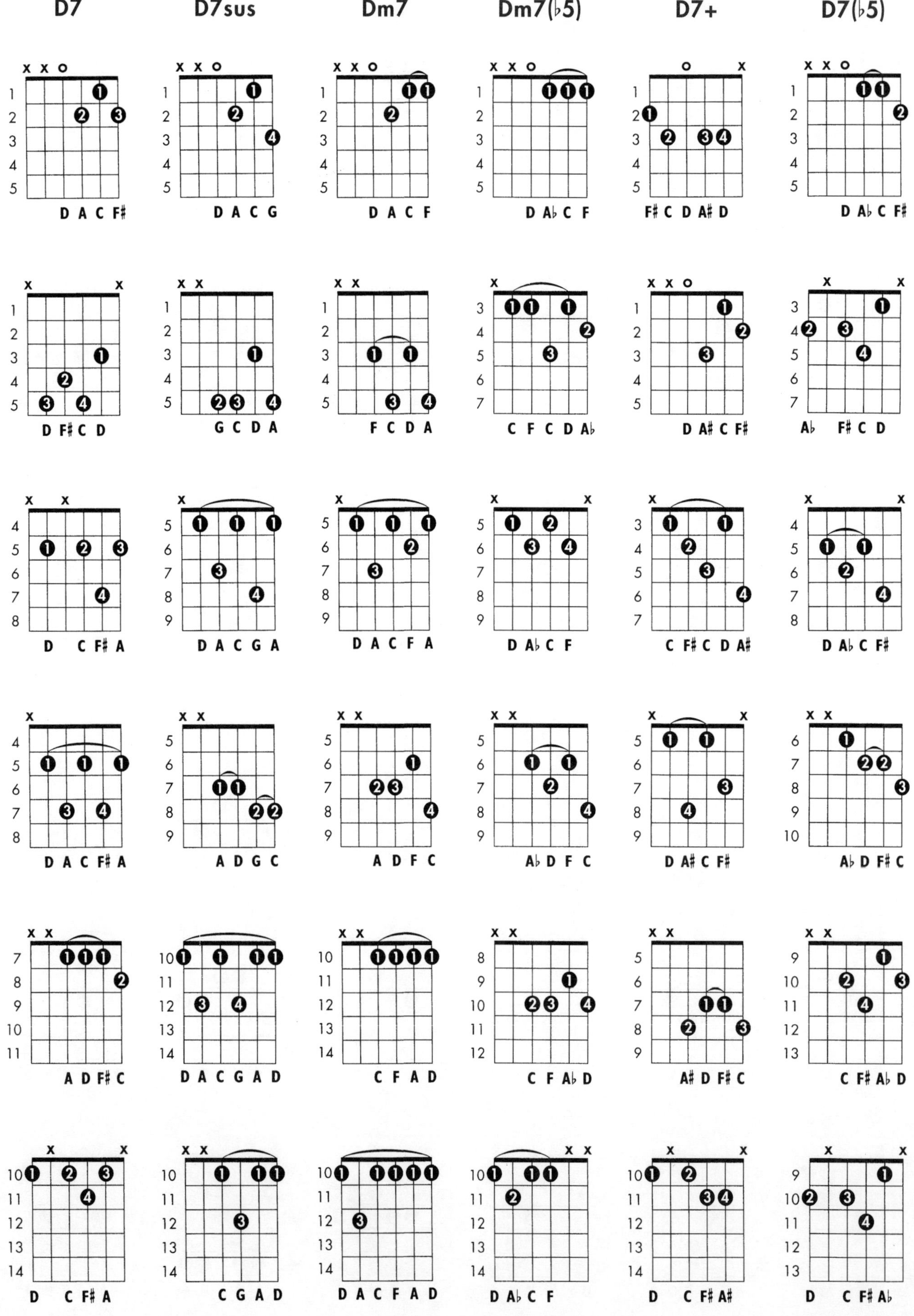

D7
D7sus
Dm7
Dm7(♭5)
D7+
D7(♭5)
D A C F♯
D A C G
D A C F
D A♭ C F
F♯ C D A♯ D
D A♭ C F♯
D F♯ C D
G C D A
F C D A
C F C D A♭
D A♯ C F♯
A♭ F♯ C D
D C F♯ A
D A C G A
D A C F A
D A♭ C F
C F♯ C D A♯
D A♭ C F♯
D A C F♯ A
A D G C
A D F C
A♭ D F C
D A♯ C F♯
A♭ D F♯ C
A D F♯ C
D A C G A D
C F A D
C F A♭ D
A♯ D F♯ C
C F♯ A♭ D
D C F♯ A
C G A D
D A C F A D
D A♭ C F
D C F♯ A♯
D C F♯ A♭

D

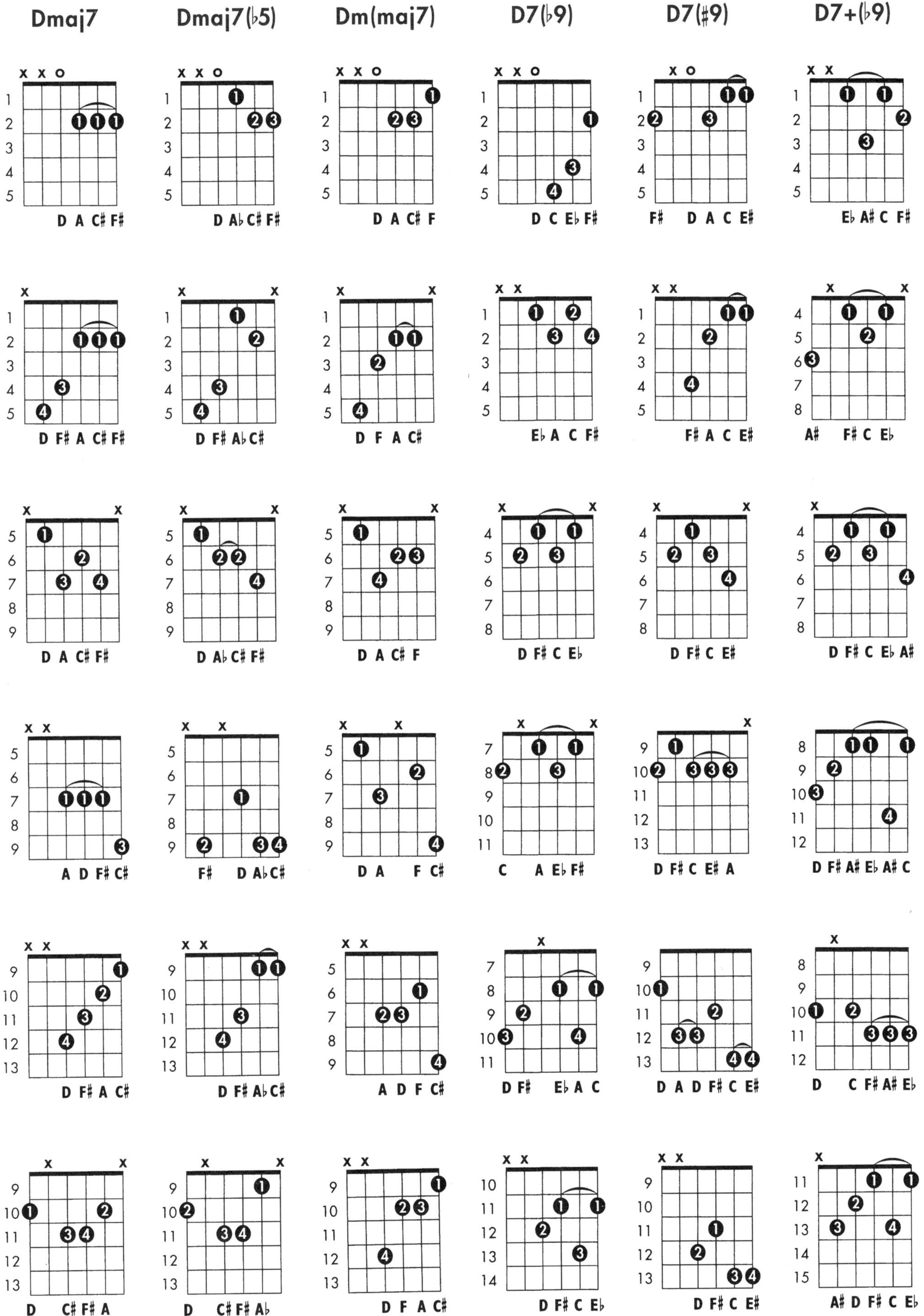
Dmaj7
Dmaj7(♭5)
Dm(maj7)
D7(♭9)
D7(♯9)
D7+(♭9)
D A C♯ F♯
D A♭ C♯ F♯
D A C♯ F
D C E♭ F♯
F♯ D A C E♯
E♭ A♯ C F♯
D F♯ A C♯ F♯
D F♯ A♭ C♯
D F A C♯
E♭ A C F♯
F♯ A C E♯
A♯ F♯ C E♭
D A C♯ F♯
D A♭ C♯ F♯
D A C♯ F
D F♯ C E♭
D F♯ C E♯
D F♯ C E♭ A♯
A D F♯ C♯
F♯ D A♭ C♯
D A F C♯
C A E♭ F♯
D F♯ C E♯ A
D F♯ A♯ E♭ A♯ C
D F♯ A C♯
D F♯ A♭ C♯
A D F C♯
D F♯ E♭ A C
D A D F♯ C E♯
D C F♯ A♯ E♭
D C♯ F♯ A
D C♯ F♯ A♭
D F A C♯
D F♯ C E♭
D F♯ C E♯
A♯ D F♯ C E♭

E♭

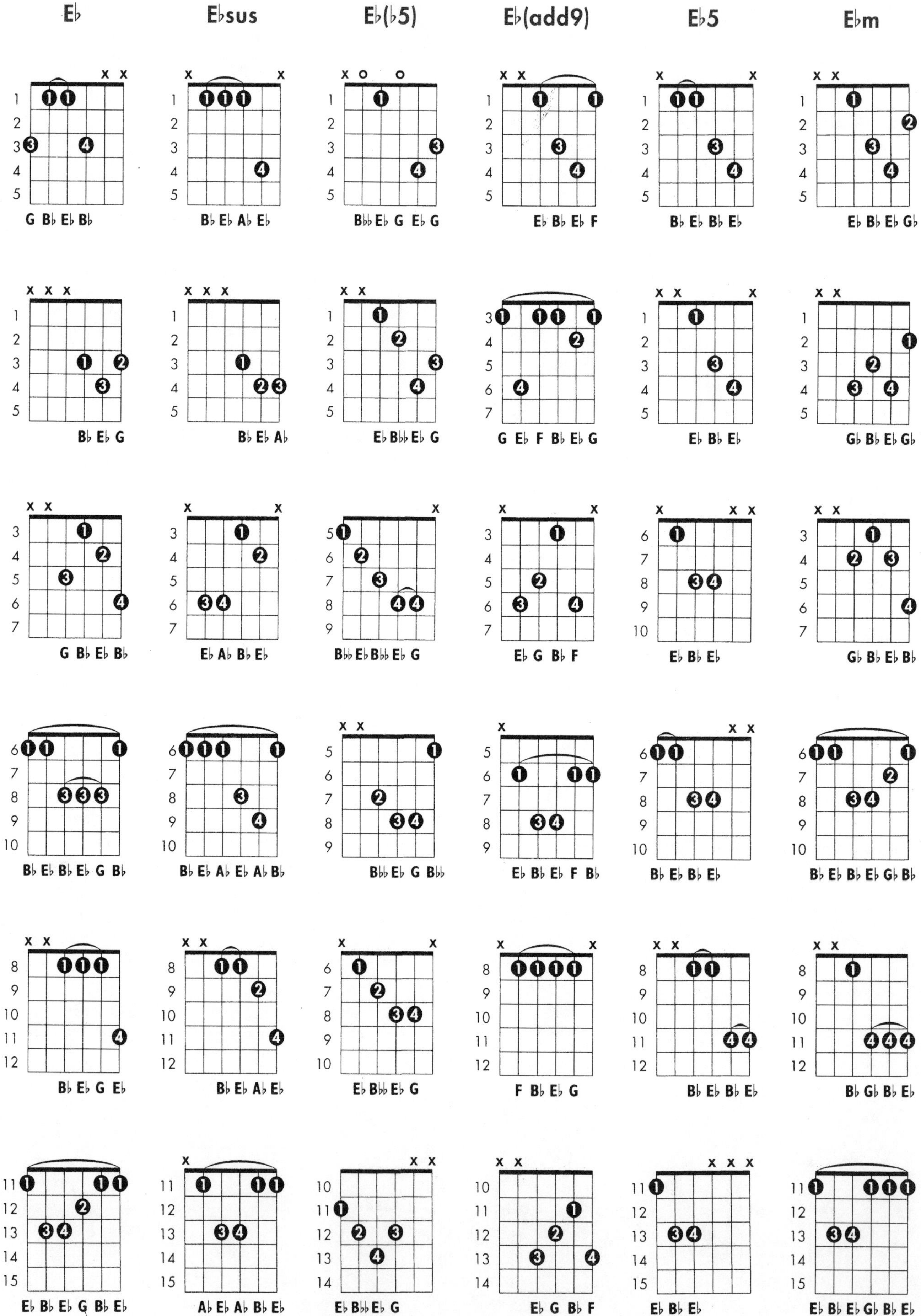
E♭
E♭sus
E♭(♭5)
E♭(add9)
E♭5
E♭m
G B♭ E♭ B♭
B♭ E♭ A♭ E♭
B♭♭ E♭ G E♭ G
E♭ B♭ E♭ F
B♭ E♭ B♭ E♭
E♭ B♭ E♭ G♭
B♭ E♭ G
B♭ E♭ A♭
E♭ B♭♭ E♭ G
G E♭ F B♭ E♭ G
E♭ B♭ E♭
G♭ B♭ E♭ G♭
G B♭ E♭ B♭
E♭ A♭ B♭ E♭
B♭♭ E♭ B♭♭ E♭ G
E♭ G B♭ F
E♭ B♭ E♭
G♭ B♭ E♭ B♭
B♭ E♭ B♭ E♭ G B♭
B♭ E♭ A♭ E♭ A♭ B♭
B♭♭ E♭ G B♭♭
E♭ B♭ E♭ F B♭
B♭ E♭ B♭ E♭
B♭ E♭ B♭ E♭ G♭ B♭
B♭ E♭ G E♭
B♭ E♭ A♭ E♭
E♭ B♭♭ E♭ G
F B♭ E♭ G
B♭ E♭ B♭ E♭
B♭ G♭ B♭ E♭
E♭ B♭ E♭ G B♭ E♭
A♭ E♭ A♭ B♭ E♭
E♭ B♭♭ E♭ G
E♭ G B♭ F
E♭ B♭ E♭
E♭ B♭ E♭ G♭ B♭ E♭

E♭

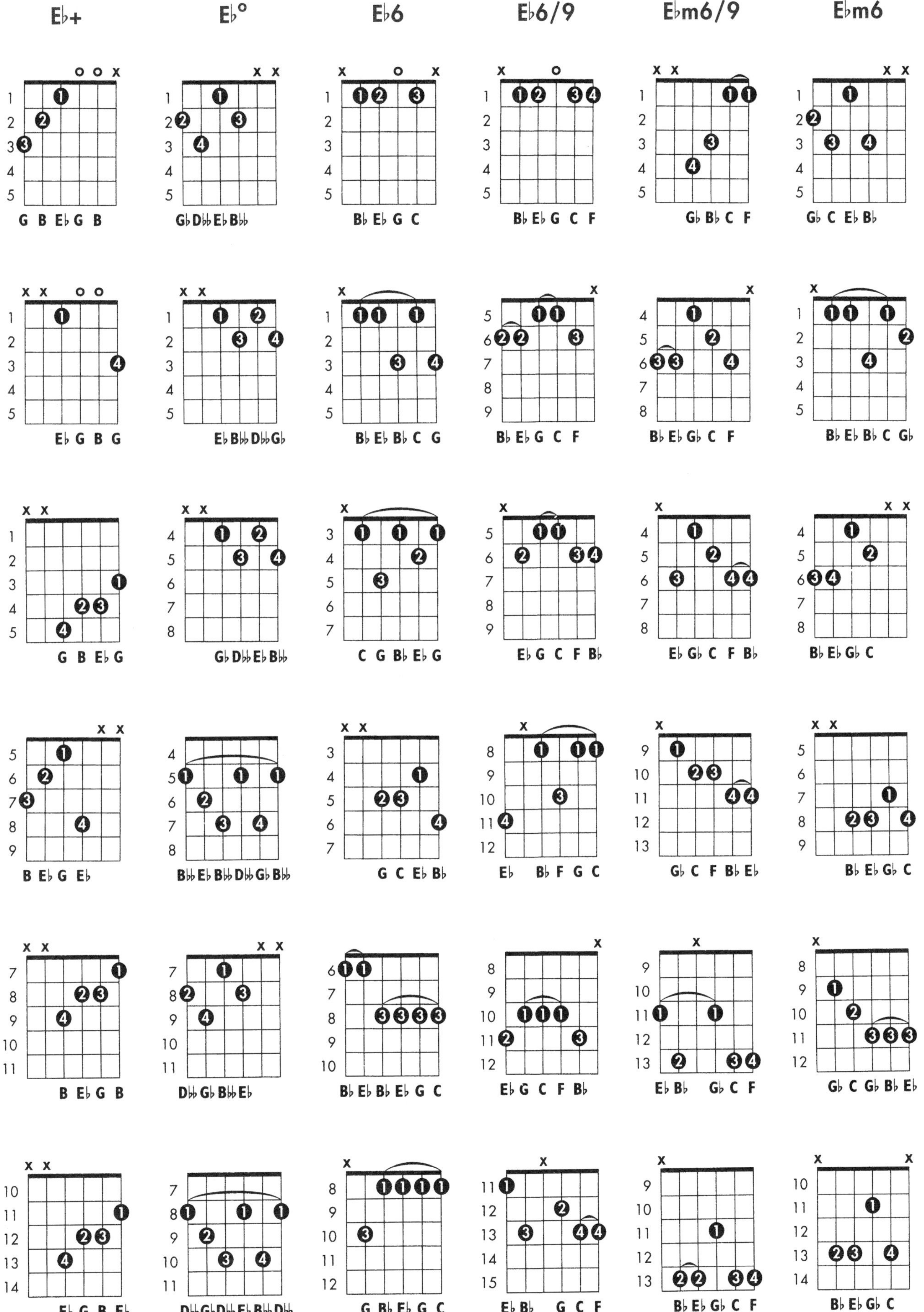
E♭+
E♭°
E♭6
E♭6/9
E♭m6/9
E♭m6
G B E♭ G B
G♭ D♭♭ E♭ B♭♭
B♭ E♭ G C
B♭ E♭ G C F
G♭ B♭ C F
G♭ C E♭ B♭
E♭ G B G
E♭ B♭♭ D♭♭ G♭
B♭ E♭ B♭ C G
B♭ E♭ G C F
B♭ E♭ G♭ C F
B♭ E♭ B♭ C G♭
G B E♭ G
G♭ D♭♭ E♭ B♭♭
C G B♭ E♭ G
E♭ G C F B♭
E♭ G♭ C F B♭
B♭ E♭ G♭ C
B E♭ G E♭
B♭♭ E♭ B♭♭ D♭♭ G♭ B♭♭
G C E♭ B♭
E♭ B♭ F G C
G♭ C F B♭ E♭
B♭ E♭ G♭ C
B E♭ G B
D♭♭ G♭ B♭♭ E♭
B♭ E♭ B♭ E♭ G C
E♭ G C F B♭
E♭ B♭ G♭ C F
G♭ C G♭ B♭ E♭
E♭ G B E♭
D♭♭ G♭ D♭♭ E♭ B♭♭ D♭♭
G B♭ E♭ G C
E♭ B♭ G C F
B♭ E♭ G♭ C F
B♭ E♭ G♭ C

E♭

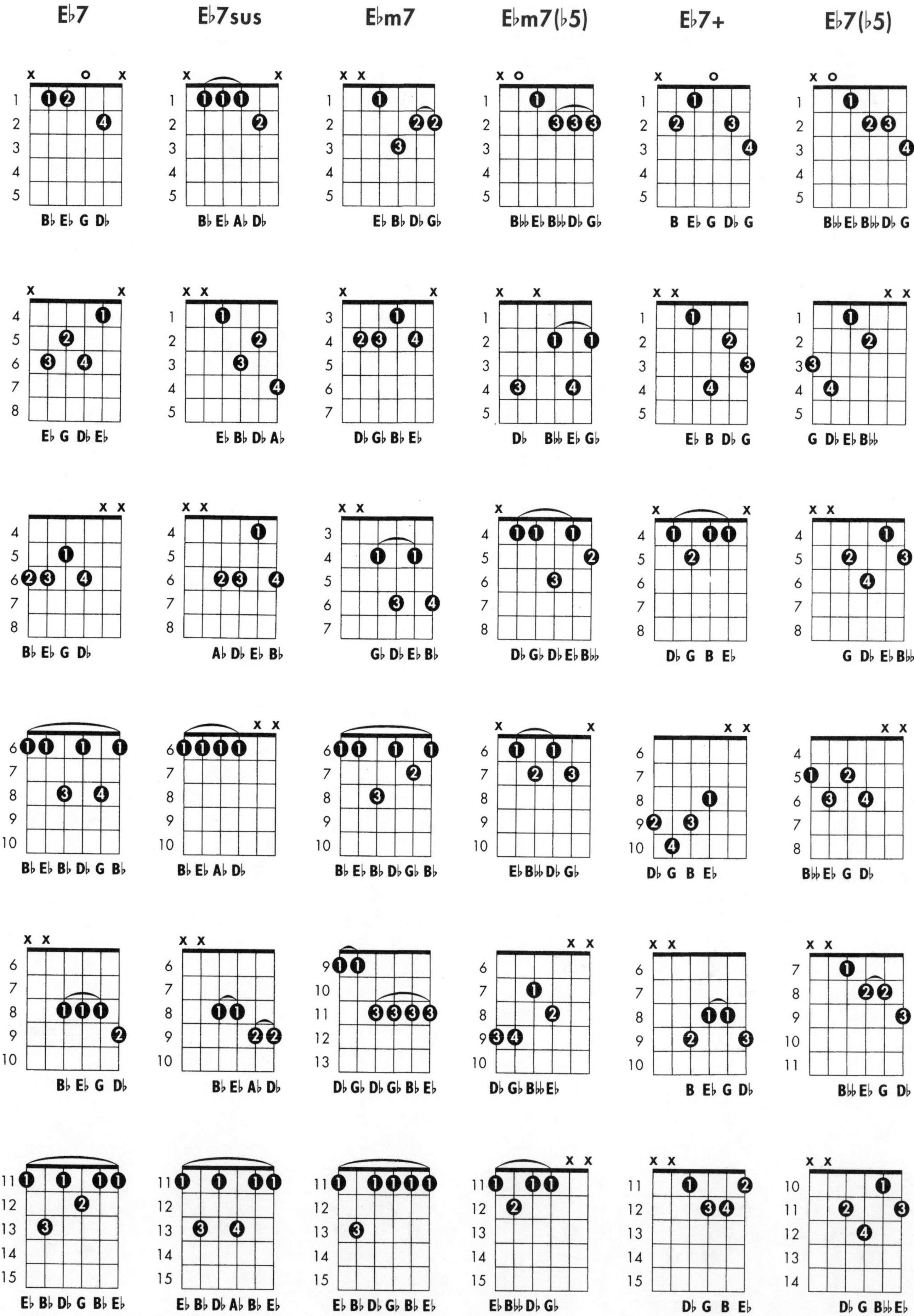

E♭

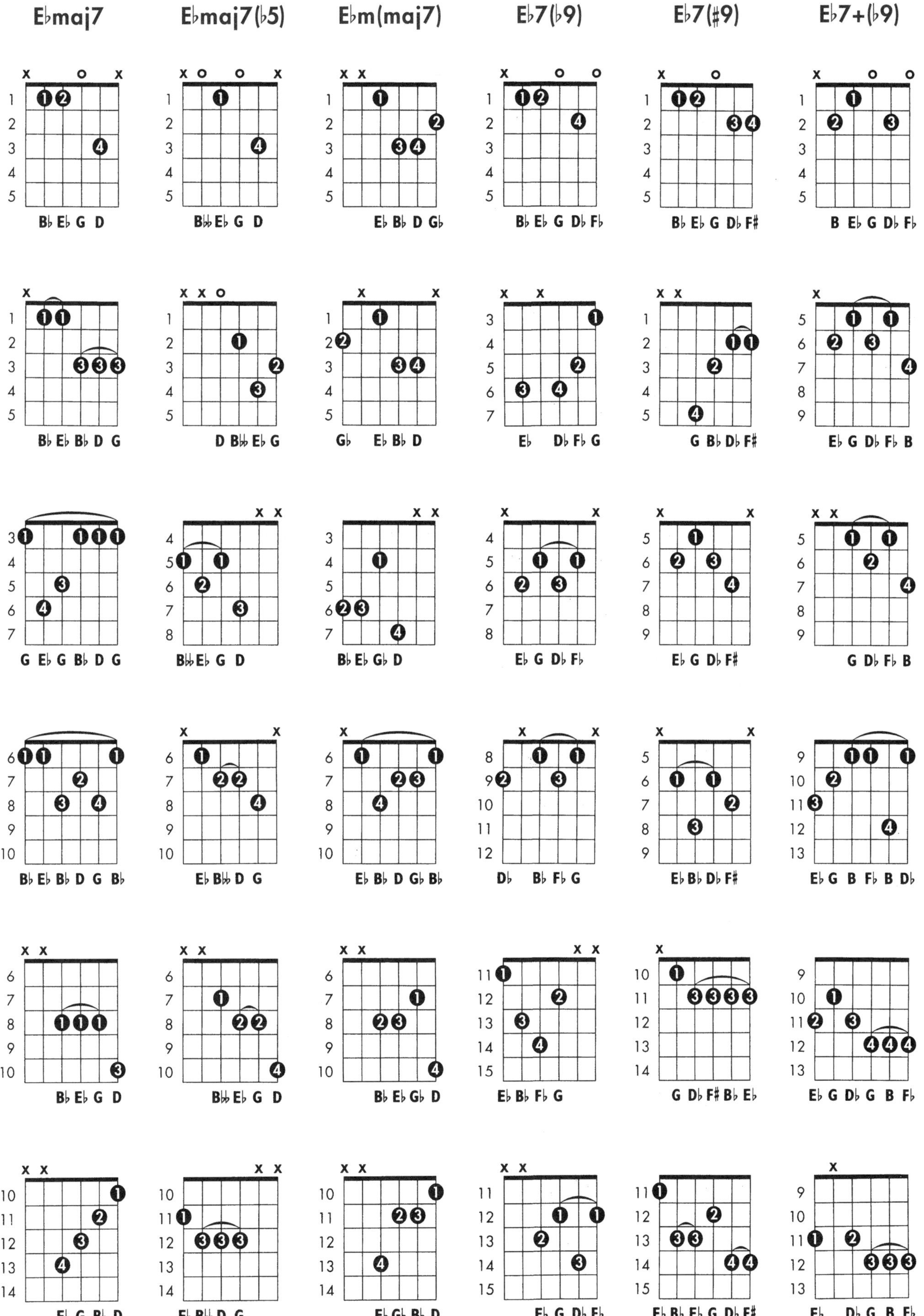

E

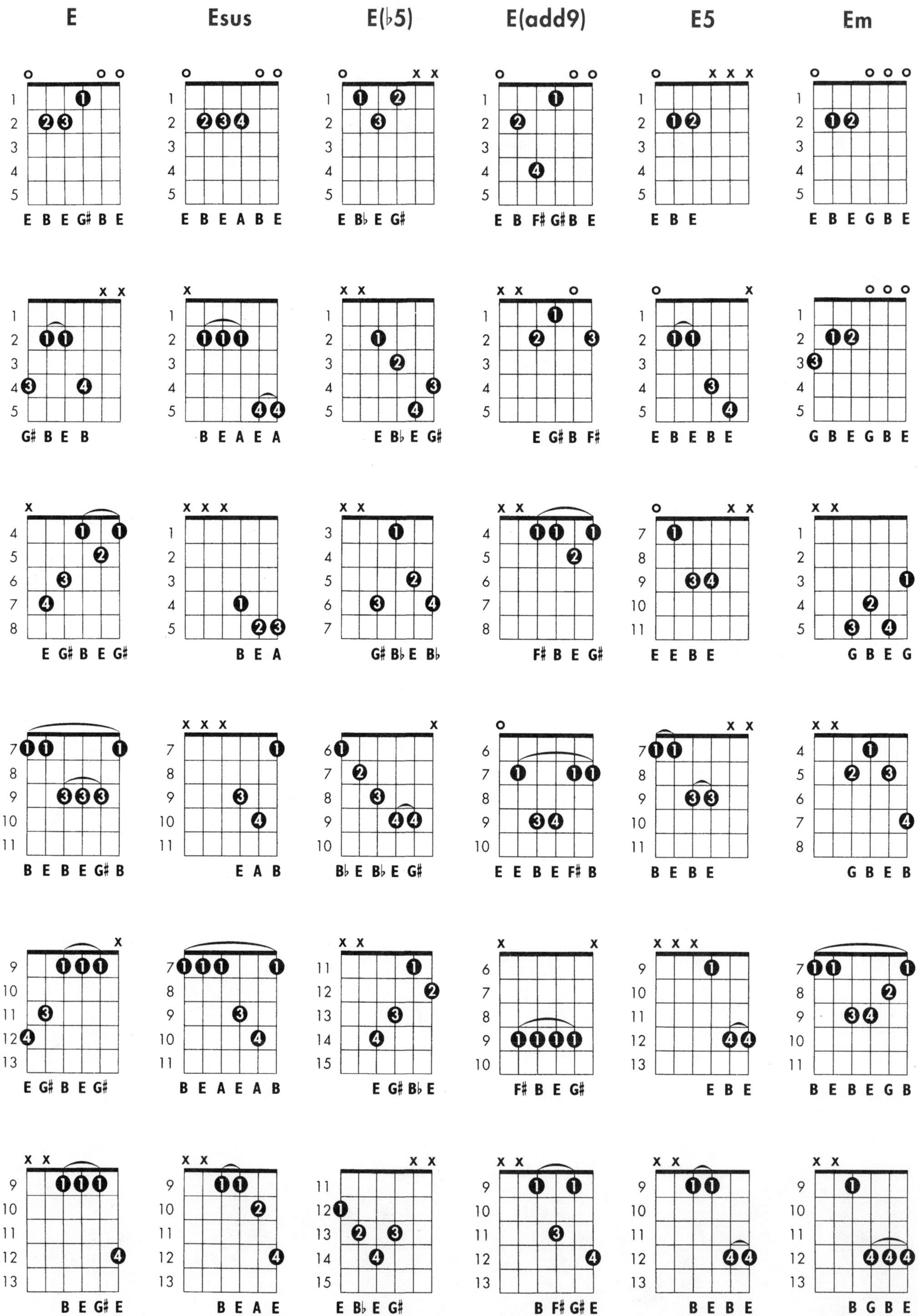

E
Esus
E(♭5)
E(add9)
E5
Em
E B E G♯ B E
E B E A B E
E B♭ E G♯
E B F♯ G♯ B E
E B E
E B E G B E
G♯ B E B
B E A E A
E B♭ E G♯
E G♯ B F♯
E B E B E
G B E G B E
E G♯ B E G♯
B E A
G♯ B♭ E B♭
F♯ B E G♯
E E B E
G B E G
B E B E G♯ B
E A B
B♭ E B♭ E G♯
E E B E F♯ B
B E B E
G B E B
E G♯ B E G♯
B E A E A B
E G♯ B♭ E
F♯ B E G♯
E B E
B E B E G B
B E G♯ E
B E A E
E B♭ E G♯
B F♯ G♯ E
B E B E
B G B E

E

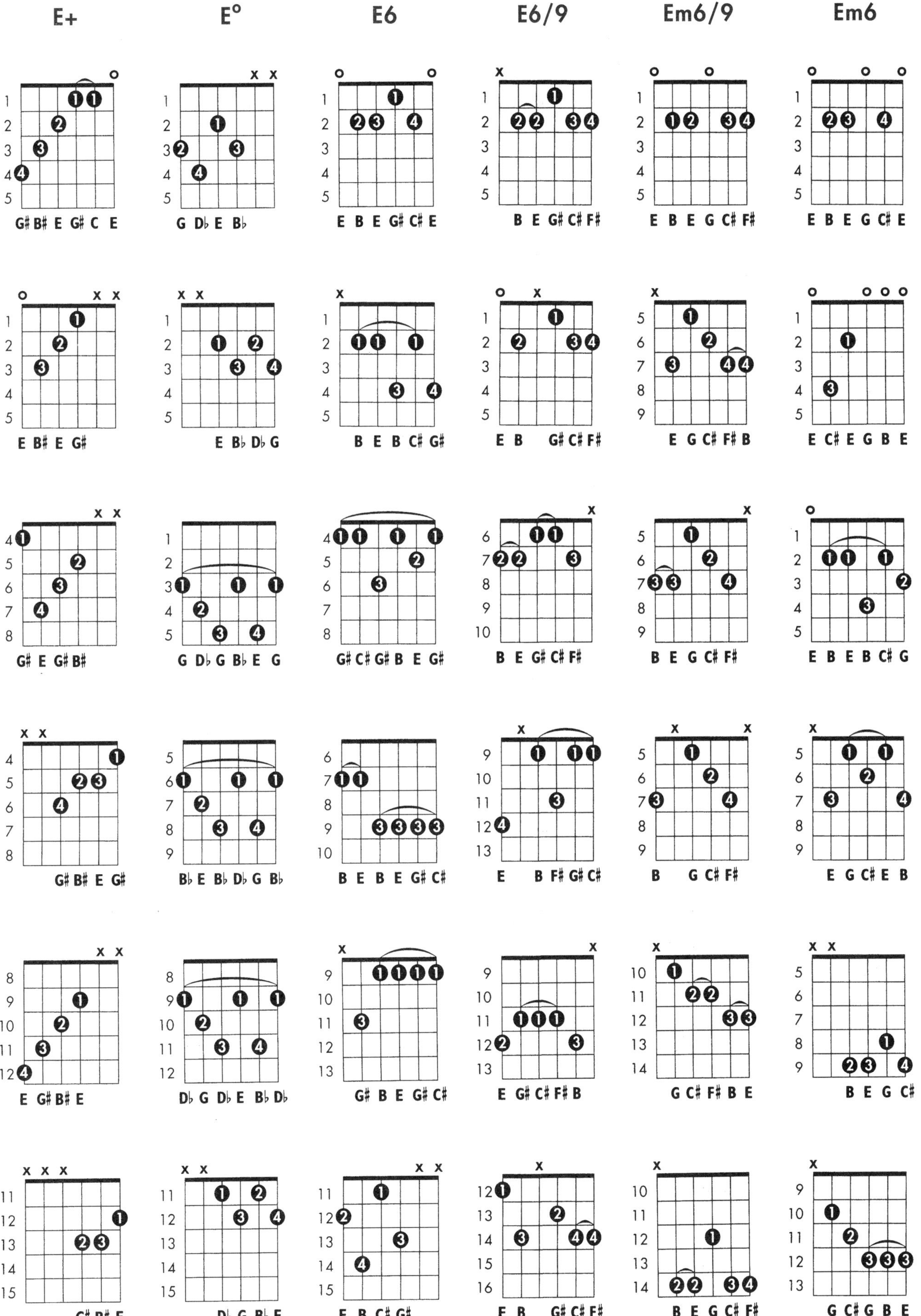

E

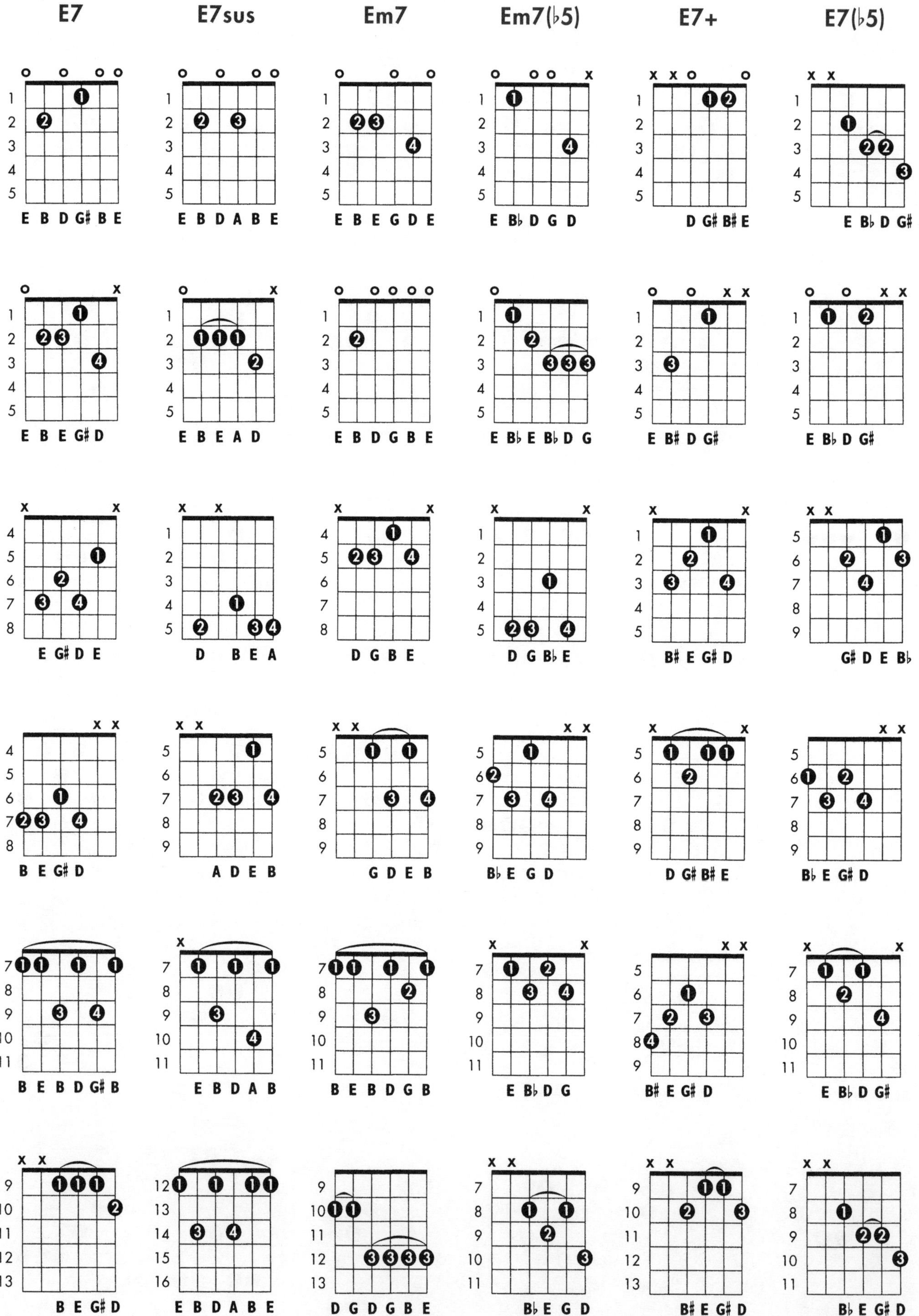
E7
E7sus
Em7
Em7(♭5)
E7+
E7(♭5)
E B D G# B E
E B D A B E
E B E G D E
E B♭ D G D
D G# B# E
E B♭ D G#
E B E G# D
E B E A D
E B D G B E
E B♭ E B♭ D G
E B# D G#
E B♭ D G#
E G# D E
D B E A
D G B E
D G B♭ E
B# E G# D
G# D E B♭
B E G# D
A D E B
G D E B
B♭ E G D
D G# B# E
B♭ E G# D
B E B D G# B
E B D A B
B E B D G B
E B♭ D G
B# E G# D
E B♭ D G#
B E G# D
E B D A B E
D G D G B E
B♭ E G D
B# E G# D
B♭ E G# D

E

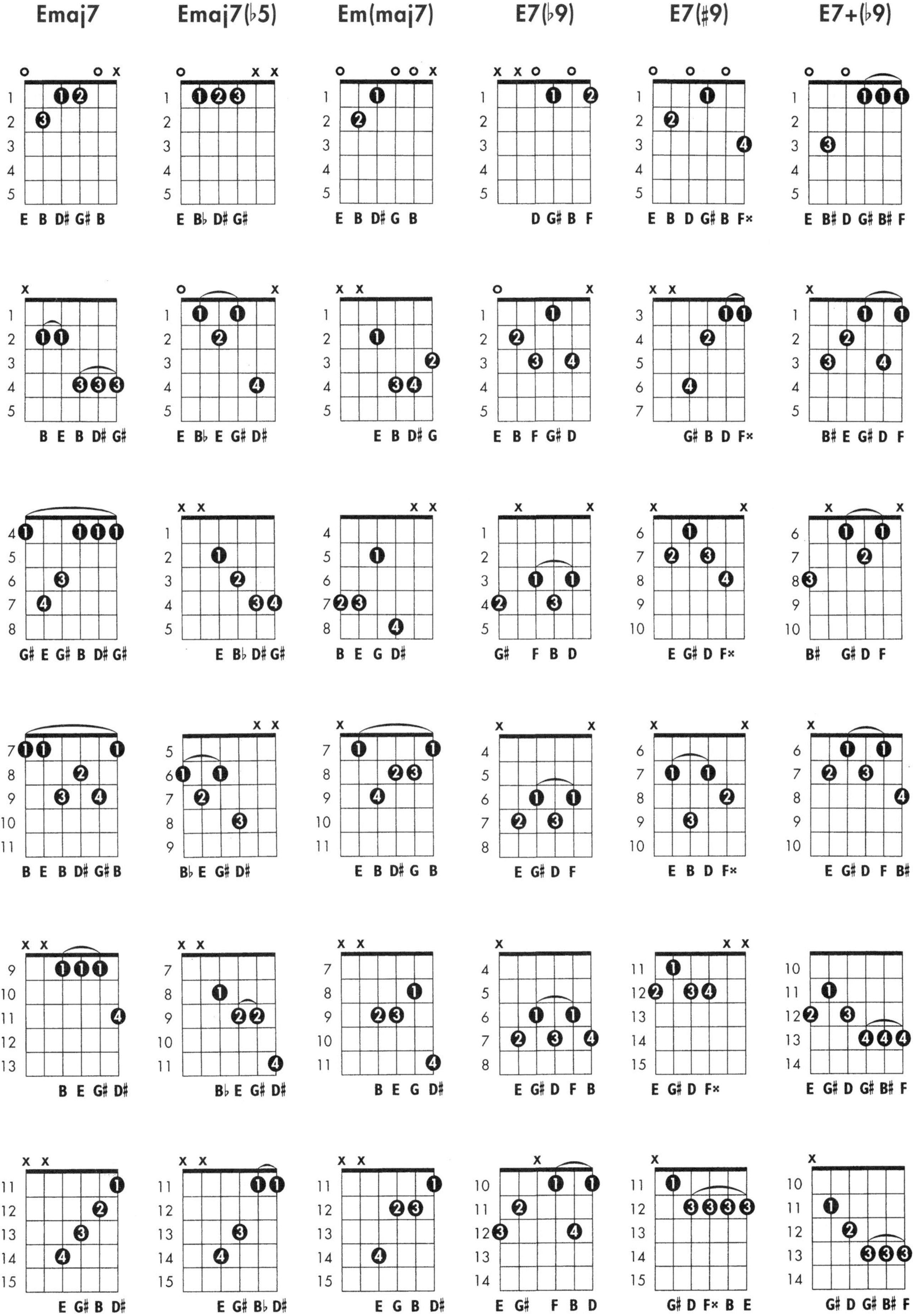

F

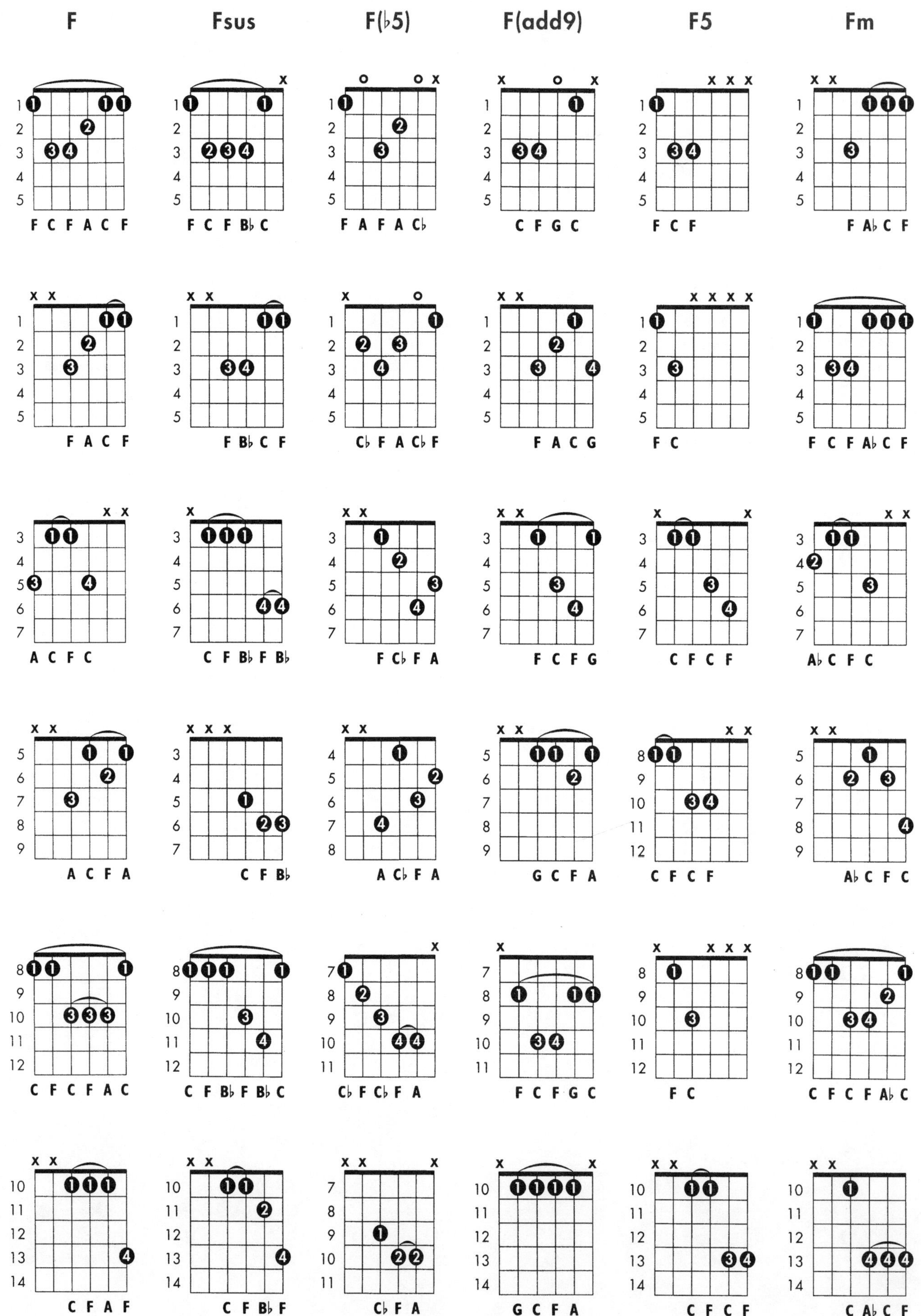

F

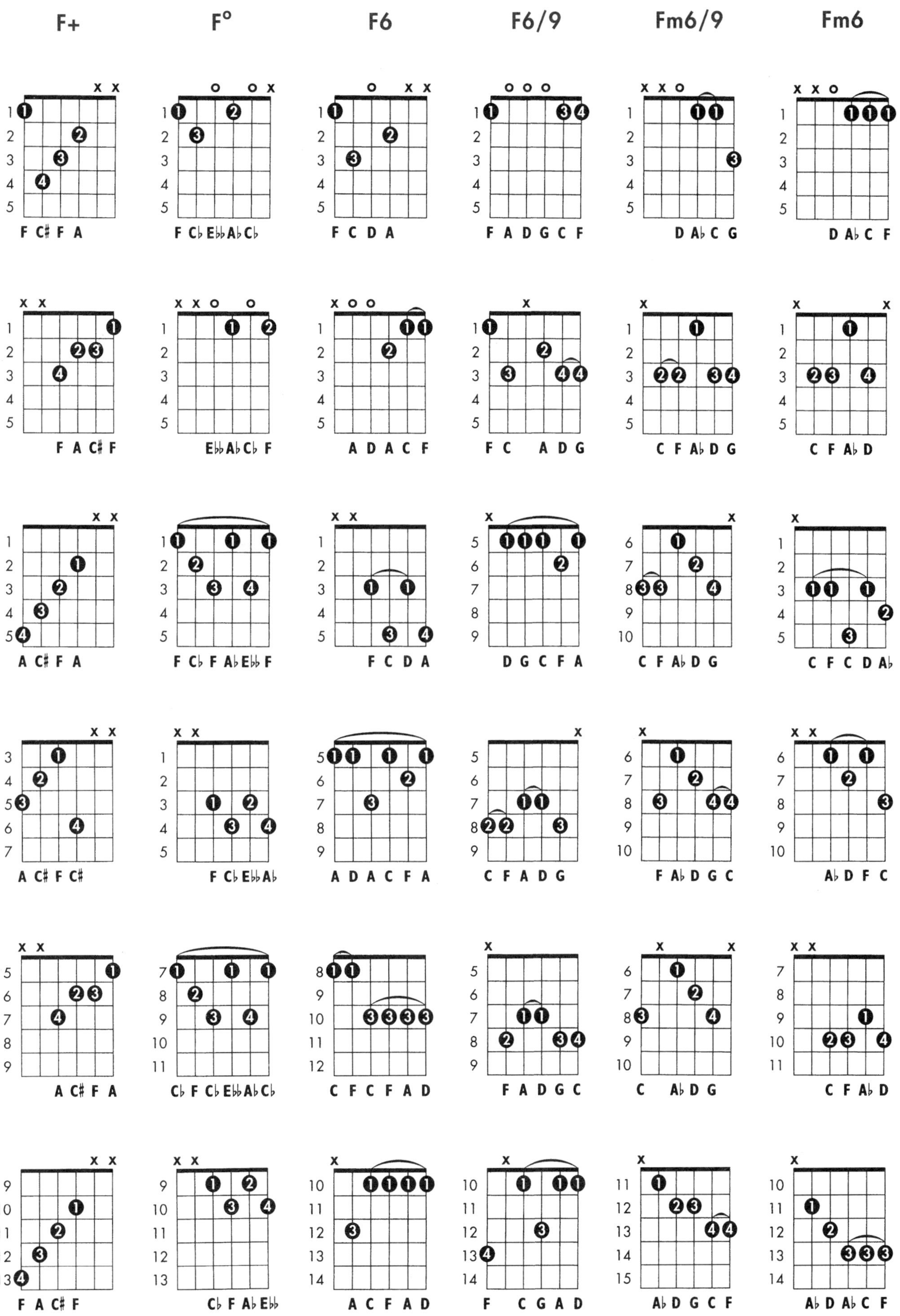
F+
F°
F6
F6/9
Fm6/9
Fm6
F C♯ F A
F C♭ E♭♭ A♭ C♭
F C D A
F A D G C F
D A♭ C G
D A♭ C F
F A C♯ F
E♭♭ A♭ C♭ F
A D A C F
F C A D G
C F A♭ D G
C F A♭ D
A C♯ F A
F C♭ F A♭ E♭♭ F
F C D A
D G C F A
C F A♭ D G
C F C D A♭
A C♯ F C♯
F C♭ E♭♭ A♭
A D A C F A
C F A D G
F A♭ D G C
A♭ D F C
A C♯ F A
C♭ F C♭ E♭♭ A♭ C♭
C F C F A D
F A D G C
C A♭ D G
C F A♭ D
F A C♯ F
C♭ F A♭ E♭♭
A C F A D
F C G A D
A♭ D G C F
A♭ D A♭ C F

F

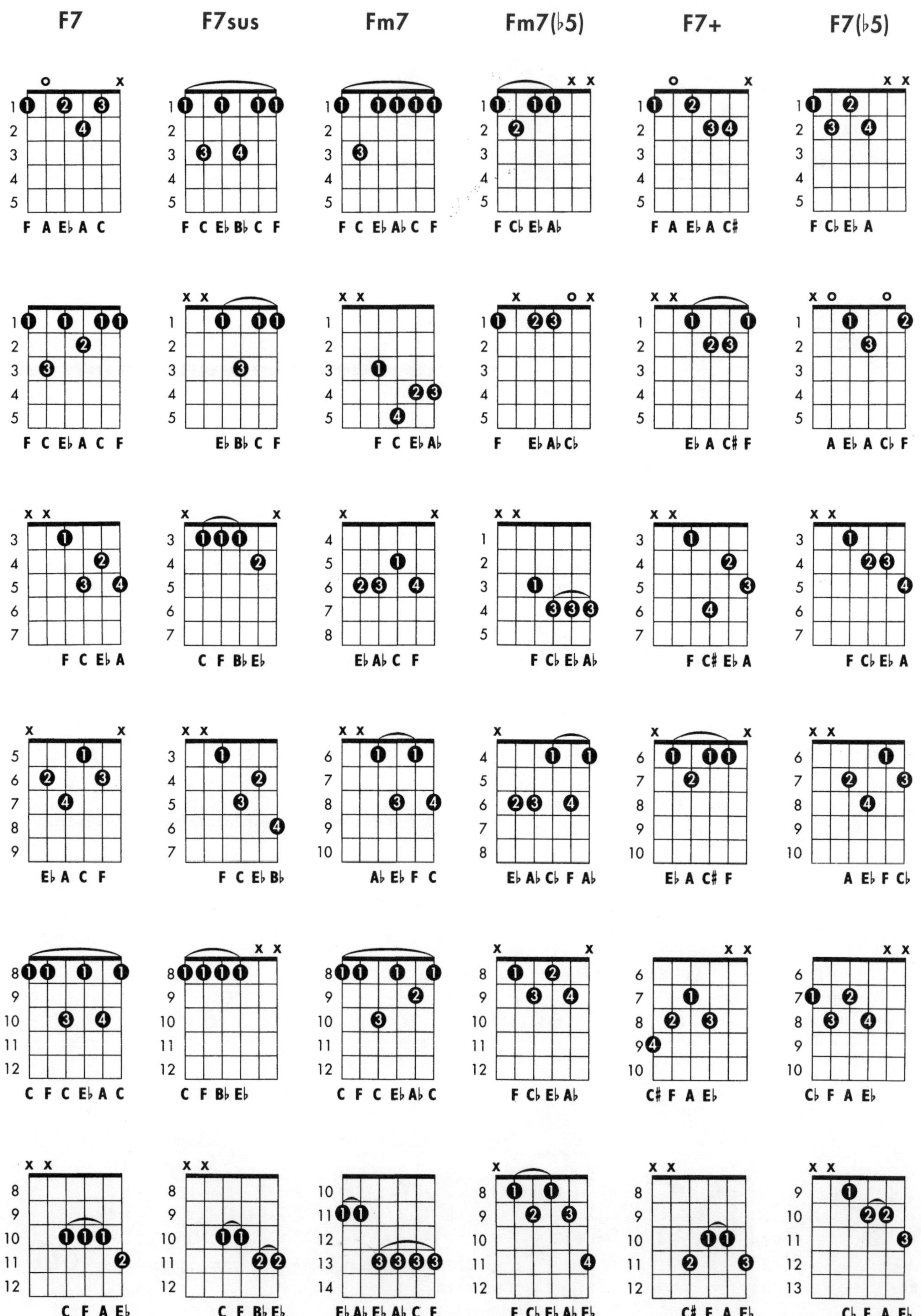
F7
F7sus
Fm7
Fm7(♭5)
F7+
F7(♭5)
F A E♭ A C
F C E♭ B♭ C F
F C E♭ A♭ C F
F C♭ E♭ A♭
F A E♭ A C♯
F C♭ E♭ A
F C E♭ A C F
E♭ B♭ C F
F C E♭ A♭
F E♭ A♭ C♭
E♭ A C♯ F
A E♭ A C♭ F
F C E♭ A
C F B♭ E♭
E♭ A♭ C F
F C♭ E♭ A♭
F C♯ E♭ A
F C♭ E♭ A
E♭ A C F
F C E♭ B♭
A♭ E♭ F C
E♭ A♭ C♭ F A♭
E♭ A C♯ F
A E♭ F C♭
C F C E♭ A C
C F B♭ E♭
C F C E♭ A♭ C
F C♭ E♭ A♭
C♯ F A E♭
C♭ F A E♭
C F A E♭
C F B♭ E♭
E♭ A♭ E♭ A♭ C F
F C♭ E♭ A♭ E♭
C♯ F A E♭
C♭ F A E♭

F

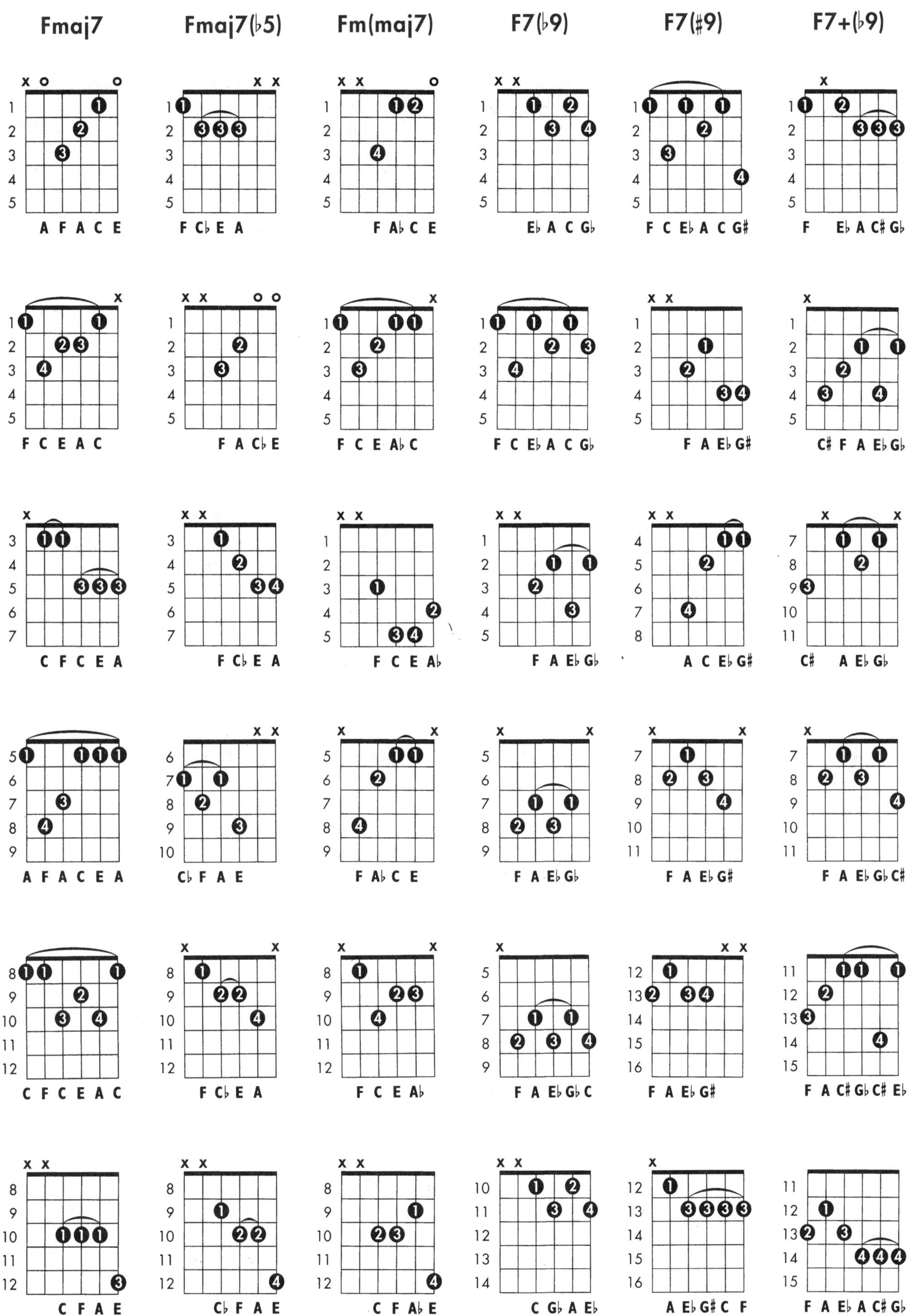
Fmaj7
Fmaj7(♭5)
Fm(maj7)
F7(♭9)
F7(♯9)
F7+(♭9)
A F A C E
F C♭ E A
F A♭ C E
E♭ A C G♭
F C E♭ A C G♯
F E♭ A C♯ G♭
F C E A C
F A C♭ E
F C E A♭ C
F C E♭ A C G♭
F A E♭ G♯
C♯ F A E♭ G♭
C F C E A
F C♭ E A
F C E A♭
F A E♭ G♭
A C E♭ G♯
C♯ A E♭ G♭
A F A C E A
C♭ F A E
F A♭ C E
F A E♭ G♭
F A E♭ G♯
F A E♭ G♭ C♯
C F C E A C
F C♭ E A
F C E A♭
F A E♭ G♭ C
F A E♭ G♯
F A C♯ G♭ C♯ E♭
C F A E
C♭ F A E
C F A♭ E
C G♭ A E♭
A E♭ G♯ C F
F A E♭ A C♯ G♭

F♯

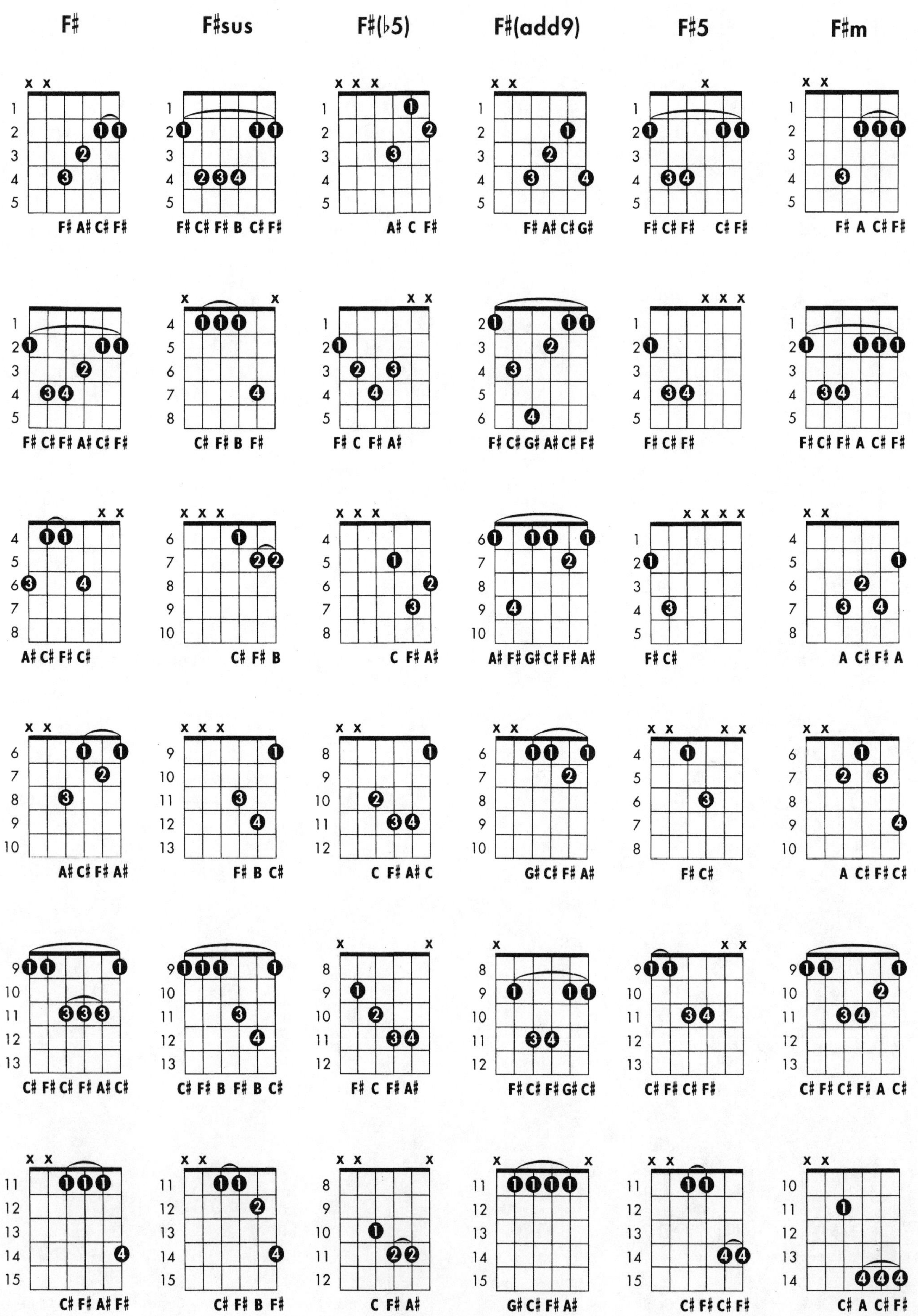
F♯
F♯sus
F♯(♭5)
F♯(add9)
F♯5
F♯m
F♯ A♯ C♯ F♯
F♯ C♯ F♯ B C♯ F♯
A♯ C F♯
F♯ A♯ C♯ G♯
F♯ C♯ F♯ C♯ F♯
F♯ A C♯ F♯
F♯ C♯ F♯ A♯ C♯ F♯
C♯ F♯ B F♯
F♯ C F♯ A♯
F♯ C♯ G♯ A♯ C♯ F♯
F♯ C♯ F♯
F♯ C♯ F♯ A C♯ F♯
A♯ C♯ F♯ C♯
C♯ F♯ B
C F♯ A♯
A♯ F♯ G♯ C♯ F♯ A♯
F♯ C♯
A C♯ F♯ A
A♯ C♯ F♯ A♯
F♯ B C♯
C F♯ A♯ C
G♯ C♯ F♯ A♯
F♯ C♯
A C♯ F♯ C♯
C♯ F♯ C♯ F♯ A♯ C♯
C♯ F♯ B F♯ B C♯
F♯ C F♯ A♯
F♯ C♯ F♯ G♯ C♯
C♯ F♯ C♯ F♯
C♯ F♯ C♯ F♯ A C♯
C♯ F♯ A♯ F♯
C♯ F♯ B F♯
C F♯ A♯
G♯ C♯ F♯ A♯
C♯ F♯ C♯ F♯
C♯ A C♯ F♯

F♯

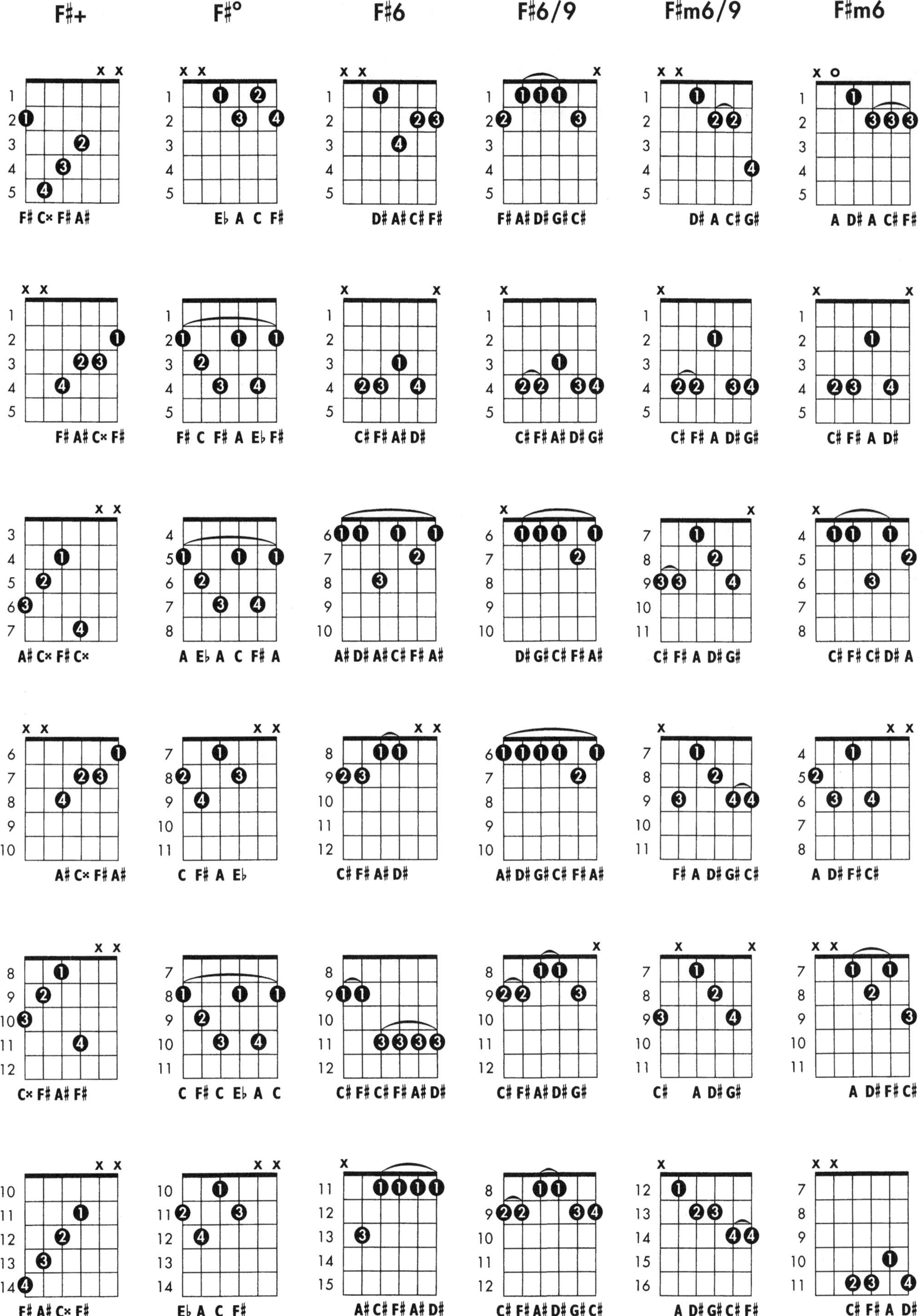
F♯+
F♯°
F♯6
F♯6/9
F♯m6/9
F♯m6
F♯ C× F♯ A♯
E♭ A C F♯
D♯ A♯ C♯ F♯
F♯ A♯ D♯ G♯ C♯
D♯ A C♯ G♯
A D♯ A C♯ F♯
F♯ A♯ C× F♯
F♯ C F♯ A E♭ F♯
C♯ F♯ A♯ D♯
C♯ F♯ A♯ D♯ G♯
C♯ F♯ A D♯ G♯
C♯ F♯ A D♯
A♯ C× F♯ C×
A E♭ A C F♯ A
A♯ D♯ A♯ C♯ F♯ A♯
D♯ G♯ C♯ F♯ A♯
C♯ F♯ A D♯ G♯
C♯ F♯ C♯ D♯ A
A♯ C× F♯ A♯
C F♯ A E♭
C♯ F♯ A♯ D♯
A♯ D♯ G♯ C♯ F♯ A♯
F♯ A D♯ G♯ C♯
A D♯ F♯ C♯
C× F♯ A♯ F♯
C F♯ C E♭ A C
C♯ F♯ C♯ F♯ A♯ D♯
C♯ F♯ A♯ D♯ G♯
C♯ A D♯ G♯
A D♯ F♯ C♯
F♯ A♯ C× F♯
E♭ A C F♯
A♯ C♯ F♯ A♯ D♯
C♯ F♯ A♯ D♯ G♯ C♯
A D♯ G♯ C♯ F♯
C♯ F♯ A D♯

F♯

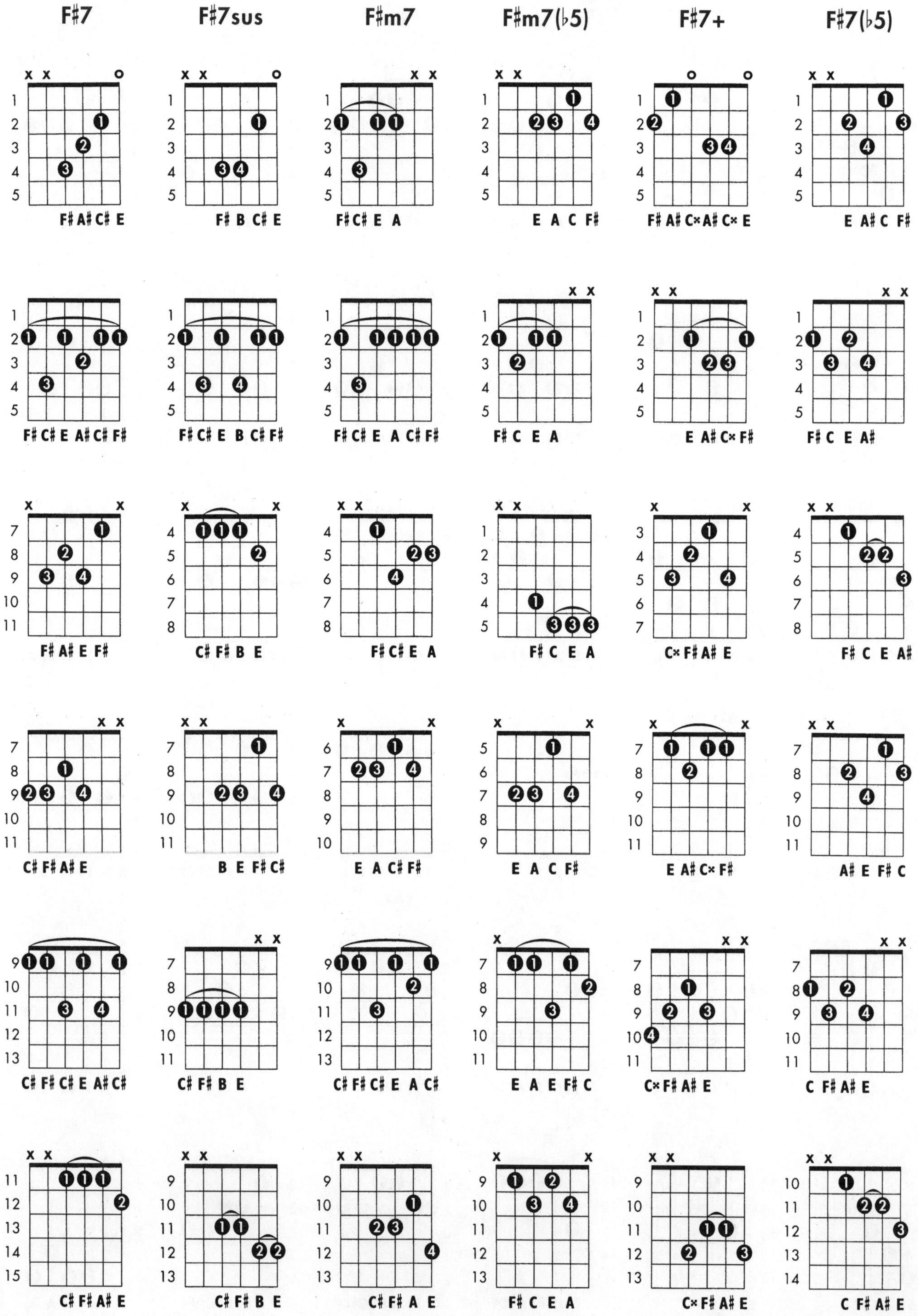

F♯

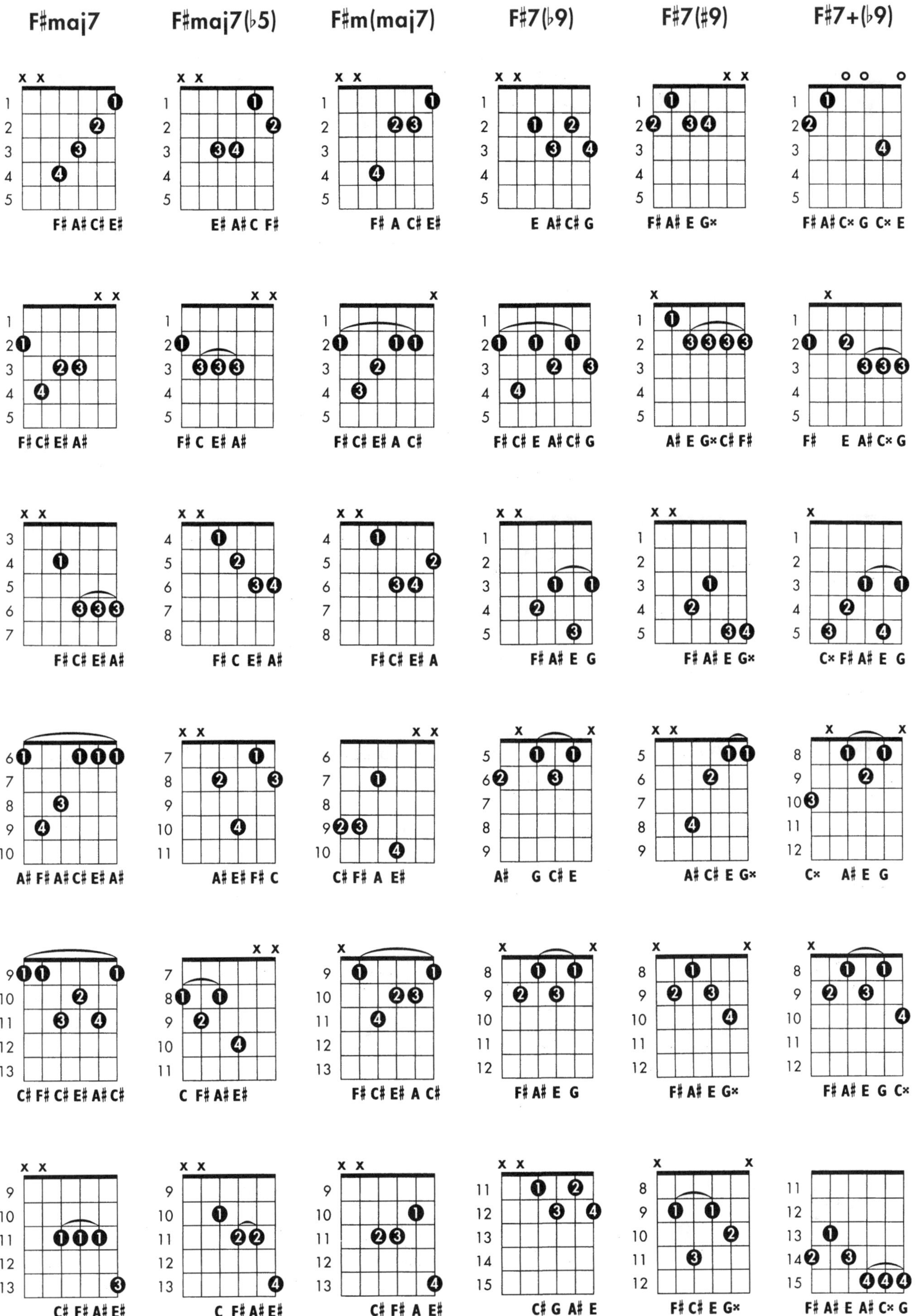

F♯maj7
F♯maj7(♭5)
F♯m(maj7)
F♯7(♭9)
F♯7(♯9)
F♯7+(♭9)
F♯ A♯ C♯ E♯
E♯ A♯ C F♯
F♯ A C♯ E♯
E A♯ C♯ G
F♯ A♯ E G×
F♯ A♯ C× G C× E
F♯ C♯ E♯ A♯
F♯ C E♯ A♯
F♯ C♯ E♯ A C♯
F♯ C♯ E A♯ C♯ G
A♯ E G× C♯ F♯
F♯ E A♯ C× G
F♯ C♯ E♯ A♯
F♯ C E♯ A♯
F♯ C♯ E♯ A
F♯ A♯ E G
F♯ A♯ E G×
C× F♯ A♯ E G
A♯ F♯ A♯ C♯ E♯ A♯
A♯ E♯ F♯ C
C♯ F♯ A E♯
A♯ G C♯ E
A♯ C♯ E G×
C× A♯ E G
C♯ F♯ C♯ E♯ A♯ C♯
C F♯ A♯ E♯
F♯ C♯ E♯ A C♯
F♯ A♯ E G
F♯ A♯ E G×
F♯ A♯ E G C×
C♯ F♯ A♯ E♯
C F♯ A♯ E♯
C♯ F♯ A E♯
C♯ G A♯ E
F♯ C♯ E G×
F♯ A♯ E A♯ C× G

G

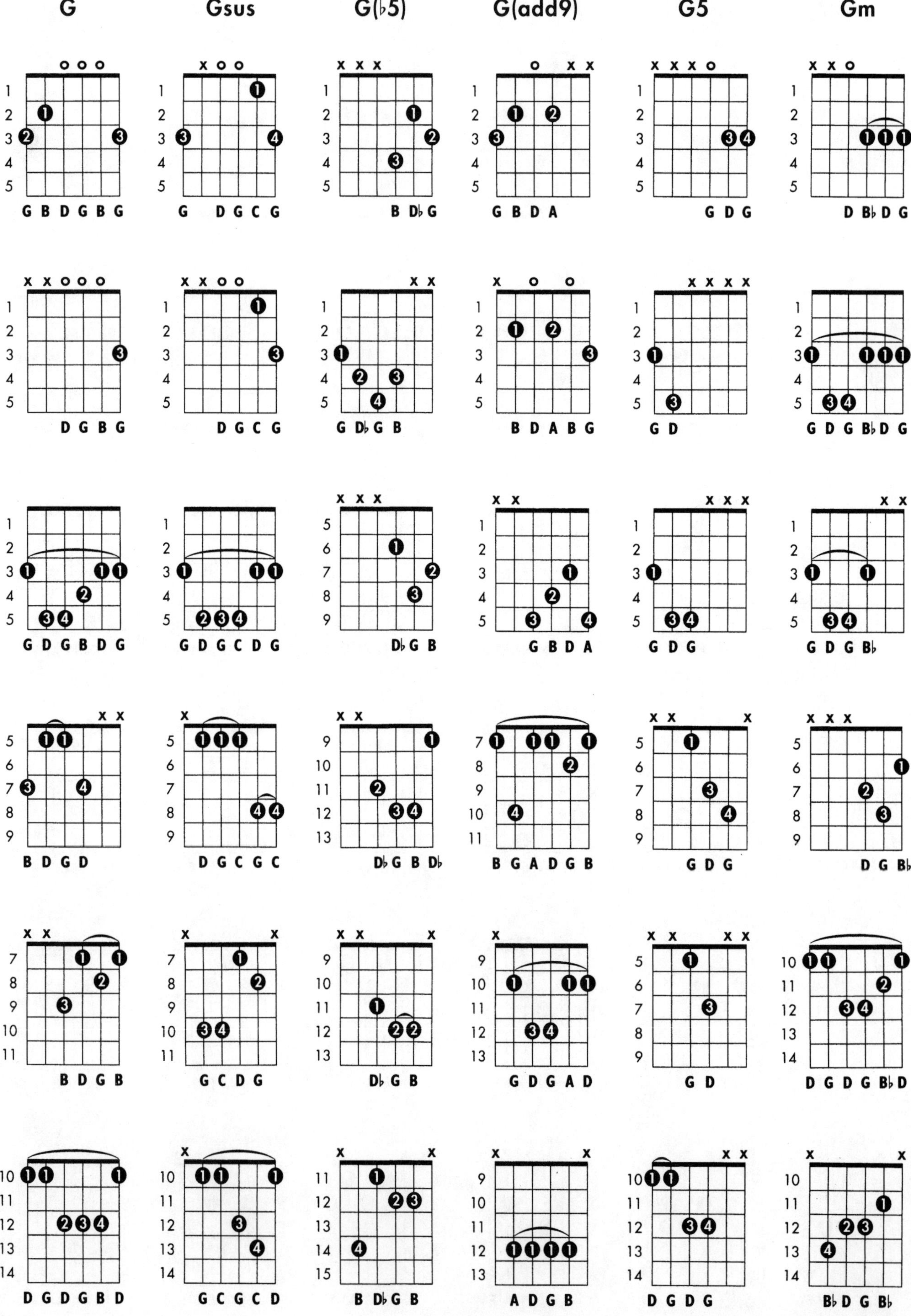
G
Gsus
G(♭5)
G(add9)
G5
Gm
G B D G B G
G D G C G
B D♭ G
G B D A
G D G
D B♭ D G
D G B G
D G C G
G D♭ G B
B D A B G
G D
G D G B♭ D G
G D G B D G
G D G C D G
D♭ G B
G B D A
G D G
G D G B♭
B D G D
D G C G C
D♭ G B D♭
B G A D G B
G D G
D G B♭
B D G B
G C D G
D♭ G B
G D G A D
G D
D G D G B♭ D
D G D G B D
G C G C D
B D♭ G B
A D G B
D G D G
B♭ D G B♭

G

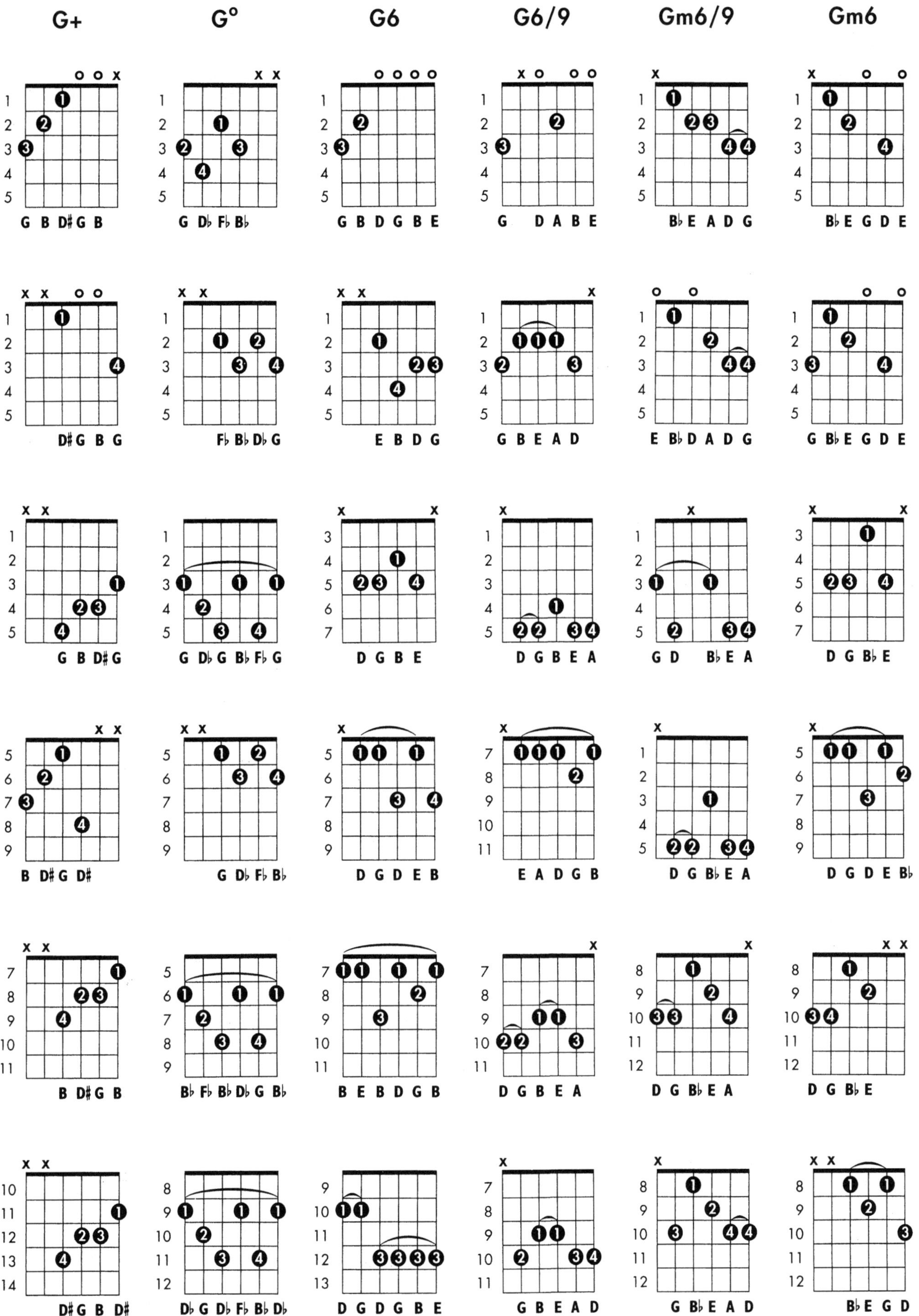

G

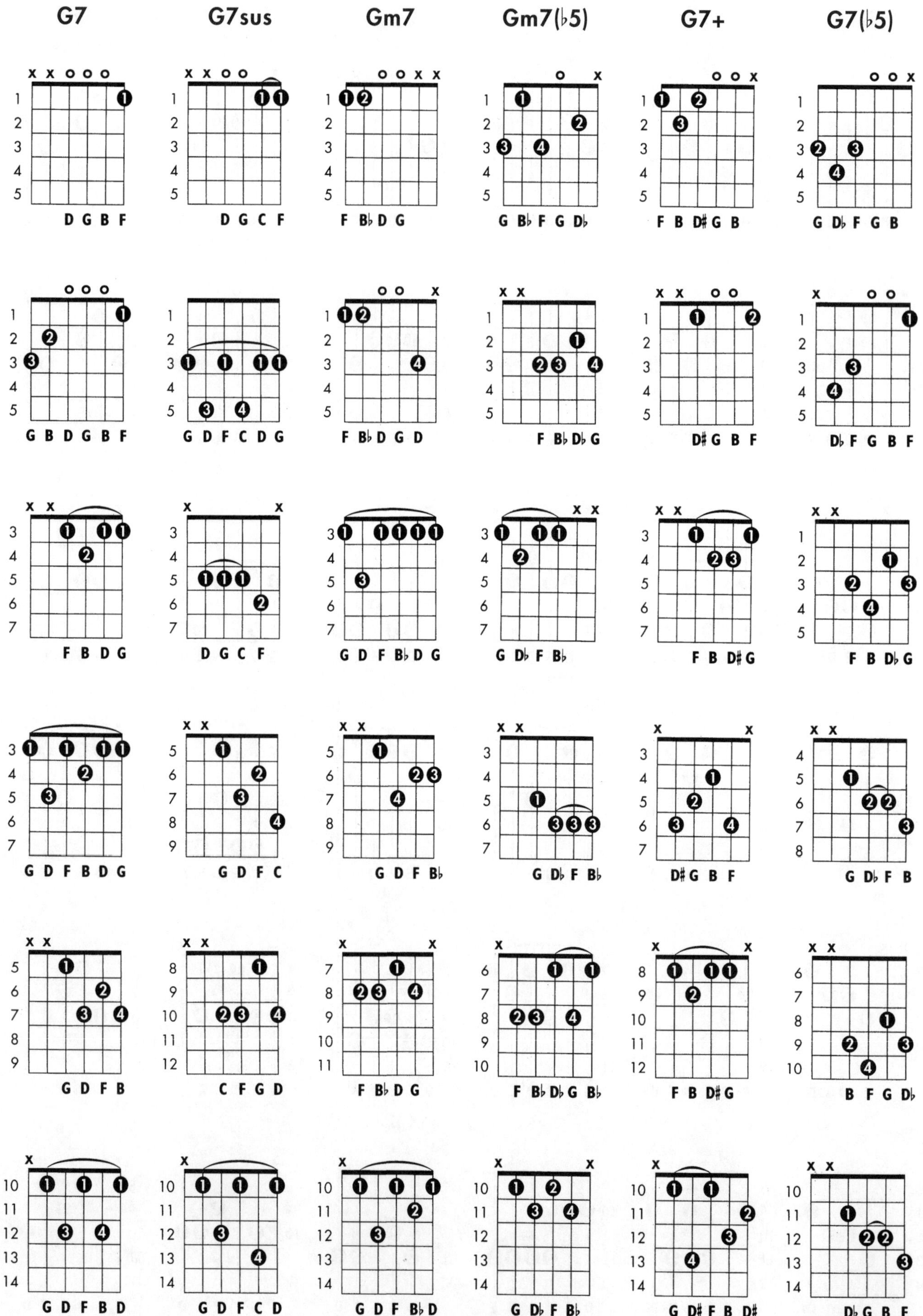
G7
G7sus
Gm7
Gm7(♭5)
G7+
G7(♭5)
D G B F
D G C F
F B♭ D G
G B♭ F G D♭
F B D♯ G B
G D♭ F G B
G B D G B F
G D F C D G
F B♭ D G D
F B♭ D♭ G
D♯ G B F
D♭ F G B F
F B D G
D G C F
G D F B♭ D G
G D♭ F B♭
F B D♯ G
F B D♭ G
G D F B D G
G D F C
G D F B♭
G D♭ F B♭
D♯ G B F
G D♭ F B
G D F B
C F G D
F B♭ D G
F B♭ D♭ G B♭
F B D♯ G
B F G D♭
G D F B D
G D F C D
G D F B♭ D
G D♭ F B♭
G D♯ F B D♯
D♭ G B F

G

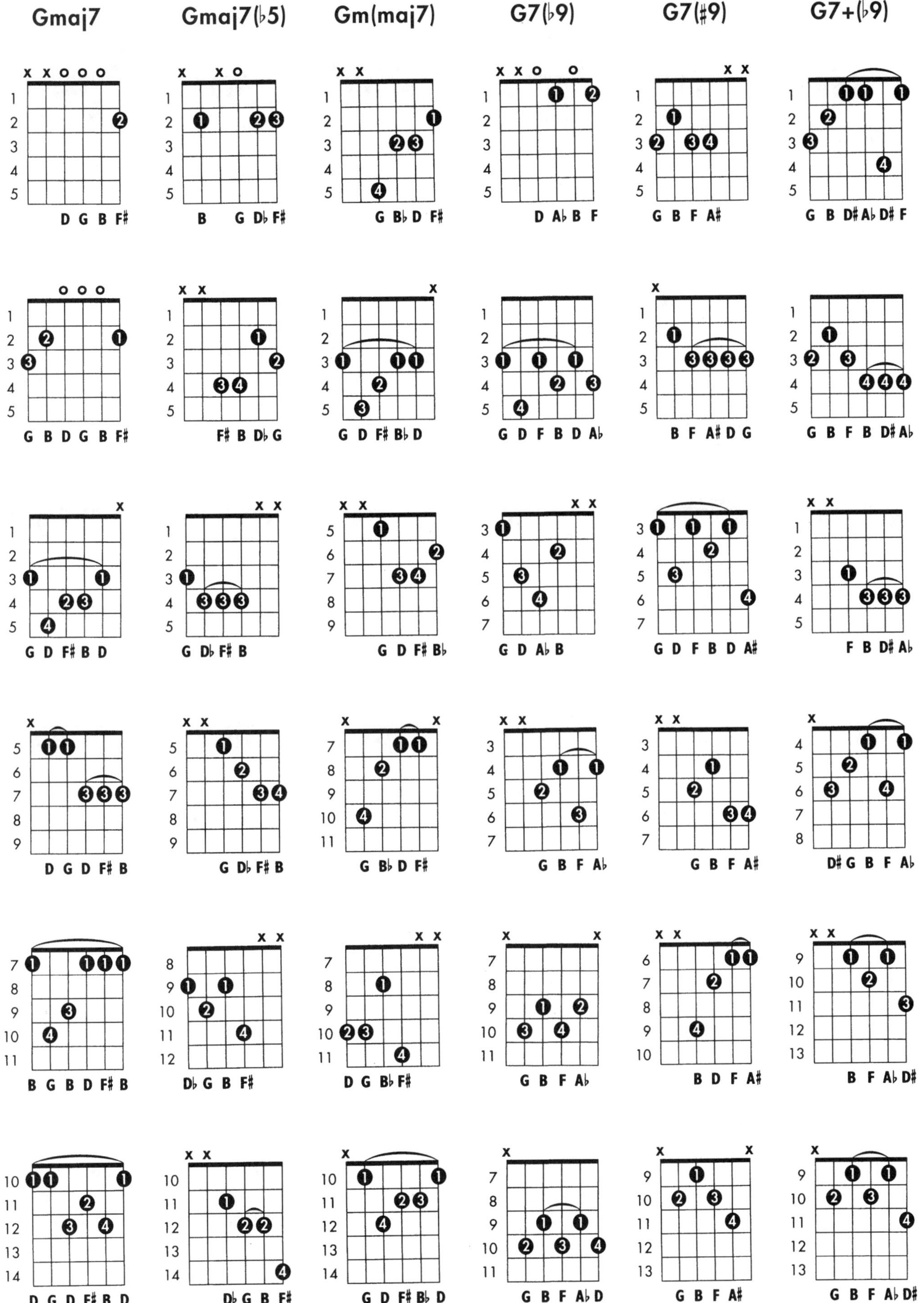
Gmaj7
Gmaj7(♭5)
Gm(maj7)
G7(♭9)
G7(♯9)
G7+(♭9)
D G B F♯
B G D♭ F♯
G B♭ D F♯
D A♭ B F
G B F A♯
G B D♯ A♭ D♯ F
G B D G B F♯
F♯ B D♭ G
G D F♯ B♭ D
G D F B D A♭
B F A♯ D G
G B F B D♯ A♭
G D F♯ B D
G D♭ F♯ B
G D F♯ B♭
G D A♭ B
G D F B D A♯
F B D♯ A♭
D G D F♯ B
G D♭ F♯ B
G B♭ D F♯
G B F A♭
G B F A♯
D♯ G B F A♭
B G B D F♯ B
D♭ G B F♯
D G B♭ F♯
G B F A♭
B D F A♯
B F A♭ D♯
D G D F♯ B D
D♭ G B F♯
G D F♯ B♭ D
G B F A♭ D
G B F A♯
G B F A♭ D♯

A♭

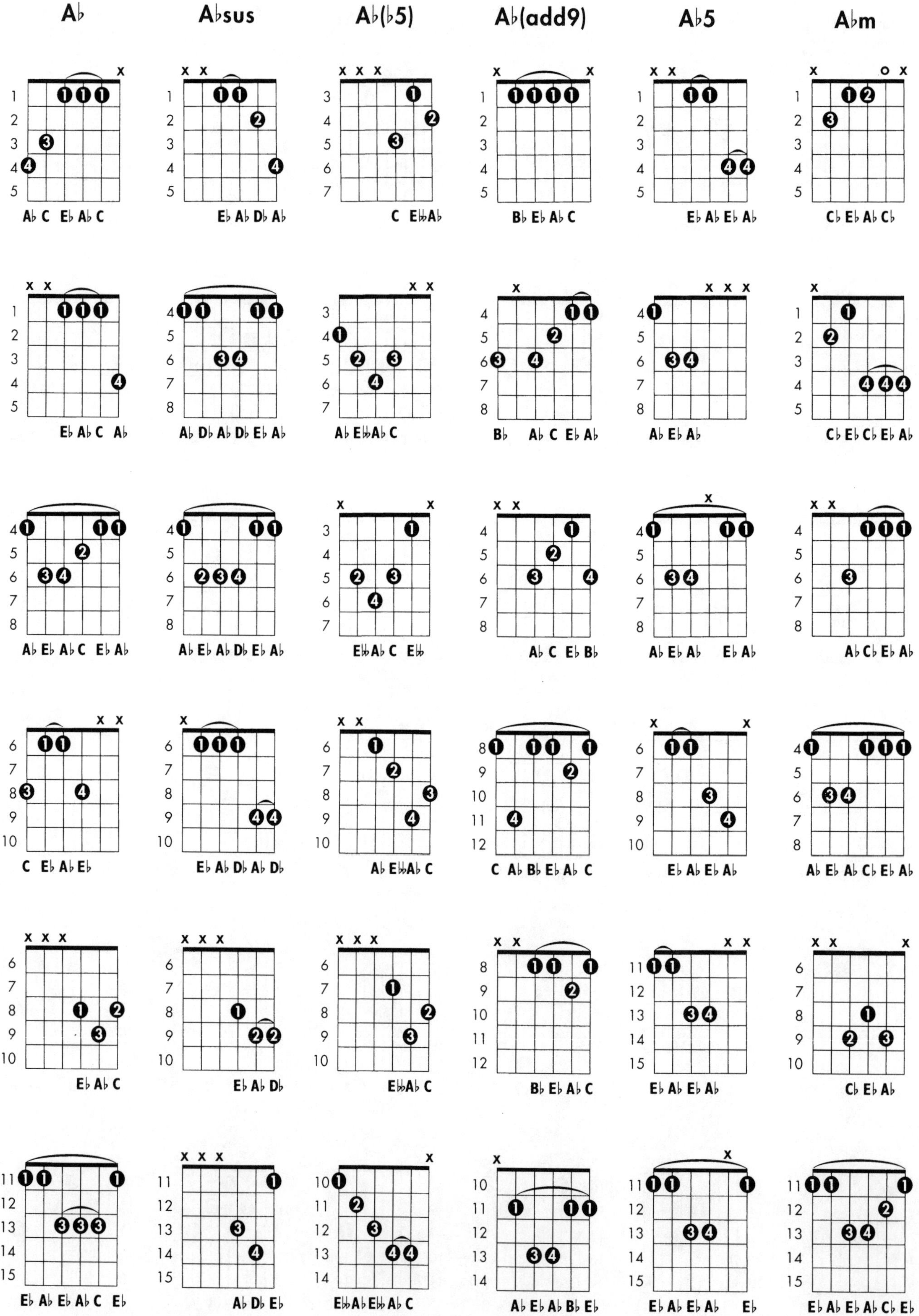

A♭

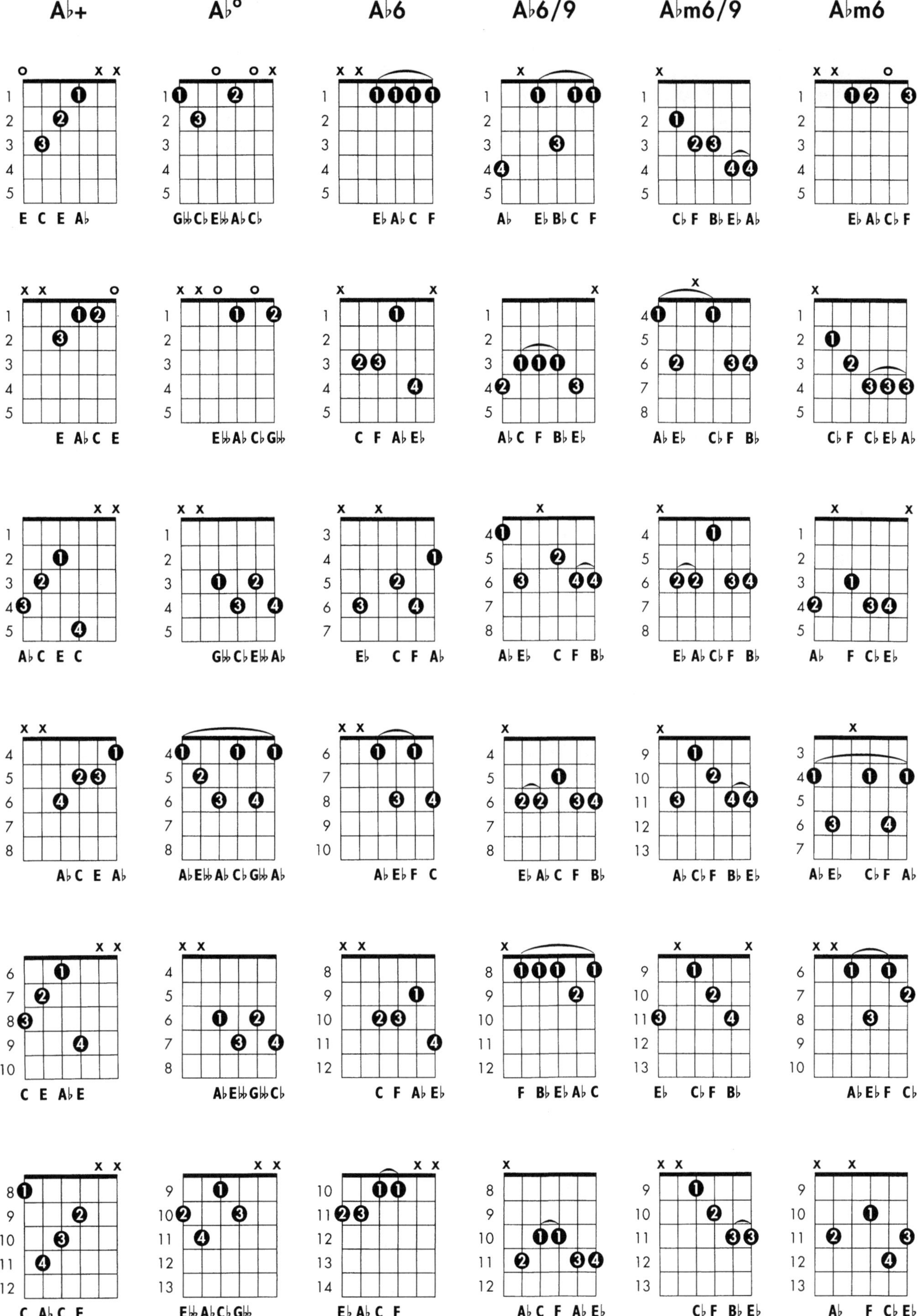
A♭+
A♭°
A♭6
A♭6/9
A♭m6/9
A♭m6
E C E A♭
G♭♭ C♭ E♭♭ A♭ C♭
E♭ A♭ C F
A♭ E♭ B♭ C F
C♭ F B♭ E♭ A♭
E♭ A♭ C♭ F
E A♭ C E
E♭♭ A♭ C♭ G♭♭
C F A♭ E♭
A♭ C F B♭ E♭
A♭ E♭ C♭ F B♭
C♭ F C♭ E♭ A♭
A♭ C E C
G♭♭ C♭ E♭♭ A♭
E♭ C F A♭
A♭ E♭ C F B♭
E♭ A♭ C♭ F B♭
A♭ F C♭ E♭
A♭ C E A♭
A♭ E♭♭ A♭ C♭ G♭♭ A♭
A♭ E♭ F C
E♭ A♭ C F B♭
A♭ C♭ F B♭ E♭
A♭ E♭ C♭ F A♭
C E A♭ E
A♭ E♭♭ G♭♭ C♭
C F A♭ E♭
F B♭ E♭ A♭ C
E♭ C♭ F B♭
A♭ E♭ F C♭
C A♭ C E
E♭♭ A♭ C♭ G♭♭
E♭ A♭ C F
A♭ C F A♭ E♭
C♭ F B♭ E♭
A♭ F C♭ E♭

A♭

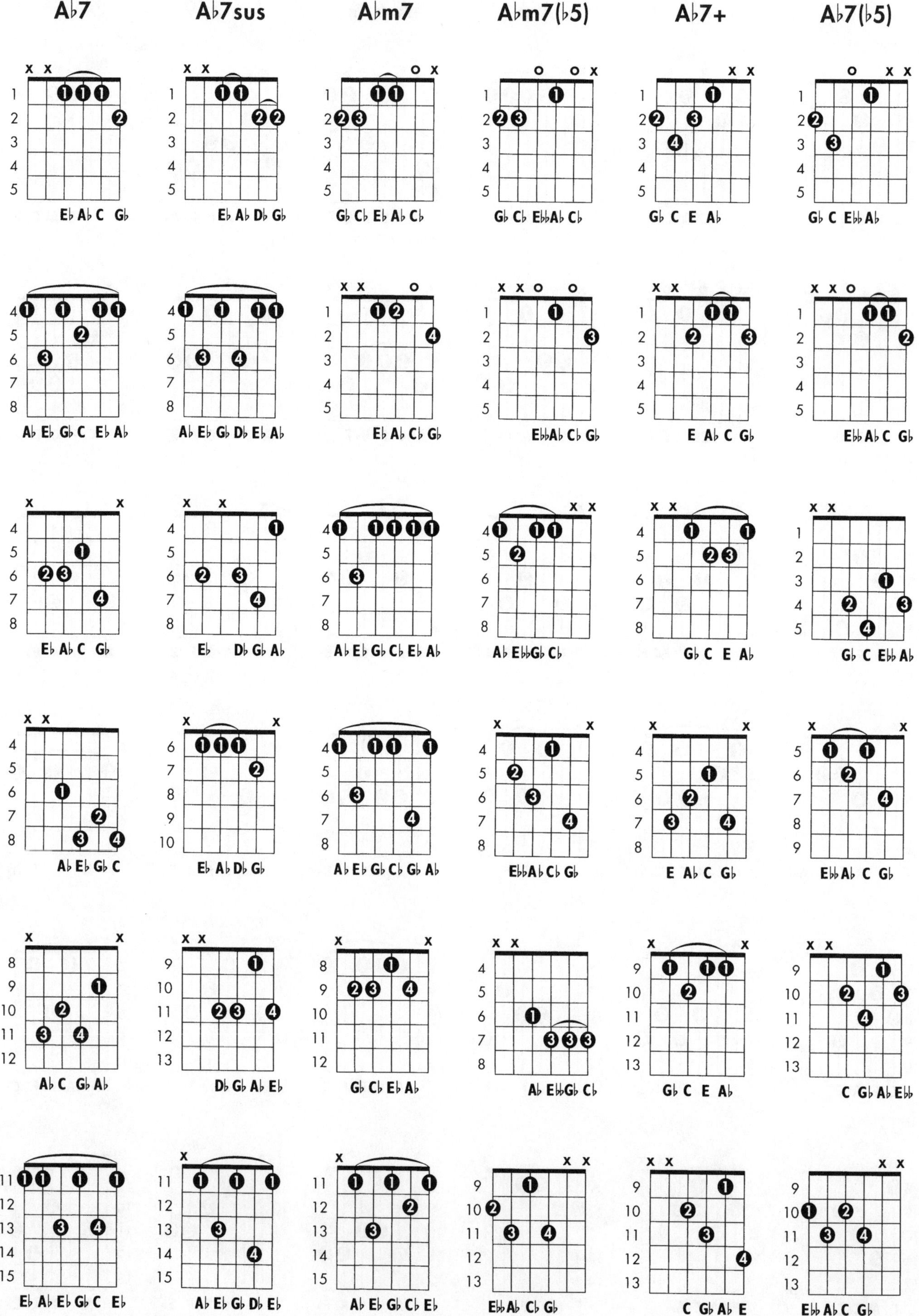
A♭7
A♭7sus
A♭m7
A♭m7(♭5)
A♭7+
A♭7(♭5)
E♭ A♭ C G♭
E♭ A♭ D♭ G♭
G♭ C♭ E♭ A♭ C♭
G♭ C♭ E♭♭ A♭ C♭
G♭ C E A♭
G♭ C E♭♭ A♭
A♭ E♭ G♭ C E♭ A♭
A♭ E♭ G♭ D♭ E♭ A♭
E♭ A♭ C♭ G♭
E♭♭ A♭ C♭ G♭
E A♭ C G♭
E♭♭ A♭ C G♭
E♭ A♭ C G♭
E♭ D♭ G♭ A♭
A♭ E♭ G♭ C♭ E♭ A♭
A♭ E♭♭ G♭ C♭
G♭ C E A♭
G♭ C E♭♭ A♭
A♭ E♭ G♭ C
E♭ A♭ D♭ G♭
A♭ E♭ G♭ C♭ G♭ A♭
E♭♭ A♭ C♭ G♭
E A♭ C G♭
E♭♭ A♭ C G♭
A♭ C G♭ A♭
D♭ G♭ A♭ E♭
G♭ C♭ E♭ A♭
A♭ E♭♭ G♭ C♭
G♭ C E A♭
C G♭ A♭ E♭♭
E♭ A♭ E♭ G♭ C E♭
A♭ E♭ G♭ D♭ E♭
A♭ E♭ G♭ C♭ E♭
E♭♭ A♭ C♭ G♭
C G♭ A♭ E
E♭♭ A♭ C G♭

A♭

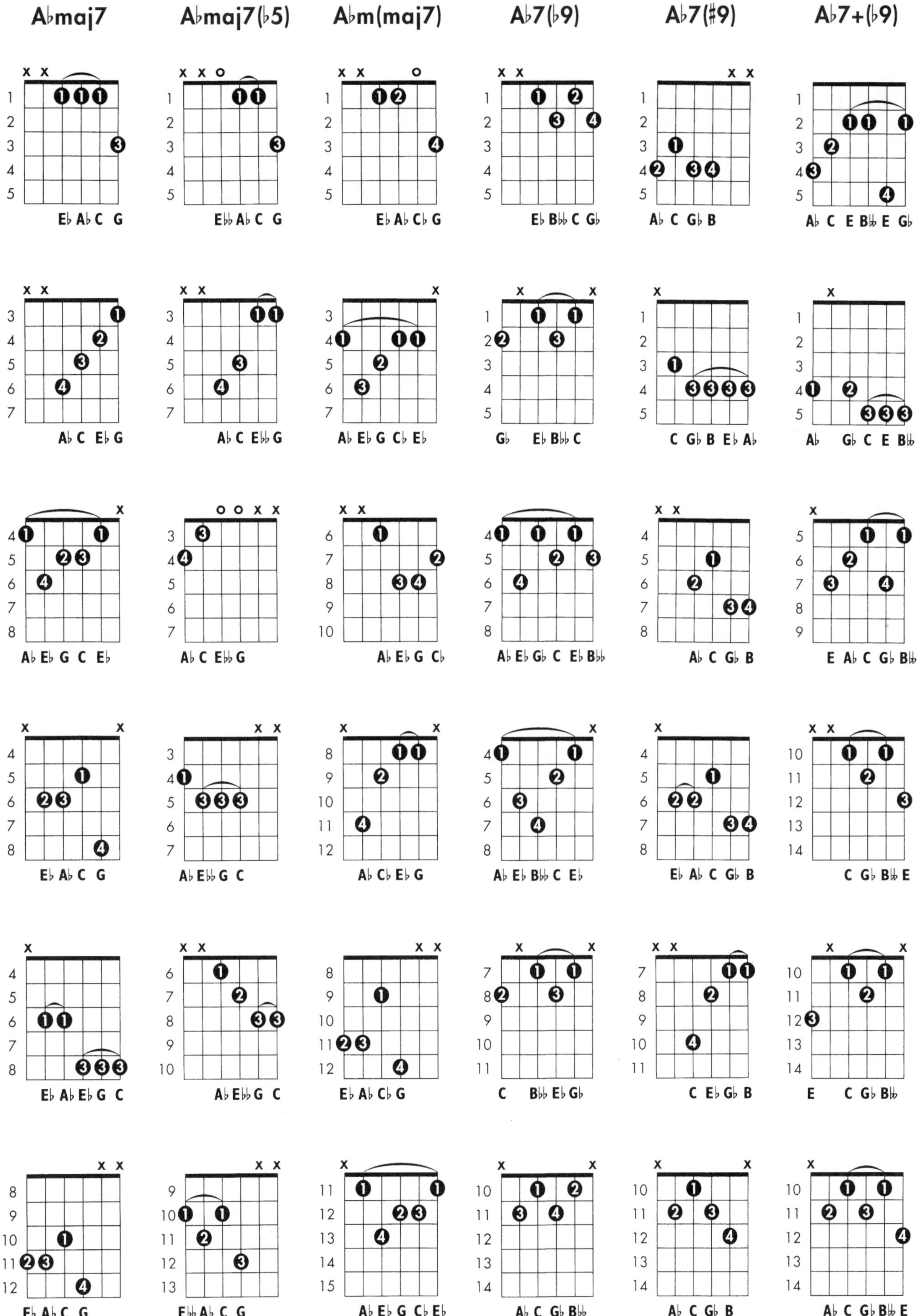
A♭maj7
A♭maj7(♭5)
A♭m(maj7)
A♭7(♭9)
A♭7(♯9)
A♭7+(♭9)
E♭ A♭ C G
E♭♭ A♭ C G
E♭ A♭ C♭ G
E♭ B♭♭ C G♭
A♭ C G♭ B
A♭ C E B♭♭ E G♭
A♭ C E♭ G
A♭ C E♭♭ G
A♭ E♭ G C♭ E♭
G♭ E♭ B♭♭ C
C G♭ B E♭ A♭
A♭ G♭ C E B♭♭
A♭ E♭ G C E♭
A♭ C E♭♭ G
A♭ E♭ G C♭
A♭ E♭ G♭ C E♭ B♭♭
A♭ C G♭ B
E A♭ C G♭ B♭♭
E♭ A♭ C G
A♭ E♭♭ G C
A♭ C♭ E♭ G
A♭ E♭ B♭♭ C E♭
E♭ A♭ C G♭ B
C G♭ B♭♭ E
E♭ A♭ E♭ G C
A♭ E♭♭ G C
E♭ A♭ C♭ G
C B♭♭ E♭ G♭
C E♭ G♭ B
E C G♭ B♭♭
E♭ A♭ C G
E♭♭ A♭ C G
A♭ E♭ G C♭ E♭
A♭ C G♭ B♭♭
A♭ C G♭ B
A♭ C G♭ B♭♭ E

Guitar Fingerboard Chart

Frets 1–12

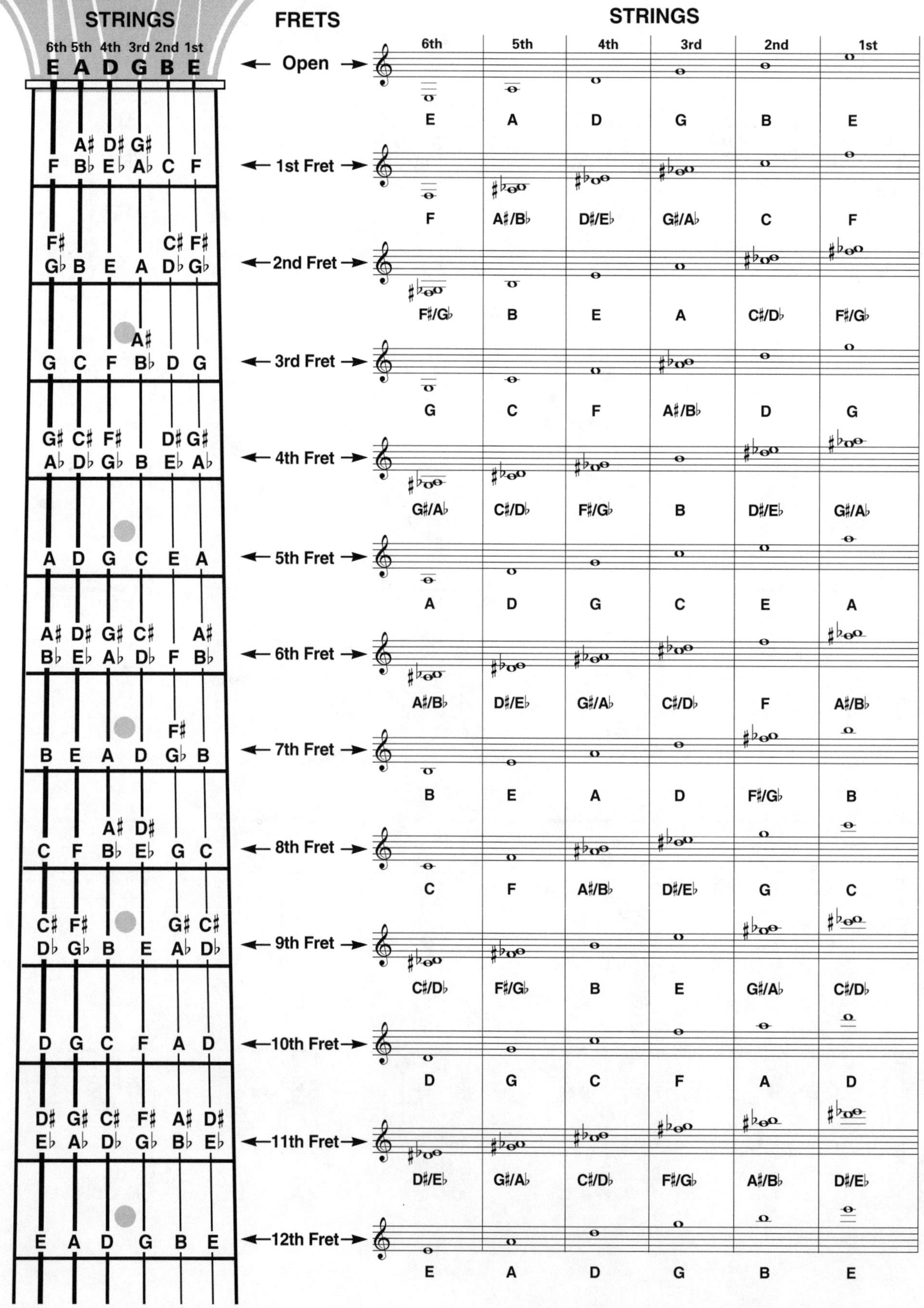

STRINGS	6th	5th	4th	3rd	2nd	1st
Open	E	A	D	G	B	E
1	F	A♯ B♭	D♯ E♭	G♯ A♭	C	F
2	F♯ G♭	B	E	A	C♯ D♭	F♯ G♭
3	G	C	F	A♯ B♭	D	G
4	G♯ A♭	C♯ D♭	F♯ G♭	B	D♯ E♭	G♯ A♭
5	A	D	G	C	E	A
6	A♯ B♭	D♯ E♭	G♯ A♭	C♯ D♭	F	A♯ B♭
7	B	E	A	D	F♯ G♭	B
8	C	F	A♯ B♭	D♯ E♭	G	C
9	C♯ D♭	F♯ G♭	B	E	G♯ A♭	C♯ D♭
10	D	G	C	F	A	D
11	D♯ E♭	G♯ A♭	C♯ D♭	F♯ G♭	A♯ B♭	D♯ E♭
12	E	A	D	G	B	E

FRETS	STRINGS: 6th	5th	4th	3rd	2nd	1st
← Open →	E	A	D	G	B	E
← 1st Fret →	F	A♯/B♭	D♯/E♭	G♯/A♭	C	F
← 2nd Fret →	F♯/G♭	B	E	A	C♯/D♭	F♯/G♭
← 3rd Fret →	G	C	F	A♯/B♭	D	G
← 4th Fret →	G♯/A♭	C♯/D♭	F♯/G♭	B	D♯/E♭	G♯/A♭
← 5th Fret →	A	D	G	C	E	A
← 6th Fret →	A♯/B♭	D♯/E♭	G♯/A♭	C♯/D♭	F	A♯/B♭
← 7th Fret →	B	E	A	D	F♯/G♭	B
← 8th Fret →	C	F	A♯/B♭	D♯/E♭	G	C
← 9th Fret →	C♯/D♭	F♯/G♭	B	E	G♯/A♭	C♯/D♭
← 10th Fret →	D	G	C	F	A	D
← 11th Fret →	D♯/E♭	G♯/A♭	C♯/D♭	F♯/G♭	A♯/B♭	D♯/E♭
← 12th Fret →	E	A	D	G	B	E

Dedication and Acknowledgements

With the *Girls Guitar Method*, you have just entered into the exclusive "Girls Who Play Guitar Club." I, myself, joined this secret club as a little girl who had big, huge dreams of learning how to play guitar and becoming a rock star. But without girl guitar books or girl guitars, I still learned how to play guitar and that's how I became part of the club. My hope is that with the help of this book and guitars designed for girls you will keep playing the guitar and not give up! Even if your fingers hurt or if it seems really, really hard, keep trying–our club is pulling for you! Why? Because playing music is one of the coolest, fun, entertaining, wonderful, amazing, expressive and moving things you can do in your life.

Tish Ciravolo

This book is lovingly dedicated to my two girls, Nicole and Sophia; the playful memory of my best friend in high school who taught me how to play guitar, Barbara Haughey; and every girl out there who finds the courage to pick this instrument. Remember–Girls Rule!

Thanks to Michael Ciravolo and the visionary staff at Schecter Guitars for the creation of Daisy Rock Guitars; thanks to Ron Manus and his amazing team at Alfred Publishing for making this book a reality.